Fishing Utah

An Angler's Guide to More than 170 Prime Fishing Spots

Second Edition

BRETT PRETTYMAN

THE LYONS PRESS
GUILFORD, CONNECTICUT
AN IMPRINT OF THE GLOBE PEQUOT PRESS

To my Dad who taught me his love for the sport; to my Mom who took me when Dad could not; to my wife, Brooke, who has the most beautiful fly cast I've seen; to my children, William and Lucie, for letting me relive the wonder of discovering angling; and to Jim, the best angler I know, for letting me tag along.

To buy books in quantity for corporate use or incentives, call **(800) 962–0973** or e-mail **premiums@GlobePequot.com**.

The Lyons Press is an imprint of The Globe Pequot Press.

Text design by Casey Shain
Maps created by Tim Kissel © Morris Book Publishing, LLC
All inside photos by Brett Prettyman unless otherwise noted.

Library of Congress Cataloging-in-Publication data is available.
ISBN 978-1-59921-226-5

Printed in the United States of America
10 9 8 7 6 5 4 3 2 1

Contents

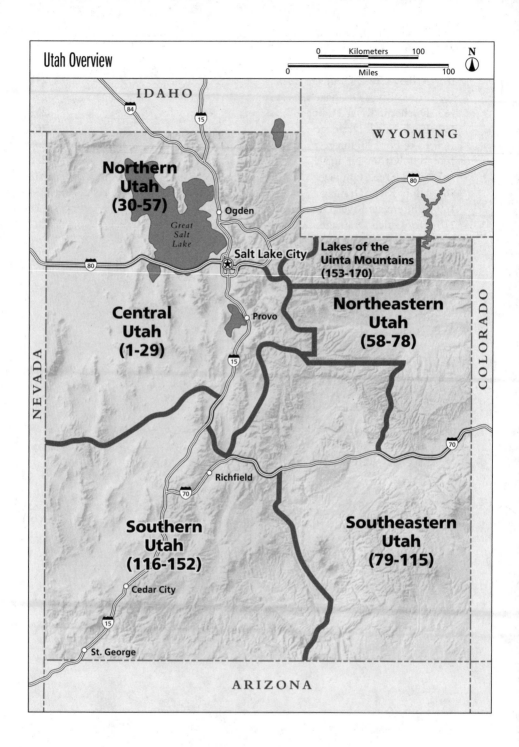

Acknowledgments

More than seventeen years of covering fishing for the *Salt Lake Tribune* and a lifetime of angling provided just enough information to start this book. The experience of other anglers and the knowledge of the biologists who manage Utah's fisheries make up the rest.

Special thanks goes to Jim Gunderson of Fish Tech Outfitters, who filled in the voids and provided tips on the best ways to catch fish at each location. His name probably should be on the book. Tom Wharton, longtime outdoor editor of the *Salt Lake Tribune* and a great friend, was also a major contributor.

Fishing buddies Pete Idstrom, Roy Hawk, Ron Colby, Ray Schelble, and George Sommer also provided input. Technical help came from my father-in-law, Larry Barrigar; my mother, Pam Mcleese; and my wife, Brooke.

Employees of the Utah Division of Wildlife Resources, past and present, also deserve much of the credit for the comprehensive detail in the book. The list is long, but they all deserve thanks: Kent Sorenson, Charlie Thompson, Dale Hepworth, Chad Crosbie, Louis Berg, Tom Pettengill, Joe Valentine, Roger Wilson, Steve Brayton, Roger Schneidervin, Wayne Gustaveson, Mike Ottenbacher, Kirk Mullins, Ed Johnson, Craig Schaugaard, Mark Hadley, Scott Root, Don Archer, Paul Birdsey, Richard Hepworth, Ted Hallows, Chuck Chamberlain, Walt Donaldson, Ron Stewart, Lowell Marthe, and Lindy Higham. Thank you to all.

Legend

Interstate Highway	(15) (215)	Fishing Site	● 1
U.S. Highway	(12) (191)	Town/City	○ Logan
tate Highway	(41) (150)	Campground	▲
County Road	(CR 603)	Trailhead	Ⓣ
Forest Road	[2302]	Pass	)(
Interstate	⟹	Dam	—
Paved Road	⇢	Bridge	)(
Gravel Road	⟹	Point of Interest	■
Dirt Road	======⟹	Guard Station	▲
Trail	- - - - -	Peak	X
Lake		Boat Ramp	▼
River/Creek		Compass	N ◑
State Boundary	- - - - - - -	Scale	0 Kilometers 100 / 0 Miles 100
Region Boundary	▬▬▬▬		

Introduction

Welcome to Utah, the second-driest state in the nation. Now grab a rod and hit the water, because despite its lack of precipitation, the Beehive State offers an incredible amount of angling opportunity. Fisheries were serendipitously created all over the state as Utahns built reservoirs to store precious water. Excellent flatwater and tailwater fisheries are the result.

More than 900,000 anglers fish Utah waters each year. They spend an estimated $468 million in the state on their sport. Because the state has limited stream and river habitat, about 75 percent of Utah's fishing occurs on lakes and reservoirs.

There is a common misconception that Utahns are abandoning trout in favor of warm-water species like bass and walleye. What officials have found is that anglers are spending more time pursuing warm-water species than they used to, but that about 75 percent of Utah anglers still classify themselves as trout fishers.

Utah anglers are also becoming more aware of the value of catch-and-release fishing. Wildlife officials have found ever-increasing support for reduced limits and special regulations. Most anglers no longer view a fishing license as a right to keep a limit. Officials say up to 75 percent of all fish caught are released.

This changed attitude has allowed the Division of Wildlife Resources (DWR) to change management strategies. To an increasing degree, the 85.5 miles of Utah Class I trout streams and a large portion of the 316 miles of Class II waters are no longer stocked with hatchery-raised fish. When anglers no longer keep fish, wild populations have a chance to flourish.

There is a flip side to the benefits of catch-and-release fishing. It can actually hurt fisheries that have ample populations and need fish to be harvested. Such circumstances exist with the striped bass at Lake Powell and the lake trout at Flaming Gorge. On the other hand, the catch-and-release ethic has helped create blue-ribbon fishing on the Green River below Flaming Gorge and on the Provo River.

Despite this trend toward releasing fish, officials have reduced the trout limit to four on most major fisheries. The regulations cited in this book come from the 2007 Utah Fishing Proclamation produced by the Division of Wildlife Resources.

As officials struggle to find the right balance at each location, regulations will continue to change yearly. Always pick up a few fishing proclamations when buying a license. Keep one with your gear, one in the car, and one at home for easy reading. It may help keep you from getting a ticket.

If you have specific questions about a certain fishery, call the DWR office in the region you plan to fish. The numbers are: Central office in Springville (801-491-5678); Northern office in Ogden (801-476-2740); Northeastern office in Vernal (435-781-9453); Southeastern office in Price (435-781-9453); Southern office in Cedar City (435-865-6100); and the Salt Lake office (801-538-4700).

There are a number of DWR-produced brochures available on specific Utah waters. DWR also has a comprehensive Web site—www.wildlife.utah.gov. You can purchase a fishing license online, read the weekly fishing report, and check fishing regulations to find out if any emergency fishing rules have been created.

Of course, there are a number of fishing stores across the state that provide an excellent resource with current conditions and productive methods.

Planning a Trip

Too many anglers forget the dangers of sunburn when fishing. A hat and sunglasses will help protect fishers from direct sunlight, but reflecting sunlight from the water is also intense. Always use sunscreen, even on cloudy days.

Mosquitoes can be a major hassle, especially when fishing high-elevation locales like the Uinta and Boulder Mountains. Insect repellent is always on the must-pack list. Ticks are common in Utah. Close personal inspections should be made during and after fishing excursions.

In the summer months, always carry water, even for short trips. Dehydration leads to headaches, which can easily ruin an excursion. Also, prepare for sudden and strong thunderstorms. Pack rain gear. It is always better to have it and never use it than to long for it in a downpour.

For current information on fishing conditions, visit www.wildlife.utah.gov/hotspots. It's also a good idea to call or stop by the local fishing store to find out what is working at your destination.

Always leave information with someone explaining where you are going, where you will be staying, and how long you will be gone.

Take the Children Fishing

A child's first fishing experience should be positive. Heading home cold, wet, hungry, and without any fish to show off is not the best way to introduce youngsters to the sport. Start them off in a comfortable environment on a lake or stream which has a high success rate. Perch, bluegill, and crappie are usually a safe bet when taking children fishing. Avoid taking them to fee areas their first time, as they might later on assume regular fishing should be as productive.

Keep it simple and be patient. Nothing will turn a child off of fishing more quickly than a grumpy adult telling them they are doing everything wrong. Show them how it is done and then let them experiment before showing them again.

Starting young would-be anglers off with bait may seem the simple answer, but the truth is children become bored waiting for something to happen. Instead, try starting them off with a small lure to keep their interest up. If you must use bait, suspend it below a bobber to give children something to watch.

Prepare children mentally by explaining that fishing isn't only about catching trout, bass, walleye, or perch. Tell them fishing is about sharing outdoor experiences with family and friends and that landing a fish is a bonus.

Teach them the ethics of fishing. Explain to them the benefits of catch-and-release fishing and illustrate to them by example the value in leaving a fishing site litter-free. Take time and be patient and you will likely end up with a fishing companion for life.

Ice Fishing

Many Utah anglers make the mistake of putting their rods away once the snow starts falling. Prepared winter anglers experience some of the most productive fishing of the year through the ice. Anglers stuck on shore during the summer months have access to the entire reservoir when it is covered with ice.

Of course, safety is the first concern. Three inches of ice usually supports one person on foot, but most anglers wait until the ice is 4 inches thick before venturing on it. Six to 7 inches of ice supports large groups of anglers. New ice is stronger than old ice, and slushy ice is only half as strong as clear ice.

Scofield Reservoir is traditionally the first major fishery to produce ice safe enough to fish on. It usually happens by mid-December. Most of the other major ice-fishing destinations become safe the week between Christmas and New Year's.

Call your favorite fishing store or check the Division of Wildlife's fishing report on the Internet to find out when it is safe to head to your favorite winter fishing destination.

Campground Reservations

To make reservations at Utah's State Parks, call (800) 322-3770 or visit www.reserve america.com.

To book a campground at a Forest Service site, call (877) 444-6777. Reservations can also be made on the Internet at www.recreation.gov.

Fishing Access for Disabled Persons

To enable people with disabilities the opportunity to enjoy fishing where they otherwise may not be able to, state agencies have created locations around Utah where anglers can fish from a wheelchair, although not always by ADA standards.

Here is a list of the sites and specific accommodations:

Northern Utah
- Bountiful Pond—fishing pier and some access to the water
- Clinton Pond—some access to the water
- Farmington Pond—fishing pier
- Logan River—two fishing piers, one at First Dam and one at Logan City Park
- Mabey Pond (Clearfield)—anglers can park at the water's edge
- Mirror Lake—wheelchair access around most of the lake
- Ogden River Parkway (mouth of Ogden Canyon to Washington Boulevard)—physically challenged access
- Perception Park (Highway 39, east of Pineview Reservoir)—two fishing piers and wheelchair-accessible sites to the river

- Pioneer Park Pond (Brigham City)—sidewalk around the pond and a bridge that serves as a fishing pier
- South Fork, Ogden River—trail and fishing platforms

Central Utah
- Adventure Learning Park Pond—asphalt trail circles the pond and provides access to a gazebo
- Canyon View Park Pond (Spanish Fork)—fishing pier and access to a low dike
- Community Reservoir—dirt trail to the dam
- Draper Pond—asphalt path from two parking lots provides access to a bridge area
- Highland Glen Park (Highland)—docks and physically challenged access
- Jordan River Parkway—access points at various places along the parkway; one of the best places is the new Willow Pond in Murray
- Mill Hollow Reservoir—limited access trail around the lake (mostly gravel, with some hardened surfaces)
- Palisade State Park—three wheelchair access points
- Payson Lakes—fishing pier and a paved trail along the shoreline
- Provo River, just above Olmstead Diversion—fishing pier
- Rainbow Reservoir (at the Deseret Chemical Depot)—cement ramp from the parking area to the lake, with a guard rail around the fishing area
- Salem Pond—fishing pier
- Silver Lake (near Brighton)—board walk that provides fishing access
- Spanish Oaks Reservoir (Spanish Fork)—wheelchair ramp to the elevated reservoir and a paved path that surrounds the reservoir
- Spring Lake (in the city of Spring Lake, south of Payson)—dirt road that comes within 10 feet of the lake shore in many spots
- Strawberry Reservoir, Haws Point area—boardwalk trails and cement walkways
- Tibble Fork Reservoir—wheelchair access to the reservoir
- Utah Lake State Park, north jetty—fishing pier
- Vivian Park Pond—fishing pier
- Yearns Reservoir—dirt trail to the dam
- Yuba State Park, Oasis Campground—dock area that is wheelchair accessible

Northeastern Utah
- Currant Creek Reservoir—wheelchair access areas
- Diamond Mountain Lakes—concrete boat ramps, oil-treated gravel roads, and parking lots allow some limited access
- Flaming Gorge Reservoir, Antelope Flat—cement boat ramp that provides fishing access
- Flaming Gorge Reservoir, Sheep Creek—cement boat ramp that provides fishing access
- Green River, Tailrace (just below Flaming Gorge Dam)—wheelchair access
- Green River, Little Hole (about 7 miles downstream from Flaming Gorge Dam)—wheelchair access on the third ramp and dock (south); also has a side-

walk access (north) that has fairly accessible fishing, depending on the level of the water

- Lake Canyon Lake—parking area that's within a few feet of the water's edge
- Sheep Creek Lake—parking area that's within a few feet of the water's edge
- West Greens Lake—fishing pier; also, wheelchair access in the northeast corner of the lake

Southeastern Utah

- Benches Pond—300-foot walkway provides access to much of the pond
- Gigliotti Pond (Helper City)—concrete trail from the parking area provides access to four fishing stations near the water's edge, two of which are shaded, one signed for use by physically challenged anglers
- Huntington North Reservoir—concrete boat ramp and floating pier provide limited access
- Millsite Reservoir—concrete boat ramp and floating pier provide limited access
- Recapture Reservoir—boat ramp provides limited access
- Scofield State Park—concrete boat ramp, trail, and fishing pier provide excellent access
- Scofield Reservoir, Beaver Dam area (opens to fishing the second Saturday in July)—paved walkway provides limited access to the northern end of the reservoir

Southern Utah

- Beaver River—paved parking lot and ramp to the river at several spots
- Lake Powell, Wahweap Marina—covered fishing pier
- Little Reservoir—concrete trail provides access to two fishing piers
- Pine Valley Reservoir—paved trail that leads to a fishing pier with a railing
- Skyline Drive Pond (St. George)—trail and fishing pier
- Tawa Ponds (Snow Canyon Parkway, St. George)—wheelchair access around most of the two ponds

Hatcheries

The first state-owned hatchery in Utah opened December 30, 1899, in Murray. After more than a hundred years of service, the state's hatchery system annually produces 850,000 pounds and 10 to 12 million fish.

Some hatcheries allow tours for groups by appointment.

J. Perry Egan Brood Station, 2550 South Bicknell Circle, Bicknell; (435) 425-3547. Tours by appointment only.

Mammoth Creek Hatchery, 1318 South Fish Hatchery, Hatch; (435) 735-4200.

Fountain Green Hatchery, 700 North Big Springs Road, Fountain Green; (435) 445-3472.

Mantua Hatchery, 555 East Fish Hatchery Road, Mantua; (435) 723-6579. Tours by appointment only.

Glenwood Hatchery, 5700 East Hatchery Road, Glenwood; (435) 896-5218.

Midway Hatchery, 907 South Center Street, Midway; (435) 654-0282.
Kamas Hatchery, 2722 East Mirror Lake Highway, Kamas; (435) 783-4883.
Springville Hatchery, 1000 North Main, Springville; (435) 489-4421.
Loa Hatchery, 2100 North 300 West, Loa; (435) 836-2858.
Whiterocks Hatchery, HCR 67, north of Whiterocks; (435) 353-4855.

Whirling Disease

Since the discovery of whirling disease in a private hatchery in southern Utah in 1991, officials have been learning how to cope with the sometimes-fatal condition that affects trout and salmon.

The whirling disease parasite attacks the cartilage tissue of a fish's head and spine, causing head deformities and twisted spines in fish that survive the early stages. Because Utah fisheries rely primarily on fish planted by the DWR rather than native-born fish, whirling has not had the effect here that it has in other states.

Still, in areas where whirling has been confirmed, officials are planting brown trout rather than rainbows. Browns have shown a resistance to whirling disease, while rainbows seem especially susceptible to the parasite.

For nine years the state hatchery system avoided infection, but in a span of five years, from 2000 to 2005, three hatcheries—Midway, Mammoth Creek, and Springville—tested positive. The result was thousands of pounds of lost trout and millions of dollars in cleansing and forced renovations to deal with the disease. It is only a matter of time before another hatchery tests positive.

With the help of Trout Unlimited, the DWR has installed signs on streams and lakes to alert anglers where whirling disease has been found. The signs also include information on ways to prevent spreading the parasite.

Anglers should clean all equipment—including boats, trailers, waders, boots, float tubes, and fins—before leaving an area they've fished. The parasite is carried by a host worm that resides in mud. Dry equipment in the sun before using it again. Cleaning waders and boots with a 10 percent solution of chlorine bleach is also a good idea.

Do not transport live fish between bodies of water. It's illegal, and whirling disease has most likely been transmitted to previously clean Utah waters this way. If you witness what you believe to be an illegal planting, call the Help Stop Poaching Hotline at (800) 662-3337. Fish entrails should be disposed of properly in trash bins, or by burning or burial. Do not throw entrails in lakes or streams; you may be passing whirling disease back into the system. Whirling disease is not transferable to humans. It is safe to eat trout or salmon that carry the parasite.

New Zealand Mud Snail

First discovered in Idaho's Snake River in 1987, the New Zealand mud snail is spreading quickly across the West. Utah's first documented case of the small, invasive, and prolific snail came in 2001 on the state's famed Green River below Flaming Gorge Reservoir.

The snail is a threat because it supplants many of the aquatic invertebrates that trout eat by eating the same food and seeking refuge in the same places. Trout, as of yet, have not discovered the hard-shelled snail to be a desirable food item.

Since the discovery in 2001, New Zealand mud snails have been found at twenty locations in twelve stream basins of northern Utah. Notable locations where the snails have become established include the Provo River, Weber River, Ogden River, Strawberry River, Logan River, Little Bear River, and East Canyon Creek.

Anglers are believed to be the predominate carrier of the snails from one fishery to the next. State wildlife officials ask anglers to thoroughly clean mud and vegetation from waders, boats, and fishing gear and, if possible, completely dry equipment before leaving the area. A hot-water bath (120° F) will kill mud snails, and spraying equipment with Formula 409 or a similar soap solution before drying will increase effectiveness.

Mercury Warnings

While mercury warnings have been around for a long time in other states, the health alerts about eating too much fish from certain waters is a new thing to Utah anglers. The number of waters with warnings is small, but more extensive testing on more popular fisheries is sure to lengthen the list in the coming years. For updated information about mercury warnings on Utah fisheries, visit the Utah Department of Environmental Quality Web site at www.deq.utah.gov/issues/mercury.

Landing a Record

Every angler dreams of catching a record-size fish. Utah offers some great opportunities to do exactly that.

To qualify for a state record, the fish must have been caught by one angler (only) while fishing legally. Separate record categories exist for set line, archery, and spear fishing. There is also a catch-and-release record program.

The process for having a trophy fish recognized is simple but precise. The fish must be positively and properly identified. The Division of Wildlife Resources is the sole judge. Have the fish documented by DWR personnel as soon as possible. If an official is not available, the angler must present a close-up, side-view color photo with the fish lying near a legible measuring stick. The picture and measurement should take place before the fish is frozen.

Only one weighing is required, but the scales used must be inspected and certified. The weighing must be witnessed by two Utah residents older than eighteen years and not members of the anglers' party or family. Witnesses must provide their address, phone number, and a written statement saying that the weighing took place on certified scales and attesting to the true weight of the fish.

Officials say the most common mistake anglers with trophy fish make is waiting too long to have the fish weighed. Fish lose weight by dehydration. Anglers also need to realize fish taken from Flaming Gorge Reservoir, Lake Powell, and Bear

Kelly Parry and his daughter, Karlee, pose with the state record tiger muskie caught July 4, 2006 from Pineview Reservoir. The fish was 49 inches long and weighed 33 pounds, 10 ounces.

Lake will be recognized if taken legally from any portion of the water if the fish are weighed in Utah and anglers follow specified rules.

The fish must have been legally taken following the regulations in the current Utah Fishing Proclamation. Any information indicating that it was not legally taken will be grounds for disqualification. The fish must have been caught from a public fishery where the public has free access. Each qualifying fish must be submitted individually within thirty days of the catch.

Rules for setting a catch-and-release record are similar, but the program is largely based on an honor system, with the emphasis on the live release of the fish. Records are based entirely on the length of a fish. If there is any information, either from the photo or from witnesses, that the fish was stressed, detained, abused, or transported from the capture site, the application will be denied. The fish should be measured, photographed, and released as quickly as possible without injury. Preferably the fish should not be removed from the water.

The fish should be measured to the nearest ¼ inch. Measure from the tip of the snout (with the mouth closed) to the tip of the tail, along the side of the body. Witness information and a clear side-view color photograph must be submitted with the application. The witness must be present on the water during the measurement and release of the fish.

Current Angling Record Fish for the State of Utah*

SPECIES	YEAR	WEIGHT	LENGTH	GIRTH	FISHERMAN	LOCATION
Bass, Largemouth	1974	10 lb 2 oz	24¼ in	20 in	Sam Lamanna	Lake Powell
Bass, Smallmouth	1996	7 lb 6 oz	22 in	16½ in	Alan Iorg	Midview Res. (Lake Borham)
Bass, Striped	1991	48 lb 11 oz	45 in	31¼ in	Travis T. Jenson	Lake Powell
Bass, White	1970	4 lb 1 oz			John R. Welcker	Utah Lake
Bluegill	1993	2 lb 7 oz	11½ in	14⅝ in	Jack Rask	Mantua Reservoir
Bullhead, Black	1999	3 lb 4 oz	16 in	13 in	Jack Gilgen	Cutler Reservoir
Carp	1993	32 lb 0 oz			Couger Elfervig	Lake Powell
Catfish, Channel	1978	32 lb 8 oz	39¾ in	22 in	LeRoy Mortensen	Utah Lake
Chub, Utah	1987	1 lb 11 oz	13¼ in	11 in	Ray Johnson	Starvation Reservoir
Crappie, Black	1993	3 lb 2 oz	17¼ in	14 in	Mike Flickinger	Quail Creek Reservoir
Grayling	1998	1 lb 12 oz	17¼ in	8¾ in	Terry J. Fieldsted	Big Dog Lake - South Slope Uintas
Muskellunge, Tiger	2006	33 lb 9 oz	49 in	21½ in	Kelly Parry	Pineview Reservoir
Perch, Sacramento	1993	4 lb 5 oz	17 in	15 in	Harlan G. Thomas	Garrison Res. (Pruess Lake)
Perch, Yellow	1984	2 lb 11 oz	15⅛ in	9¾ in	Ray Johnson	Sevier Bridge Reservoir
Pike, Northern	2002	25 lb 0 oz	43½ in	19 1/2 in	Henry Fenning	Yuba Reservoir
Salmon, Kokanee	1995	6 lb 0 oz	25 in	16 in	Todd Chikaraishi	Strawberry Reservoir
Sucker, Utah	2003	6 lb 6 oz	25½ in	13¼ in	Jamin C. Buttars	Weber River
Sucker, White	1992	2 lb 8 oz	19¼ in	9½ in	Ray Johnson	Flaming Gorge Reservoir
Sunfish, Green	2003	15.5 oz	10¼ in	10 in	Sean Buchanan	Glassman Pond
Trout, Albino	1989	9 lb 2 oz	24¾ in	17 in	Nick Manning	Joes Valley Reservoir
Trout, Brook	1971	7 lb 8 oz			Milton Taft	Boulder Mountain
Trout, Brown	1977	33 lb 10 oz	40 in	25 in	Robert Bringhurst	Flaming Gorge Reservoir
Trout, Brownbow	2000	1 lb 0 oz	15 in		Benjamin Spencer Harward	Mill Meadows
Trout, Cutthroat	1930	26 lb 12 oz			Mrs. E. Smith	Strawberry Reservoir
Trout, Golden	1977	14 oz	14½ in		Breck Tuttle	Atwood Creek
Trout, Lake	1988	51 lb 8 oz	45⅛ in	31¾ in	Curt Bilbey	Flaming Gorge Reservoir
Trout, Rainbow	1979	26 lb 2 oz			Del Canty	Flaming Gorge Reservoir
Trout, Splake	2006	17 lb 4 oz	36 ½ in	21⅛ in	Stacy S. Willden	Fish Lake
Trout, Tiger	2007	10 lb 12 oz	29 ½ in	17⅛ in	Michael David Moon	Pallisade Lake Palisade Lake
Walleye	1991	15 lb 9 oz	31¾ in	20¾ in	Jeffery Tanner	Provo River
Whitefish, Bonneville	1982	4 lb 4 oz	21 in	13¾ in	Deon Sparks	Bear Lake
Whitefish, Mountain	1997	4 lb 12 oz	21½ in	14 in	Roy L. Montoya	Deer Creek Reservoir
Wiper	2007	9 lb 12 oz	26⅛ in	19¼ in	Rob Valdez	Willard Bay

*Updated April 17, 2008

Current Spear Fishing Record Fish for the State of Utah*

SPECIES	YEAR	WEIGHT	LENGTH	GIRTH	FISHERMAN	LOCATION
Bass, Smallmouth	2007	4 lb 0 oz	17⅞ in	11 ½ in	Michael Weyland	Flaming Gorge Reservoir
Bass, Largemouth	2003	6 lb 0 oz	19⅓ in	17¼ in	Jason Mull	Steinaker Lake
Bluegill	2004	8 oz	8¼ in	8¾ in	Jon Konrad	Steinaker Reservoir
Carp	2007	27 lb 12 oz	34 in		David L Hemphill Jr.	Starvation Reservoir
Chub, Utah	2005	1 lb 0 oz	12¾ in	8⅛ in	Shane Forrester	Starvation Reservoir
Muskellunge, Tiger	2006	14 lb 7 oz	37½ in	16½ in	Matt Boyd	Fish Lake
Perch, Yellow	1988	5 oz	8¼ in	5½ in	Rud Warner	Fish Lake
Sucker, Utah	2003	4 lb 15 oz	23 in	11 in	Mike McGuire	Fish Lake
Trout, Brown	1983	21 lb 12 oz	35½ in	21¾ in	Bruce Boyd	Fish Lake
Trout , Lake	2003	2 lb 4 oz	20 in	9⅛ in	Mike McGuire	Fish Lake
Trout, Rainbow	1992	3 lb 8 oz	19 in	9½ in	Paul Gibson	Fish Lake
Trout , Splake	2005	13 lb 5 oz	30¾ in	20½ in	Stacy S. Willden	Fish Lake
Walleye	2002	11 lb 6 oz	31 in	18 in	Mike McGuire	Deer Creek Reservoir

Current Setline Record Fish for the State of Utah*

SPECIES	YEAR	WEIGHT	LENGTH	GIRTH	FISHERMAN	LOCATION
Catfish, Channel	1975	31 lb 0 oz	39 in	20½ in	Dorothy Lorenzen	Utah Lake

Current Archery Record Fish for the State of Utah*

SPECIES	YEAR	WEIGHT	LENGTH	GIRTH	FISHERMAN	LOCATION
Carp	1991	27 lb 0 oz	34 in	23¾ in	Ray D. Johnson	Great Salt Lake Marshes
Sucker, Utah	1992	4 lb 5 oz	19¾ in	12 in	David W. Stuart	Utah Lake
Sucker, White	1992	2 lb 7 oz	18½ in	9¼ in	Ray Johnson	Flaming Gorge Reservoir

Current Catch and Release Record Fish for the State of Utah*

SPECIES	DATE	LENGTH	FISHERMAN	LOCATION
Bass, Largemouth	03/29/98	27 in	Dennis Miller	Quail Lake
Bass, Smallmouth	07/04/03	23½ in	Clifford Sackett Jr.	Jordanelle Reservoir
Bass, Striped	05/11/00	32½ in	Marty Peterson	Lake Powell
Bass, White	05/07/05	19 in	Clint Lance	Salem Pond
Bluegill	10/05/07	11⅝ in	Derek Haryyman	Pelican Lake
Bullhead, Black	06/15/97	13½ in	Shawn Clement	Kaysville Ponds
Carp	09/02/03	35½ in	Lance Egan	Starvation Reservoir
Catfish, Channel	04/08/03	34 in	Blair Peterson	Davis Community Pond
Chub, Utah	06/21/97	14¼ in	Sue McGhie Troff	Flaming Gorge Reservoir
Crappie, Black	05/20/07	16 in	Dustin Gunrud	Pineview Reservoir
Grayling	07/17/99	19 in	Russell Lee, Jr.	Uinta Mountains
Muskellunge Tiger	11/28/98	53¼ in	Ray Johnson	Pineview Reservoir
Perch, Sacramento	05/28/00	15 in	Lance Egan	Pruess Lake

*Updated April 17, 2008

SPECIES	DATE	LENGTH	FISHERMAN	LOCATION
Perch, Yellow	03/04/00	15¼ in	Brad Cutler	Yuba Reservoir
Pike, Northern	06/13/98	49¼ in	Logan Hacking	Lake Powell
Salmon, Kokanee	05/29/04	26⅝ in	Ray Johnson	Flaming Gorge
Sucker, Utah	08/12/05	27 in	John Sanders	Middle Provo River
Sucker, White	04/26/97	19 in	Kirk Ray Johnson	Flaming Gorge
Sunfish, Green	05/29/00	10½ in	Jack Vincent	Pelican Lake
Trout, Albino	04/28/04	29 in	Duncan Bernstein	Ogden River
Trout, Brake				
Trout, Brook	12/06/97	23 in	Travis L. Clark	Boulder Mountain
Trout, Brown	05/26/01	32 in	Cody Mortensen	Jordanelle Reservoir
Trout, Brownbow	06/13/97	12¼ in	Kirk Johnson	Mill Meadow Reservoir
Trout, Cutthroat	12/07/02	30 in	Blaine Beazer	Bear Lake
Trout, Golden	06/05/07	10½ in	Jeffrey Gallagher	Echo Lake
Trout, Lake	07/09/98	46½ in	Ray Johnson	Flaming Gorge
Trout, Rainbow	12/30/00	29 in	Enich Mockli	East Canyon
Trout, Splake	10/19/03	20½ in	Ryan Barnes	Joe's Valley Reservoir
Trout, Tiger	11/25/07	24 in	Nicholas Granato	Palisade Reservoir
Walleye	04/04/02	31½ in	Enich Mockli	Starvation Reservoir
Whitefish, Bonneville	12/04/00	19¼ in	Scott Tolentino	Bear Lake
Whitefish, Mountain	06/20/04	24 in	Craig Shriner	Weber River
Wiper	07/08/05	25 in	Dale P. Tracy	Willard Bay

Utah's Game Fish

Rainbow Trout

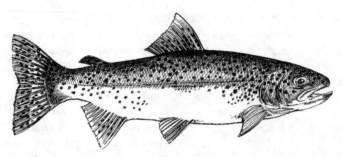

There is no more abundant and wide-ranging species of fish in Utah than the rainbow trout. The state's Division of Wildlife Resources (DWR) annually plants more than 750,000 pounds of rainbows in the state's waters. There are a few wild rainbow populations, but if there is one fish Utah anglers do not practice catch-and-release with, it is the rainbow trout.

In a number of the state's most heavily fished waters, like lakes in the Uinta Mountains, 20 percent of the rainbows planted are albino rainbow trout. Some lakes are planted twice a week and are what DWR officials call put-and-take fisheries. Biologists put the rainbows in the water and freezer-stuffing anglers take them out.

Rainbows are hard fighters and have a tendency to leap when hooked. They are easily recognized by the pink band running on both sides of the fish from head to tail. Rainbow trout in streams and those spawning in the spring are darker and have more intense colors than those in lakes.

It is the species' ability to adapt to a large range of environmental conditions and its willingness to take a variety of bait that makes it the most common trout in the state. Rainbow trout is a firm, flaky meat, and depending on the environment, it provides excellent table fare.

Rainbows do not compete well with rough fish like the Utah chub. Rainbow trout under 2 pounds feed on zooplankton, insects, and crustaceans. Fish over 2 pounds feed on other fish. The key to successful rainbow fishing is light line (4- to 6-pound test) and small hooks (sizes 10 to 14).

Bait is the most effective method for catching rainbows in Utah. Power Bait, salmon eggs, cheese, and night crawlers tipped with marshmallow are what most people call traditional trout baits. Trolling in water 10 to 40 feet deep with pop gear, flatfish, or a spinner tipped with a night crawler is a reliable method on hot summer days.

Because rainbows tend to feed on aquatic insects, fishing with wet flies near weed beds can be a great way to catch them. Dark woolly buggers and damselfly nymphs are popular flies. Fishing from a float tube is an easy way to access the fish when weed growth makes shore angling difficult.

Scofield and Flaming Gorge Reservoirs, Panguitch and Fish Lakes, and lakes along the Mirror Lake Highway (Highway 150) in the Uinta Mountains are great places to fish for rainbow.

Brown Trout

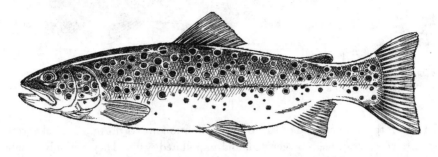

The native trout of Europe, browns were widely introduced to North America in 1883. They reproduce naturally in streams and are often associated with deep, undercut banks and pools choked with woody debris.

Brown trout were planted in Utah before 1900. They have since become one of the state's most important trout species. Browns are more tolerant of warm and silty water than other trout, but they need a lot of space and are susceptible to habitat loss. For browns, the presence of gravel for spawning beds is critical. Wild brown trout populations are found throughout the state's rivers and streams, with some trophy fish occasionally caught in reservoirs.

Browns are olive-brown with yellowish sides. The belly color is dusky yellow but may be creamy white. They typically have some orange or red spots on their sides, which are often encircled with light yellow or white, and they have dark spots on the back and sides.

Adult browns are voracious eaters of large food items such as crayfish and other fish, especially trout. They sometimes feed on aquatic and terrestrial insects. Browns are elusive and tend to hold in deep holes on smaller streams. They feed actively at twilight and through the night.

Browns are one of the most difficult trout to catch. One of the best times to fish for them is in the fall when they are preparing to spawn. Lure anglers should use minnow or trout-imitating lures in low light conditions. Fly fishers do well with streamers. Some anglers chase trophy-size browns in reservoirs by trolling with large minnow-imitating lures. Among baits, night crawlers, grasshoppers, and frozen minnows work well.

In northern Utah, the Green, Provo, and Weber Rivers all contain excellent populations of brown trout. In the southern half of the state, try Lower Fish Creek, Huntington Creek, and the Fremont River.

Lake Trout

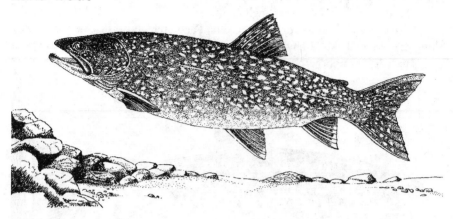

Utah is at the southern end of lake trout distribution in North America. Lake trout require cold, clear, well-oxygenated, and unpolluted water. They are only caught with frequency at Flaming Gorge Reservoir and Fish Lake.

These are the biggest trout in Utah. Fishing for lake trout is more costly than for other trout because of the special techniques and equipment required. In the summer, they often move as deep as 120 feet. However, they move into the shallows to spawn in the fall and will often invade the shallows to feed in the spring, when the water is still cool.

The lake trout's diet consists almost entirely of small fish. Lake trout populations in Flaming Gorge and Fish Lake have decimated populations of Utah chubs—their primary food source. At the Gorge, big lakers have taken to feeding on kokanee salmon. At Fish Lake, they eat planted rainbows.

Trolling deep with large flatfish or minnow-imitating lures will often produce lake trout. Vertically jigging with spoons and plastic jigs also works. A fish finder is a big help in locating the deep-ranging fish.

Cutthroat Trout

If you have seen the fish on some Utah license plates, you have seen a cutthroat trout. The cutthroat is the only trout native to the state and is the official state fish. It is the second-most common fish stocked in Utah, with about 3 million planted each summer.

State officials are taking different approaches to cutthroat stocking. For example, Bear Lake cutthroat are being planted at lakes and reservoirs around the state to help control rough fish populations, so rainbows can sustain themselves. Yellowstone cutthroat were used for a long time by state officials to create game fish opportunities, but the DWR has phased them out in favor of two trout native to Utah: Colorado cutthroat and Bonneville cutthroat. Biologists have taken eggs and milt from remnant Bonneville and Colorado cutthroat and are planting the fish in streams and rivers in their historic ranges. Strawberry Reservoir and Bear Lake are two popular Bonneville cutthroat fisheries.

Cutthroat are typically quite a bit longer than they are deep. The have light spotting and a red or orangish slash on the throat. They feed on aquatic and terrestrial insects and fish. Fishing for the predators is effective with a variety of methods. They will take some baits, but artificial lures and flies are much more dependable. Lures, flies, and jigs that resemble minnows are the most efficient. Cutthroat in lakes tend to stay away from shorelines, except in late fall and just as the ice is coming off in the spring. These are excellent times to fish for them from the shore. Leech patterns, minnow-imitating lures, and tube jigs can all work at these times.

Summer fishing for cutthroat consists of trolling Rapalas, flatfish, large needlefish, and Triple Teazers down to 50 feet. Pop gear with a worm attached also works. Ice fishing in winter is also possible: try jigs, spoons, and lures tipped with sucker meat between 15 and 20 feet below the surface.

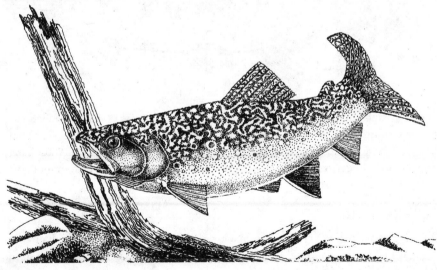

Brook Trout

This species inhabits high-elevation cold-water streams, beaver ponds, and lakes. These feisty and pretty little trout are distinguished by a gray to olive green base color with wormlike markings on their back and dorsal fin. Brookies' sides have light blue halos around pink or red spots. Their lower fins and lower tail have a white edge.

The brook trout is native to northeastern North America and ranges from Georgia to the Arctic Circle. It has been introduced to the remainder of the United States, Canada, South America, and Europe. Brook trout were introduced to Utah in 1875 near Salt Lake City. They have dispersed across the state and have had great success spawning in high mountain streams. They spawn in the fall, like browns, displaying dramatically brilliant colors.

Brookies feed on aquatic and terrestrial insects. Larger brookies will eat small fish if available, and in many lakes and streams they seem to have competitive advantages over other fish. They also have a tendency to overpopulate, especially in productive lake environments.

Brookies are easy to catch, especially in the early spring or late fall when cold water keeps them very active. They are caught on flies, small spinning lures, jigs, and worms. Fishing is good for brook trout in the high mountain lakes and streams of the Uinta and Boulder Mountains.

Golden Trout

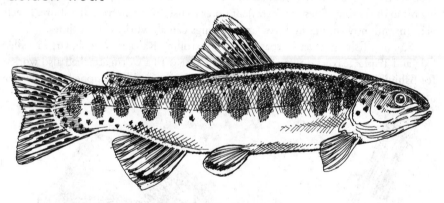

This rare and unique trout is limited to high-elevation lakes and streams and is native to northern California. It was once planted in the Uinta Mountains of Utah, but goldens are hard to obtain and the last stocking was in the mid-1980s. There may be some lingering fish, but it is highly unlikely since golden trout do not compete well with other trout.

Splake Trout

This aggressive fish is a cross between a brook trout and a lake trout. Biologists are using it to help control rough fish populations, and they have introduced the sterile hybrid in fisheries affected with whirling disease. Splake are considered excellent table fare and are a popular fish with many anglers.

Because they feed largely on fish, trolling or casting minnow-imitating lures works well for splake. They are sometimes caught by bait anglers fishing with night crawlers, dead minnows, or Power Bait from shore.

Ice fishing is one of the best ways to catch a splake. Fish Lake and Joe's Valley Reservoir both offer excellent ice-fishing opportunities for splake. Try jigging medium to large spoons and ice flies tipped with a wax worm or sucker meat down to 60 feet.

Tiger Trout

Biologists were not sure what they would get when they crossed a brown trout and a brook trout, but anglers sure like the unique-looking result. Since their first planting in Utah, anglers have asked for more tiger trout across the state.

Actually, anglers have been bringing in naturally produced tiger trout to the DWR for several years, trying to find out what they were. Browns and brookies in the upper reaches of the Blacksmith Fork had produced natural hybrid offspring, a rare occurrence. Only a small percentage of the artificially produced hybrids make it to plantable size, but anglers love them. The aptly named trout bears wormlike patterns over most of its body, and it is an aggressive fish.

Huntington Reservoir, Scofield Reservoir, Joe's Valley Reservoir, Mill Hollow, and Palisade Reservoir are good places to fish for tiger trout. They have also been introduced in some lakes of the Uinta Mountains. They will hit small, flashy spoons, dark-colored wet flies, and bright-colored streamer patterns.

Kokanee Salmon

This is a landlocked subspecies of sea-running sockeye salmon. They have a dark blue back with silvery sides and very few spots. Kokanee salmon look similar to trout until they mature and prepare for the spawn, typically in their third or fourth fall, at which time both male and female kokanee begin to turn a brilliant red. The lower jaw of the male becomes hooked, and a pronounced hump forms on its back.

The fish swim up the tributaries they hatched in or were planted in to spawn and then die. People gather along the tributaries of Strawberry Reservoir and Flaming Gorge Reservoir to watch the kokanee spawn from late September through October. Flaming Gorge also has a unique population of of shore-spawning kokanee. These fish produce more than 90 percent of the kokanee in the massive reservoir.

Kokanee eat zooplankton and travel in large schools. It is rare for a shore angler to catch a kokanee. They are best pursued from a boat because they are usually found in open water. Trolling with downriggers or leaded line is the best way to reach them. Fish at 40 to 60 feet with bright-colored lures. A popular method is to use a dodger trailing a needlefish, a Triple Teazer, or spinners. Troll at faster speeds for kokanee than you would for trout, and try to vary the action by zigzagging occasionally.

Grayling

This colorful member of the salmon family is found in a dozen or so high-elevation lakes. They are distinguished by a large dorsal fin sporting a kaleidoscope of colors. The body has scattered black spots on a silver-gray base, sometimes with pink hues.

The most productive Arctic grayling fishing in the United States today is in Alaska. There are some small populations in Montana, Wyoming, and Utah. Grayling are easy to catch, as they will hit just about anything they see. Fishing for them in Utah can be fast with dry or wet flies and small spinners.

Grayling do not compete well with other fish and are often the only fish in a lake. They also have a tendency to overpopulate, which means the fish you catch may be on the small side.

Mountain Whitefish

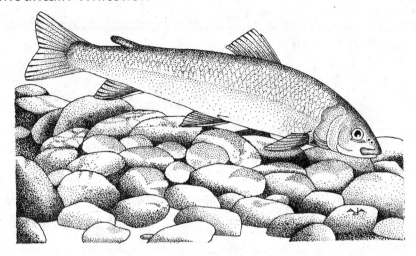

Angler attitudes on mountain whitefish vary. Some enjoy catching and eating them. Others treat the native species as a trash fish and smirk in disgust when they realize they've hooked one.

Mountain whitefish are tannish-white with a hint of silver. Not often caught in the summer, they provide good fishing in the winter when angling for trout can be slow. Healthy populations of mountain whitefish exist in the Logan, Weber, Duchesne, Provo, and Blacksmith Fork Rivers.

Bonneville Whitefish

Few anglers catch Bonneville whitefish. They are native to and restricted to Bear Lake in northern Utah and southern Idaho. Bonneville whitefish provide forage for large cutthroat and lake trout in Bear Lake.

Part of the reason anglers rarely catch Bonneville and mountain whitefish is because they have a small mouth that features an upper jaw that is longer than the lower. Some anglers catch them at Bear Lake while bouncing small red and white spoons on the bottom in deep water. They are also caught by ice anglers who use small jigs or ice flies tipped with a wax worm. Fishing for Bonneville whitefish can also be productive in the fall when they are spawning.

Bonneville Cisco

These fish provide a rare form of angling for Utahns. For two weeks each year, hundreds of thousands of Bonneville cisco head to the shallows of Bear Lake to spawn in water ranging from 40 feet to several inches. Fishermen use dip nets to scoop spawners out of the lake along rocky shorelines and jig for them with spoons on submerged rock reefs.

The popularity of dip netting waned toward the end of the 1990s, but some die-hard Bear Lake anglers still enjoy catching the cisco. The cisco are eaten and also used as bait throughout the rest of the year.

Bonneville cisco are the most numerous fish in Bear Lake and are an important food source for the cutthroat and lake trout there.

Largemouth Bass

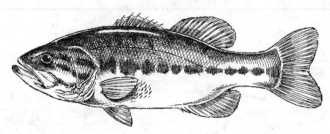

Few angling experiences compare to the sight of a big largemouth doing a tail dance on the surface trying to rid itself of a hook. For that reason, largemouth bass are arguably the most popular warm-water game fish in North America.

The fish earned its name from sporting a very large mouth, with the upper jaw of adults extending beyond the rear margin of its eyes. Largemouth are dark olive or green on the back, with light-colored sides shading down to a white belly. There is a dark horizontal band on each side of the fish.

Bass are carnivorous, eating anything that moves. At about 2 inches in length, they become active predators. Adults feed almost exclusively on other fish and large invertebrates such as crayfish. Generally, bass move to deep water or into heavy cover during the day and return to the shallows to feed at night.

Bass spawn from April through July, a good time to fish for them. Largemouth bass prefer to nest in quiet, more vegetated water than other bass. Nests are usually built in 2 to 8 feet of water. In the spring, largemouth can be caught in shallow water with spinnerbaits, spider jigs, and plastic grubs, or worms fished on the bottom in spawning areas.

In the heat of summer, largemouth head for deep water and can be caught off of points or in rock piles down to 30 feet. Fish for them with plastic grubs or tubes, diving crankbaits, and small rubber worms. Translucent lure colors in natural shades are good in the clear water of the West. A few largemouth will stay shallow year-round. They concentrate around submerged trees, aquatic vegetation, and ledges. Throw spinnerbaits, jerkbaits, and topwater lures to fish holding in shallow water.

Because of the strong interest in largemouth bass fishing, numerous clubs have formed to support the sport. Joining one may help you learn how to fish for these popular bass even more efficiently. It will at least give you a place to share your stories.

Lake Powell, Quail Creek Reservoir, Sand Hollow Reservoir, and Hyrum Reservoir have good populations of largemouth bass.

Smallmouth Bass

Smallmouth bass are one of the most sought-after game fish in North America. The fight they put forth when hooked is equaled by few other sport fish. Utah has a growing population of smallmouth, and more anglers are realizing the value of these fish with red eyes.

Deer Creek, Jordanelle, and Flaming Gorge Reservoirs and Lake Powell all hold large numbers of smallmouth. Generally dark green or brown with dark vertical bands, smallmouth body color depends largely on habitat and the depth the fish are caught from.

Smallmouth bass are aggressive and feed predominately on crayfish, fish, and insects. Lures that imitate crayfish or minnows are effective. Crankbaits, spinners, plastic baits, and topwater lures are consistent producers. Fly fishers do well for smallies stripping in leech or streamer patterns from shore or in float tubes. Smallmouth typically begin active feeding when water temperatures go above 50 degrees.

Smallmouth spawn from late April through July. During this period, mature fish move to shallow flats with gravel or weeds. The fish will aggressively strike most lures and can easily be reached by anglers from shore in most cases.

As the water warms, most smallmouth move deeper and are best caught by jigging slowly on the bottom. Smallmouth love to chase lures and will often come from 20 feet to hit topwater lures and other lures fished with a fast retrieve.

Striped Bass

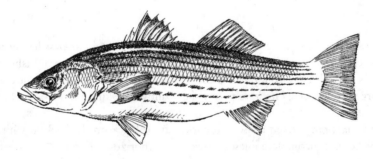

Striped bass are the largest in the bass family. They are actually a sea bass that live off the coast and move inland to spawn. Populations have been created in many freshwater environments, including Lake Powell.

Stripers are silver in color with seven or eight uninterrupted horizontal stripes on their sides. They were planted in Lake Powell in 1974 and were not expected to be able to reproduce, but they did and soon they had reduced the shad population, the primary forage fish in Lake Powell, to dangerously low levels. There is a vicious cycle between the shad and stripers that prevents the bass from reaching optimum sizes, while the shad population struggles to rebound enough to avoid crashing again.

Officials have removed the limit on stripers at Lake Powell, hoping anglers will help control their burgeoning population. If their numbers can be controlled, it is possible the striper state record of 48 pounds, 11 ounces could be broken.

Stripers provide an exciting fishing experience known as a boil. Schools of stripers chase groups of shad to the surface, causing the small fish to explode out of the water.

The violent feeding frenzy provides an excellent opportunity to catch the striped bass. Most any lure thrown next to the chaos will be inhaled shortly after hitting the water.

The most common ways to fish for stripers include casting or trolling shad-imitating lures and jigging spoons and jigs along vertical walls. It is also possible to catch stripers on a hook baited with anchovy.

White Bass

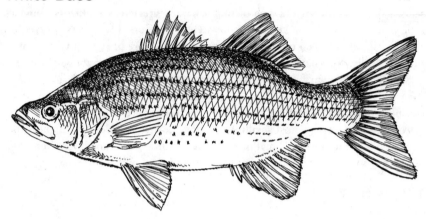

In 1956 189 white bass were planted in Utah Lake. By 1978 white bass had become the most common game fish in the large, shallow lake west of Provo. Fishing for white bass at Utah Lake is popular in the winter through the ice, and in the spring, when large groups of white bass patrol the shallows looking for schools of small fish.

White bass range from a silver to dark gray or black on the back to white on the belly. Several incomplete lines, or stripes, run horizontally on each side of the body. They are spring spawners and may grow up to 10 inches in their first year.

Effective carnivores, white bass schools will chase smaller fish to shore, trap them, and then feed on them. Anglers can take advantage of the situation by casting minnow-imitating lures from shore. Once a school has been located, successful anglers often fish the surface with spoons or spinners. White bass are excellent fighters and are considered superb table fare. The fish can be hard to locate because they move in and out of shallow water, but once found, fishing can be fast. Spring and fall are the best times to catch them. Look for them near the boat harbors and inlets at Utah Lake. Summer fishing is poor, as the fish scatter throughout the lake.

Wiper

This hybrid between a white bass and striped bass was planted in Willard Bay Reservoir to provide diversity for anglers and give the reservoir a fish-feeding predator to roam its open water.

The fact that wipers are hybrids and sterile allows biologists to control their population. If the shad population starts to suffer, wiper stocking can be discontinued at any time. But if white bass had been introduced, there easily could have been a population explosion, creating all kinds of other problems.

Like stripers, wipers create boils when they chase schools of fish to the surface. They are typically caught with small spoons, crankbaits, and jigs in shad-imitating colors.

Walleye

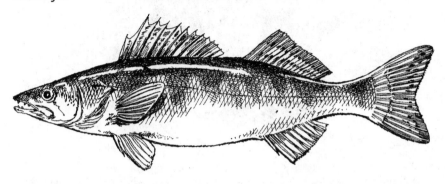

Few freshwater fish are more difficult to catch on a regular basis than the walleye. Most anglers don't want to spend the time or effort to catch the tasty fish with big eyes. Walleye are not spectacular fighters, but they are considered a prize when landed.

Walleye were introduced to Utah in 1951 and have become somewhat of a staple fish for anglers. They are hard to catch because they are primarily active at night and they tend to live on or near the bottom in open water. They are most identifiable by their large, bulging eyes, which glow in bright light, and yellow-to-greenish body mottled with dark blotches.

They are obvious carnivores, with teeth in the jaws and on the roof of the mouth. Walleye are fast growers and may attain lengths of 10 inches or more during their first year. Although young fish may consume crustaceans and various insects and their larvae, adults primarily feed on other fish.

Voracious predators, walleye are most easily caught in the spring. In fact, they are so vulnerable that most tributaries to Utah waters where they are found are closed to fishing during the spawn.

Fishing for walleye is best in the spring and fall. Troll with bottom bouncers trailing a harness-tipped spinner and worm. Plastics grubs (3 to 5 inches) tipped with a night crawler and deep-diving crankbaits will also produce fish. When active, walleye can be found on windy points, weed lines, and break lines.

Fall traditionally produces larger fish. Casting or trolling minnow-imitating crankbaits at night is especially effective at this time.

Deer Creek, Starvation, and Yuba Reservoirs, as well as Willard Bay, Lake Powell, and Utah Lake, are good places to fish for walleye. There is a statewide limit of 10 walleye, except at Willard Bay, where the limit is 6. Only 1 of the walleye taken can be longer than 24 inches.

Black Crappie

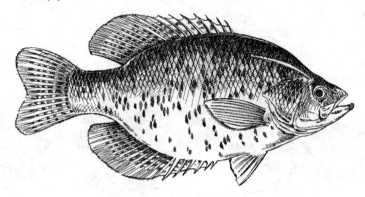

Black crappie are silver-olive with numerous black or dark green splotches on the sides. They have light, iridescent green sides and look somewhat like bass.

Crappie can get large—Utah's state record is over 3 pounds—and fishing for them can be fast. Pineview Reservoir, Quail Lake, Willard Bay, and Lake Powell all support healthy populations of black crappie.

Like other panfish, crappie are most readily caught during the spring spawn when the fish flood the brush. Spinners and jigs tipped with a night crawler are effective. Crappie are usually found in large groups, so fish the same area for a while. After the spawn, the schools leave the shallows in favor of deeper brush edges and will often suspend on ledges and over flooded trees most of the summer

Perch

Perch are likely Utah's most important panfish. Anglers and larger fish find perch meat delicious. Walleye, tiger muskie, and largemouth bass feed heavily on perch where they are available.

Perch are brassy-yellow with dark vertical bars running from the back down. Large schools of perch congregate near vegetation, where they feed on small fish, crawfish, and aquatic insects.

Most fishing for perch is done through the ice in the winter, but fishing in the summer can be productive as well. Jigging ice flies and spoons tipped with a wax worm or perch meat is a good ice-fishing technique. Fishing with small jigs and night crawlers next to or in weed beds is effective in the summer.

Fish Lake and Pineview, Hyrum, Rockport, Deer Creek, Newton, Yuba, and Jordanelle Reservoirs are excellent places to fish for perch.

Bluegill

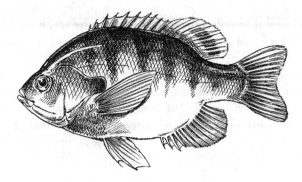

Many an angler learned the sport by catching bluegill. They are a popular panfish in Utah. Bluegill are often caught with frequency, and pound for pound, they put up as much fight as any game fish.

Bluegill may be distinguished from other panfish by the dark spot at the base of the dorsal fin and their relatively small mouth. The back and upper sides of bluegill are usually dark olive green blending to lavender, brown, copper, or orange on the sides and reddish-orange or yellow on the belly.

Pelican Lake near Vernal is known for producing big bluegill. Red Fleet, Hyrum, and Newton Reservoirs, as well as Lake Powell, all have healthy bluegill populations.

Fishing for bluegill is usually best during the spring spawn. They create nests on flats with weeds. It is not uncommon for 50 or more beds to be located in the same area. Fly fishing with surface poppers and small wet flies is a common spring-time method.

Bluegill are often caught with small spinners, plastic/feather jigs, and night crawlers on light spinning tackle. When the spawn winds down, the fish leave the shallows and head for deeper water.

Green Sunfish

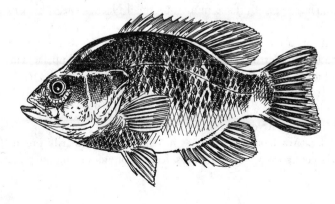

This small, aggressive member of the sunfish family is often viewed as a problem fish, largely because it has the potential for out-competing larger, more desirable sport fish. The green sunfish has the body shape of a bass, is dark green on top, and fades to a lighter green on the sides. Some scales and fins have turquoise highlights.

Green sunfish rarely grow beyond 10 inches; the state record is less than a pound. They are a versatile species that can tolerate a wide range of environmental conditions. Due to their propensity to overpopulate, green sunfish populations often become stunted, so they rarely reach a desirable size for angling.

They are found in numerous waters but are most common at Lake Powell. These fish are voracious feeders and are often hooked on lures the length of their body.

Channel Catfish

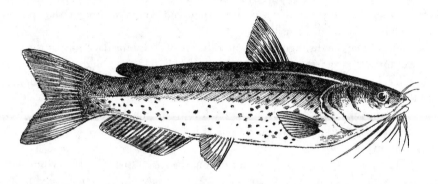

Channel catfish bottom feed in more lakes, reservoirs, and rivers than many Utahns realize. They are not the most sought-after game fish, but they do have a passionate following. Channel cats can get big—20-pounders are not uncommon in some of the more productive catfish waters. They're good to eat, and in the South, they're considered a delicacy.

Channel cats are olive brown to slate blue on the back and sides with a silvery white belly. They typically have numerous small black spots, which may fade as they get older.

Channel cats are native to North America east of the Rockies, from southern Canada south into northeastern Mexico, and east of the Appalachians with the exception of much of the coastal plain north of Florida. The species has been widely introduced in other areas and as far west as California. It first appeared in Utah in 1888, and it has become a mainstay in Utah Lake, the Bear River, Willard Bay, the Green and Colorado Rivers, and Lake Powell.

Channel catfish less than 4 inches in length feed primarily on small insects. Adults are largely scavenging omnivores, feeding on insects, mollusks, crustaceans, fish, and even some plant matter. Feeding at night is typical of large channel cats, which feed almost exclusively on other fish.

Fishing with bait on the bottom, or just off the bottom, is an effective method. Try shrimp, night crawlers, frozen minnows, and carp meat.

Bullhead Catfish

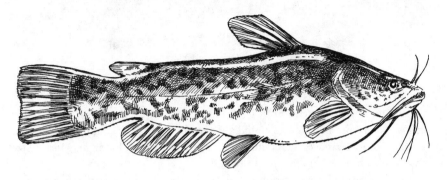

If most Utah anglers largely ignore channel catfish, even more of them don't even know about bullhead catfish. This catfish tends to remain small and doesn't have the range of channel cats. Bullheads are typically black to greenish-black on the back and range to gray or white on the belly. In muddy water, a bullhead's back may be yellowish-brown.

The species is omnivorous, feeding primarily from the bottom on a wide range of plant and animal material. Fingerlings feed almost exclusively on crustaceans. Immature aquatic insects and crustaceans often comprise a considerable proportion of the adult diet.

A variety of baits may be used to catch bullheads, but worms are usually best. Utah Lake is the best place to fish for them.

Northern Pike

This popular sport fish is known for its size and fighting ability. Pike are long and slender and have duckbill snouts. Their mouth is loaded with sharp teeth, and the lower jaw typically extends slightly beyond the upper jaw.

Pike are a solitary fish and highly effective predators. By the time a pike has reached 2 inches, it is looking for fish to feed on. Adults are opportunistic carnivores and will eat anything they can catch and swallow. Their primary diet source is fish, but they will eat frogs, crayfish, mice, and ducklings. Because they are so aggressive, pike will take large lures. Cast or troll large Rapalas and spoons to get their attention; steel leader is highly recommended.

Redmond Reservoir is the best place to catch a pike, but you'll also find them in Yuba Reservoir, Lake Powell, and the Green and Colorado Rivers.

Tiger Muskie

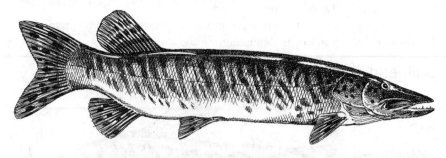

Few fish have sparked attention in Utah like the tiger muskie. The fish thrived at Pineview Reservoir, and anglers found that catching them was not as difficult as their fish-of-a-thousand-casts reputation led them to believe. Ice anglers fishing for perch even catch them on lightweight rods.

Word spread and many trout anglers converted to this warm-water species. Officials planted the sterile hybrid between a northern pike and muskellunge to help control burgeoning panfish populations in Pineview Reservoir and also to provide a unique species for Utah anglers.

Like northerns, muskies eat whatever they can find, including frogs, crayfish, and ducklings. Muskies prefer large food items. Successful anglers use spoons, spinners, Rapalas, and spinnerbaits up to 12 inches long. When hooked, tiger muskie often leap and make long runs. They frequently break the line or straighten hooks. As with northern pike, a steel leader is recommended.

Central Utah

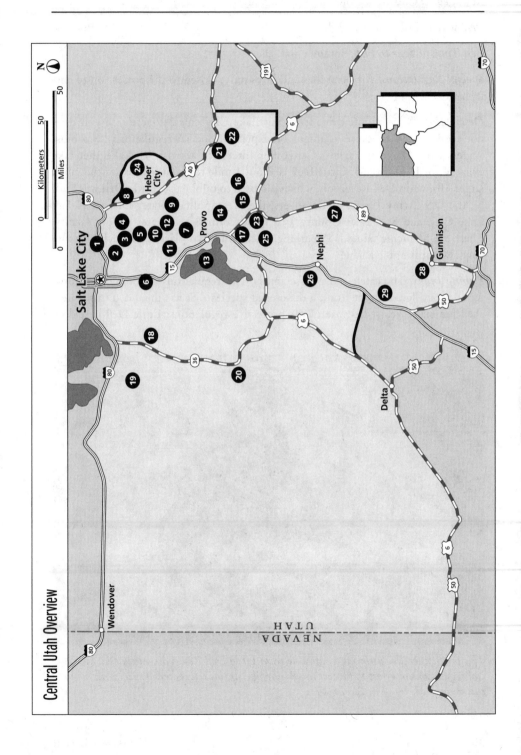

1 Little Dell Reservoir

Key Species: Cutthroat trout and brook trout.

Best Way to Fish: Lures and flies.

Best Time of Year to Fish: Summer and fall.

Special Regulations: Artificial flies and lures only; closed to the possession of cutthroat trout.

Description: A 15-minute drive from Salt Lake City, this 249-acre reservoir does not see as much pressure as might be expected. Special regulations keep most anglers away. Drive up Parley's Canyon on Interstate 80 from Salt Lake, then take exit 134 for Highway 65. Little Dell is about 1 mile to the northeast of the much larger Mountain Dell Reservoir, which is closed to public use. Little Dell was built by the U.S. Army Corps of Engineers, the Metropolitan Water District of Salt Lake City, and Salt Lake County as a flood control and water supply facility. There are 56 picnic tables, 135 parking spaces, and two places to launch boats by hand. Water is not available.

Fishing Index: The catch-and-release and no-bait regulations are designed to protect Bonneville cutthroat trout, a threatened species that has inhabited this watershed for many years. Because of the protective regulations, Little Dell is seldom

This fat Bonneville cutthroat trout came from Little Dell Reservoir. Little Dell has special regulations in effect to protect the Bonneville strain, a threatened species native to this watershed. Photo by Larry Mathis

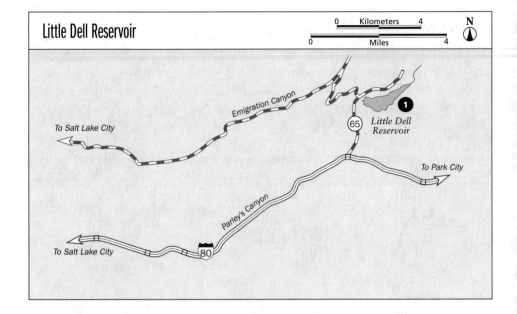

stocked with fish and angling can be spotty. The best fishing is where the creek enters the lake. Three-pound cutthroat are not uncommon in the spring. In the early fall, anglers find aggressive brook trout preparing for the spawn. Copper, gold, black, and orange spoons and spinners work well. Fly anglers do well with bright-colored streamers or dark-colored leech patterns.

2 Mill Creek

Key Species: Rainbow trout, cutthroat trout, and brown trout.

Best Way to Fish: Bait.

Best Time of Year to Fish: Summer and fall.

Special Regulations: None.

Description: Its proximity to Salt Lake makes Mill Creek popular among recreationists along the Wasatch Front. However, anglers make up a small percentage of the canyon's users. The canyon has 12 picnic areas, which make for good places to take the family for an after-work or weekend adventure. A fee is required to enter the canyon.

Fishing Index: The Division of Wildlife Resources (DWR) plants a fair number of rainbow trout in the most heavily used areas. There are also a healthy number of wild cutthroat and some brown trout in the creek. Heavy use keeps bank growth down around the picnic areas, making them a good place to try fly fishing. Dry flies are effective in the summer when the water is clear. Bait is always a good choice.

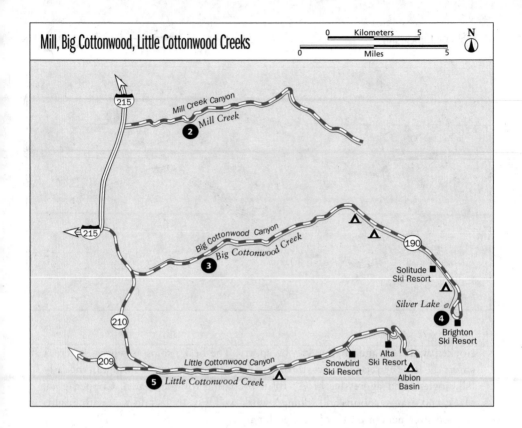

Kilometers

Miles

N

215

Mill Creek Canyon

Mill Creek

2

215

Big Cottonwood Canyon

Big Cottonwood Creek

3

190

Solitude
Ski Resort

Silver Lake

210

4

Brighton
Ski Resort

209

Little Cottonwood Canyon

Little Cottonwood Creek

5

Snowbird
Ski Resort

Alta
Ski Resort

Albion
Basin

3 Big Cottonwood Creek

See map above.

Key Species: Rainbow trout, brown trout, and brook trout.

Best Way to Fish: Bait, spinners, and flies.

Best Time of Year to Fish: Summer and fall.

Special Regulations: None.

Description: Most people only pay attention to Big Cottonwood Creek as they head to Solitude and Brighton ski resorts, or if they're on a hike in this heavily used Wasatch Front canyon. The creek runs along most of Highway 190. There are five picnic areas and three campgrounds in the canyon. The creek starts at Silver Lake near the top of the canyon.

Fishing Index: Due to large populations of brown and brook trout, the DWR has reduced the number of fish planted in Big Cottonwood Creek. The creek is on the verge of obtaining wild fish status, and one day may not be planted at all. Most anglers fish with salmon eggs and night crawlers, but a growing number of fly fishers are taking advantage of the wild browns and brookies. Shortly after runoff has diminished, the fish key in on stonefly hatches. Try trudes and stimulators at this time. As the water levels off, look for hatches of mayfly and caddis. Parachute Adams, elk hair caddis, royal humpy, renegade, stimulator, and terrestrial patterns will work through the summer. Pheasant tail and prince bead-head nymphs are good wet fly choices. Some big browns inhabit the deeper pools; try Rapalas, spinners, and streamers to catch them.

4 Silver Lake

See map on page 32.

Key Species: Rainbow trout.

Best Way to Fish: Bait and flies from shore.

Best Time of Year to Fish: Summer.

Special Regulations: None.

Description: At the top of Big Cottonwood Canyon east of Salt Lake City near the Brighton ski resort, Silver Lake has slowly developed into one of the premier urban fishing spots for Salt Lake Valley residents. The addition of a boardwalk to protect marsh and riparian habitat has made this a place for anglers in wheelchairs or parents of young children who want to take them for a nice walk and do some fishing in the process. This is a scenic high-elevation setting surrounded by pine trees and mountain peaks. For a simple family fishing outing, few places near Salt Lake City offer these kinds of amenities. There is also a nearby public campground. The Forest Service, which manages the area, has added some interpretive signs explaining the flora and fauna. There is even a small visitor center where the trail starts.

Fishing Index: Due to the heavy use this little alpine lake receives, it is stocked with catchable rainbow trout on an almost weekly basis during the summer. Most anglers simply use bait, though it is not uncommon to see a fly fisher wade into the relatively shallow waters or a float tuber trying her luck for rising trout. The good news is that the trout are plentiful and most anglers come away with a a rainbow trout or two fresh from the hatchery for their efforts.

5 Little Cottonwood Creek

See map on page 32.

Key Species: Rainbow trout and cutthroat trout.

Best Way to Fish: Bait.

Best Time of Year to Fish: Summer and fall.

Special Regulations: None.

Description: Like its sister canyon to the north, most people only view Little Cottonwood Creek as pleasant scenery on their way to skiing at Snowbird or Alta ski

Central Utah
33

resorts or on a hike in the Wasatch-Cache National Forest. At times, the creek runs close to Highway 210 in the canyon.

Fishing Index: The DWR stocks 1,000 rainbow in Little Cottonwood Creek above Snowbird each year. There is, however, little carryover from year to year. Officials believe the problem in Little Cottonwood Creek stems from mine tailings that affect the stream's ability to sustain fish. Fishing here is poor and will likely only improve if something is done to improve water quality in the canyon. Bait works for rainbows, and fly fishers have some success with dry flies.

6 Jordan River

Key Species: Channel catfish, white bass, bullhead catfish, walleye, and rainbow trout.

Best Way to Fish: Bait.

Best Time of Year to Fish: Year-round.

Special Regulations: None.

Description: This river flows 37 miles through the Salt Lake Valley from Utah Lake to the Great Salt Lake. It is named after the biblical river that flowed from a fresh-water to saltwater lake. Once one of the more polluted waters in the state, it is slowly turning into an urban gem. Many parts of an urban parkway have been completed, with paths along the entire river. There are places to park, docks for canoes, and parklike amenities along the route.

Fishing Index: Despite the fact very little management is practiced on the river, the Jordan hosts a surprising number of anglers. The river is planted with channel catfish regularly. When spring runoff is not too high, catchable rainbow trout are also planted. Some white bass have wandered down from Utah Lake, and anglers are often surprised with an occasional brown trout or carp. Walleye can also be caught. In fact, one of the fascinations with fishing the Jordan is an angler is liable to catch just about anything on a given day—even an 11-inch piranha caught near 2100 South.

   The best fishing on the Jordan River is found from 9000 South to Utah Lake because the water is cooler and fresher. However, people fish the Jordan all the way into the city. The area where the Jordan comes out of Utah Lake is popular, and so is an area off of Highway 73 between Lehi and Cedar Fort just east of Redwood Road. The addition of paved bicycle trails along much of the Jordan's course makes it an ideal urban fishery for kids, many of whom can be seen carrying fishing rods on their bicycles. Because the river is slow-moving and the banks often overgrown, fishing with bait is still the preferred method. Most anglers use heavy sinkers to keep their bait on the bottom. Catfish prefer baits such as shrimp and chicken, but many are also caught with a night crawler.

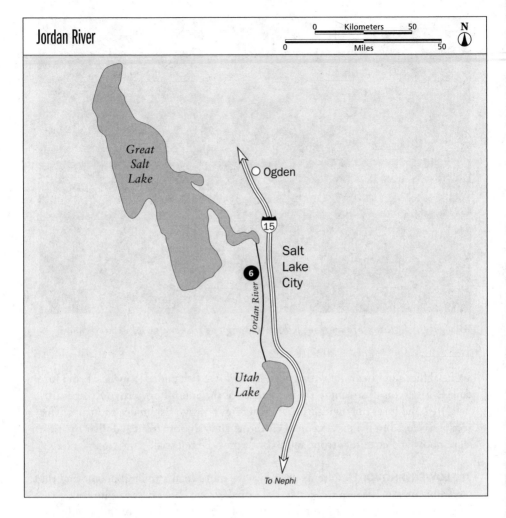

Great
Salt
Lake

○ Ogden

15

Salt
Lake
City

6

Jordan River

Utah
Lake

To Nephi

7 Provo River

Key Species: Brown trout, rainbow trout, cutthroat trout, and whitefish.

Best Way to Fish: Wading.

Best Time of Year to Fish: Year-round.

Special Regulations: East from Center Street Bridge near the entrance to Utah Lake State Park to Interstate 15 is closed to the taking of nongame fish by methods other than angling and is closed March 1 to 6:00 a.m. on May 1. Upstream from the Olmstead Diversion Dam in Provo Canyon to Deer Creek Reservoir—known as the Lower Provo to anglers—artificial flies and lures only with a trout limit of two fish under 15 inches. From the Legacy Bridge of Midway Lane (Highway 113) in Midway upstream to Jordanelle Reservoir—known as the Middle Provo to anglers—

An aged Provo River brown trout fell for this angler's trickery. Photo by Steve Herron

artificial flies and lures only with a trout limit of two fish under 15 inches. From Jordanelle Reservoir upstream to the confluence of the South Fork Provo River is artificial flies and lures only with a brown trout limit of two fish under 15 inches. This section is closed to the possession of cutthroat and rainbow trout and their hybrids; all rainbow and cutthroat trout and hybrids must be released.

7a. LOWER PROVO: Despite its proximity to more than a million people and the incredible pressure it sees as a result, the Lower Provo River deserves its ranking as a blue-ribbon fishery. This is especially true of the 6-mile section of the river below Deer Creek Reservoir Dam. From 1991 to 1995, pressure on the river increased 240 percent in Provo Canyon. This is Utah's most heavily fished river. The best time to avoid crowds is early in the week and, not surprisingly, on Sunday, when a large portion of the state's residents attend church.

Catch-and-release fishing on hardy brown trout over 15 inches is the main reason this section can handle the pressure. The river is easily accessible as it runs along U.S. Highway 189 from Orem to Deer Creek Reservoir. The canyon provides a scenic background as anglers fish holes with colorful names—the Pines, Spring Hole, the Slot, T.V. Hole (also known as Luge Run), the Trestle, and Brown's Cave. There's even one called the Presidential Suite "because it is so good that's where the president would fish if he came," say local guides. The view from the base of Bridal Veil Falls is breathtaking, and it also happens to be a good place to fish. Many anglers use Vivian Park as a meeting place. The river near the highway tunnel is also a productive area. Parking can be a problem, especially in the winter when plows

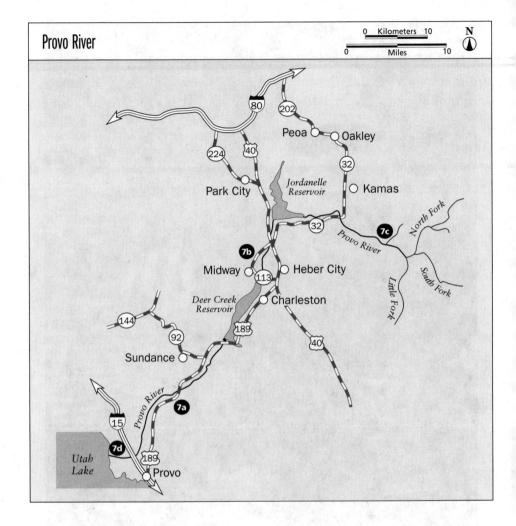

Provo River

use lots as storage areas for snow. There are occasional break-ins, so keep valuables out of sight when leaving your vehicle.

Fishing Index for the Lower Provo: Because of its easy access from the highway, the Lower Provo is one of the only places to fly fish in the winter, and it sees as many anglers in the winter as it does in the middle of summer. Fishing remains constant throughout the year, primarily due to steady flows from the dam.

When the water is low and clear, the fish will feed actively on pheasant tail nymphs, sow bugs, midge larvae, and scuds. Occasional midge and blue-winged olive mayfly hatches occur in the early spring on warm afternoons. The hatches increase as summer nears. The river can get high and murky at times during late spring. During those periods, fishing with a San Juan worm is a good bet. If you happen to be lucky enough to get into one in the spring, a stonefly hatch provides some great fishing. Hoppers can also work, especially on the upper two

Mark Forslund with a robust rainbow caught on the lower Provo River in Provo Canyon.

sections, but the bread and butter of the Lower Provo is fishing subsurface with small nymphs and emergers like sow bug, scud, hare's ear, and pheasant tail patterns. Dry fly die-hards concentrate on pale morning duns and caddis hatches. In the fall, the browns feed more aggressively. Fly fishers do well stripping large streamer patterns.

Lure anglers would do best to try silver spoons in the winter months. Rapalas fished along the edges and through deeper holes will turn up some fish. Night is also a good time to fish the Lower Provo, with large Rapalas and streamer patterns on top. Some huge browns have been caught in the dark.

7b. THE MIDDLE PROVO: The Provo River from Deer Creek Reservoir up to Jordanelle Reservoir was long overlooked by anglers because of private property, low water, and few fish. The Utah Reclamation Mitigation and Conservation Commission began work on the Provo River Restoration Project in 1999. The $30 million project involved removing dikes and reestablishing river access to the historical flood plain, restoring meandering in the river where concrete channels once existed, restoring fish habitat, and ensuring an 800- to 2,200-foot-wide corridor for angler access along the Provo River between Deer Creek and Jordanelle Reservoirs. New parking areas, access points, and restrooms were created.

Fishing Index for the Middle Provo: The culmination of the Provo River Restoration Project and ensured flows from Jordanelle Reservoir have made and will continue to make the Middle Provo one of Utah's best trout rivers. Brown trout dominate the Middle Provo. Favorite lures for those who know the river are sinking Rapalas, heavy spinners, and plastic or feather jigs. White, black, olive, and brown $1/16$- to $1/4$-ounce jigs are effective year-round. Pre-spawn browns are fond of yellow and chartreuse. Nymphing with hare's ear, pheasant tail, prince, midge pupae, and caddis patterns works year-round. Dry fly fishing is best in the summer and early fall with grasshopper, Chernobyl ant, beetle, and stimulator patterns. Many anglers trail bead-head nymphs and emergers behind these large dries. Caddis hatches in the late evenings are consistent, and occasionally there are some green drake hatches. In the spring, usually from the end of April to the first part of June, there are heavy hatches of stoneflies. Streamer fishing is a reliable method in the fall and during summer twilight periods. Bait anglers also now have a chance for the big browns of the Middle Provo due to a regulation change, which allows the use of bait on a 2-mile stretch from the Legacy Bridge in Midway down to Deer Creek Reservoir.

7c. UPPER PROVO: The Provo River from Jordanelle Reservoir upstream to its confluence with the South Fork of the Provo above Woodland, some 10 miles, is artificial fly and lure fishing only, with a limit of two brown trout under 15 inches. The river runs mostly through private property between Jordanelle and Woodland. Because this section is not a tailwater, the flow is inconsistent and susceptible to spring runoff. Good fishing is possible for rainbows and browns during their spawning periods, when they're moving from Jordanelle Reservoir into the river.

Fishing Index for the Upper Provo: Summer and early fall are the best times to fish this section. It offers some quality dry fly fishing. The fish will take a wide variety of flies on the upper section, but they sometimes focus on specific hatches. A good number of stoneflies are present in the spring. Stimulators and trudes will match these hatches. During the summer, when caddis flies and mayflies are hatching, elk hair caddis and parachute Adams are consistent producers; terrestrial patterns will also work. For small fall hatches, try blue-winged olives and Griffith's gnats. In low water, spin anglers need to use smaller lures. Fish carefully, as the trout here spook easily.

Zach and Alex Alexander enjoy a heavy smallmouth bass caught by Alex during a family fishing trip to Jordanelle Reservoir.
Photo by Adrian Alexander

7d. THE PROVO'S BAIT SECTION: The bait section of the Provo runs from the Olmstead Diversion Dam down to Utah Lake, and it also harbors nice fish as it flows through downtown Orem and Provo. It is stocked frequently with catchable rainbows. Night crawlers and salmon eggs work best, but many anglers use flies on this section as well. Walleye migrate from Utah Lake in the spring up the Provo to spawn. Some smallmouth, largemouth, and white bass can also be caught in the Provo from the lake upstream to I-15. Don't forget about the North Fork of the Provo as it flows along the Mirror Lake Highway in the Uintas. It is planted with rainbows and contains brook trout, whitefish, and browns as well. Most anglers use salmon eggs and night crawlers, but fishing with small dries can be a lot of fun and quite effective.

8 Jordanelle Reservoir

Key Species: Rainbow trout, brown trout, cutthroat trout, smallmouth bass, and largemouth bass.

Best Way to Fish: From a boat and from shore.

Best Time of Year to Fish: Year-round.

Special Regulations: Bass limit six, all bass over 12 inches must be released; yellow perch limit 50.

Description: This young reservoir is 6 miles north of Heber City off U.S. Highway 40. Two state-operated facilities provide camping, picnicking, fishing access, and a boat ramp. The Hailstone site is on the west shore of the reservoir and is reached via the Mayflower exit off US 40. Facilities at Hailstone include more than 200 camping areas, modern restrooms, showers, utility hookups, a visitor center, sandy beaches, three group-use pavilions, 41 day-use cabanas, two boat ramps (one ramp for personal watercraft), an 80-slip marina with utility hookups, fuel dispensing, marina store, and a restaurant.

The Rock Cliff site is located on the Provo River 2 miles west of Francis on Highway 32. Facilities include a nature center, boardwalks, 50 walk-in camping sites, group-use area, modern restrooms, showers, and a small boat access ramp.

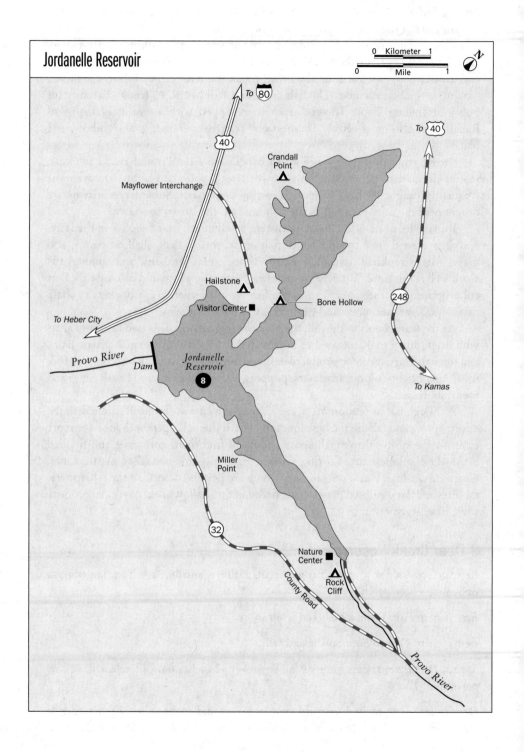

Jordanelle Reservoir

To 80

40

Crandall Point

Mayflower Interchange

Hailstone

Visitor Center

Bone Hollow

To Heber City

Provo River

Dam

Jordanelle Reservoir

8

Miller Point

32

To 40

248

To Kamas

Nature Center

Rock Cliff

County Road

Provo River

0 Kilometer 1
0 Mile 1

N

Fishing Index: Rainbow trout are the main draw at Jordanelle. The Hailstone area is traditionally the best bet for those seeking rainbows from shore. Salmon eggs and Power Bait are the top producers. In the spring and fall, many fly fishers launch float tubes from the Rock Cliff area. They strip leech patterns, bead-heads, and damselfly nymphs around the brush edges and river channel. In the summer, trolling is the best method. The fish are found from 10 to 40 feet and readily hit pop gear trailing Triple Teazers or spinners tipped with a worm. Flatfish and Rapalas can also be effective. The best colors are chartreuse, gold, rainbow, and black.

Brown trout find their way into Jordanelle from the Provo River. Each year, stories circulate of people catching browns over 8 pounds. The browns are most frequently caught by bass fishermen casting crankbaits. Some large browns are caught near the inlet each fall as the fish head up the Provo to spawn.

Jordanelle is one of the most consistent smallmouth bass fisheries in the state. Spring is a good time to find larger fish on sagebrush flats, shallow points, and gravel flats. Crankbaits, weedless plastic tubes/grubs, jerkbaits, and spinnerbaits work well at this time. Watermelon, smoke, chartreuse, white, and black are the best color options. As the water warms, the fish move to small brush pockets to chase minnows. Topwater lures can be effective when this happens.

As the water cools in the fall, the bass congregate on steep shorelines and areas with deep (down to 30 feet) water nearby. Jerkbaits, crankbaits, small plastic baits, and topwater lures become productive. If you are looking to hook bass on a fly rod, try fishing bright-colored streamers, poppers, and wet flies around brush edges and rocky shorelines.

Although not as predominant, the largemouth bass at Jordanelle are worth the effort. Spring and fall are the best times to fish for them. Largemouth look for more cover in the spring than smallmouth. You will find them near trees and flooded brush. Use spinnerbaits, floating worms, jig-n-pig, and weedless plastic tubes. Chartreuse, white, black, purple, and brown are popular colors. In the fall, topwater lures and dark-colored plastic baits fished in the shallows near cover can produce some nice largemouth.

9 Deer Creek Reservoir

Key Species: Rainbow trout, brown trout, walleye, smallmouth bass, largemouth bass, and yellow perch.

Best Way to Fish: From a boat and from shore.

Best Time of Year to Fish: Spring and fall.

Special Regulations: Bass limit six, all bass over 12 inches must be released; yellow perch limit 10.

Description: Due to its location between Provo and Heber City, Deer Creek is more popular with water sports recreationists than with anglers. During the sum-

This chunky smallmouth bass was taken from Deer Creek Reservoir, also home to rainbow and brown trout, walleye, largemouth bass, and yellow perch. Photo by Lance Egan

mer, sailboat, water ski, and personal watercraft use is intense. Deer Creek Dam is situated at the top of Provo Canyon and is fed by the middle portion of the Provo River. The blue-ribbon lower stretch of the river starts at the dam.

U.S. Highway 189 runs along the east side of the reservoir and provides free foot access from large parking areas along the highway. The Historic Heber Railway scenic train ride runs along the west shore. The entire shoreline is publicly owned. Mount Timpanogos provides a scenic backdrop to the 3,260-acre reservoir, which is also used for domestic water storage and agricultural purposes.

Deer Creek State Park facilities include a concrete boat ramp, a 35-unit campground with modern restrooms and showers, two group-use areas, sewage disposal, fish-cleaning stations, and a paved parking area. Deer Creek Island Resort provides a restaurant, boat rentals, a boat launch, gas, a swimming area, and a store.

Fishing Index: Years ago Deer Creek was the place to find big brown trout and catch a bucket of perch. A series of droughts and the predations of illegally planted walleye diminished the perch population, which had been sustaining the browns.

Some browns are still caught by anglers trolling with minnow-imitating crankbaits or by casting jigs during low-light periods and at night. Occasionally, browns are caught by shore anglers using frozen minnows or night crawlers. Each year produces browns weighing more than 10 pounds.

Rainbows are planted at 10 inches to prevent predation by the walleye. Trolling is good at 10 to 30 feet with Rapalas, flatfish, and pop gear trailing spinners or Triple

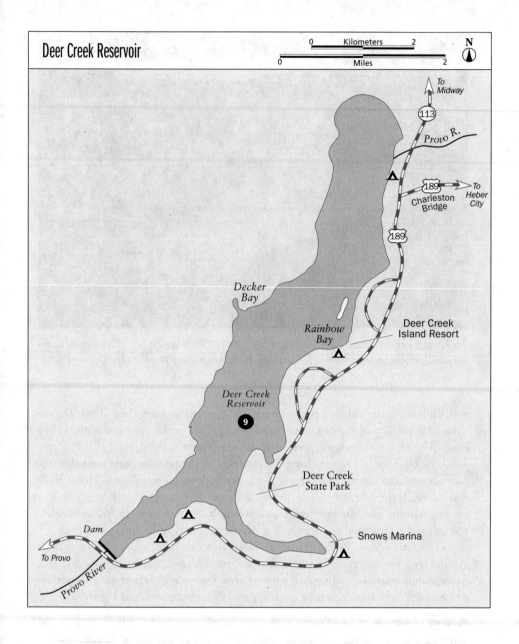

Deer Creek Reservoir

Kilometers 0 — 2
Miles 0 — 2
N

To Midway
113
Provo R.
189
Charleston Bridge
To Heber City
189
Decker Bay
Rainbow Bay
Deer Creek Island Resort
Deer Creek Reservoir
9
Deer Creek State Park
Snows Marina
Dam
To Provo
Provo River

Teazers. Power Bait, salmon eggs, and night crawlers are good choices when fishing from shore. Rainbows are caught through the ice with small spoons and jigs tipped with wax worm, salmon eggs, and Power Bait in 5 to 20 feet of water. Float tubers do well with slow-sinking fly lines near river inlets in the spring and fall. The best trout fly choices are Crystal Killers, woolly buggers, leech patterns, and streamers in black, purple, brown, white, and chartreuse.

After a long absence from the creel, anglers can once again keep perch at the reservoir. These tasty panfish are most often caught through the ice with small spoons and ice flies tipped with wax worm or perch meat. Look for the perch on gradual sloping shoreline in water up to 60 feet. The fish will be on the bottom. In the summer and fall, perch can be found near weeds and flooded brush and are best caught with night crawlers or small jigs.

Late spring and fall are the best times for walleye at Deer Creek. Troll diving crankbaits or bottom bouncers trailing a spinner harness in depths of 10 to 40 feet are effective. Windy points, weed lines, and channels can hold schools of walleye. Once a school is found, jig with bright-colored 3- to 5-inch plastic grubs. Fall traditionally produces larger walleye. Casting or trolling minnow-imitating crankbaits at night is especially effective. Fish in less than 10 feet of water near windy shorelines or points. A typical walleye at Deer Creek is 5 pounds or less, but you have a much better chance of landing a 10-pounder here than at many other walleye destinations in the state.

Fishing for large smallmouth bass is best in the spring and fall, but anglers find fast action throughout the summer. In the spring, look for shallow flats with grave or weed cover. Spinnerbaits and crankbaits in crayfish and bright colors work well. Spider jigs and other plastic baits in crayfish—smoke, black, and chartreuse—also make effective baits.

Largemouth bass tend to hold near weeds or flooded brush. In the summer, look for windy points, ledges, and weed lines. Topwater lures in low-light conditions can be fun. Use crankbaits and other plastic baits at other times. Once fall arrives, the fish move toward steep banks. Plastic jigs fished down to 30 feet should turn up some.

10 Silver Lake Flat Reservoir

See map on page 46.

Key Species: Rainbow trout.

Best Way to Fish: Bait and lures from shore.

Best Time of Year to Fish: Summer.

Special Regulations: Fishing from a boat with a motor is prohibited.

Description: This is a scenic little lake on a steep dirt road that winds up switchbacks above the more developed Tibble Fork Reservoir and Granite Flats Campground, at the end of the North Fork of American Fork Canyon Road. Located at the base of the Lone Peak Wilderness Area, Silver Lake Flat is not as crowded as the more developed Tibble Fork.

Fishing Index: This is mostly a put-and-take fishery. Anglers catch stocked rainbows, mostly fishing from shore with bait, but sometimes casting a spinner can be more productive. Few folks bother with rafts or float tubes. Shore access is good.

11 American Fork Creek

Key Species: Rainbow trout, brown trout, cutthroat trout, brook trout, and walleye.

Best Way to Fish: Bait, flies, and spinners.

Best Time of Year to Fish: Summer and fall.

Special Regulations: East from Utah Lake to Interstate 15 is closed March 1 to 6:00 a.m. May 1.

Description: The creek runs above and below Tibble Fork Reservoir in American Fork Canyon. Just 45 minutes from the Salt Lake Valley and closer to Provo, this creek is a popular destination for anglers looking to squeeze in a couple of hours of fishing. American Fork Creek is also a great place to introduce children to stream fishing. However, caution is required during early spring when high water makes the stream dangerous.

The best access is along the narrow Highway 92, which runs up the canyon, and at the campground on the opposite side of the creek. The stream is also fished along Highway 144 toward Tibble Fork Reservoir; the stream above the reservoir is accessed via Forest Road 085, a dirt road. Campgrounds and picnic areas are located along the river and near the reservoir. Open camping is allowed above the reservoir. A user fee is required to enter the canyon. Timpanogos Cave National Monument is also found in American Fork Canyon.

Fishing Index: Because of heavy pressure, the Division of Wildlife Resources (DWR) frequently plants the river with rainbows, but not until after the spring runoff. A self-sustaining population of brown trout is also present. Bait is the best

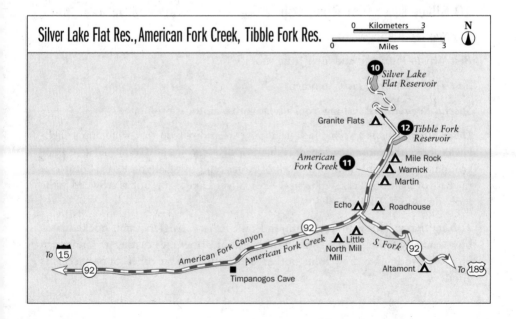

choice on the river below Tibble Fork Dam. Salmon eggs and night crawlers are especially effective. Small Rapalas and spinners fished through the deeper holes can also work for brown trout. Officials are cutting back on the frequency of rainbow plantings above the reservoir in hopes that a cutthroat population will naturally sustain itself. Some brook trout are found in the upper reaches of the creek. Fly fishing is an option, but thick brush on the banks makes casting difficult. In open areas, attractor and terrestrial patterns are good choices. Some walleye enter American Fork Creek from Utah Lake for spawning, thus the special regulations mentioned before, but few anglers fish for them on this creek.

12 Tibble Fork Reservoir *See map on page 46.*

Key Species: Rainbow trout and brown trout.

Best Way to Fish: Bait from shore.

Best Time of Year to Fish: Spring, summer, and fall.

Special Regulations: Fishing from a boat with a motor of any kind is prohibited.

Description: Tibble Fork is a small reservoir offering great views of both Lone Peak and Mount Timpanogos. It is located near Timpanogos Cave National Monument in the Uinta National Forest. The Granite Flats Forest Service campground is located nearby and features a number of group areas. A ramp offers access to about 20 percent of the shoreline. Nearby restrooms are wheelchair accessible. Small boats such as rafts and canoes are common. The setting is spectacular, and the turquoise blue waters make this a wonderful summer picnic area.

Fishing Index: As might be expected, most anglers are satisfied with using bait, spinners, or flies to catch the large quota of catchable rainbow trout stocked throughout the summer in this popular water. But there can be surprises. There are stories of 5- to 10-pound browns being caught at this little fishery. Heavy vegetation around the shoreline can give some shore anglers problems.

13 Utah Lake

Key Species: Walleye, white bass, channel catfish, bullhead catfish, largemouth bass, crappie, bluegill, and yellow perch.

Best Way to Fish: From a boat or from shore.

Best Time of Year to Fish: Spring and fall.

Special Regulations: Largemouth and smallmouth bass limit six, but all largemouth and smallmouth bass over 12 inches must be released.

Description: While most visit this 96,600-acre lake for boating, there is a great diversity of fishing here. Because it is quite shallow and at a low elevation, Utah Lake

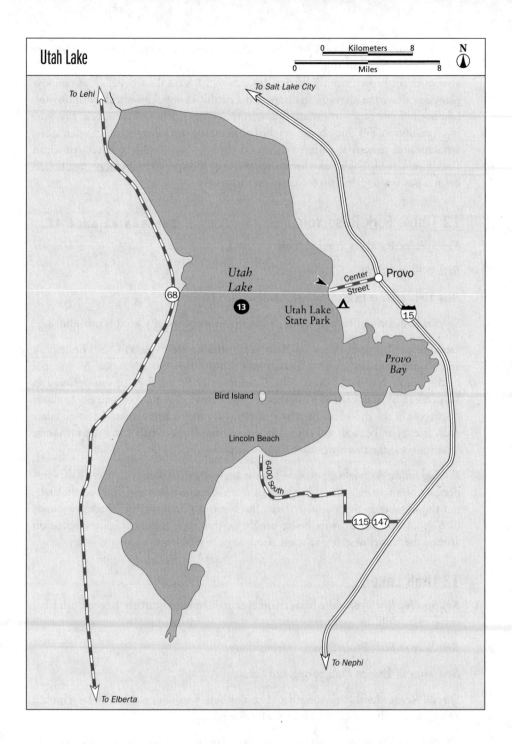

warms early in the year and provides the first opportunity of open-water spring fishing. The lake is serviced by Utah Lake State Park. To get there, take the Center Street exit 268 from Interstate 15 and head west. The road ends at the state park. Facilities include four boat ramps, a sheltered 30-acre marina, 78 seasonal/transient boat slips, restrooms, showers, 73 campsites, a fishing area for the disabled, and sewage disposal.

The American Fork Boat Harbor, a private boat ramp, provides good access on the north portion of the lake. Take I–15 exit 279 then head south to 6800 North and west to 6000 West and then south to the boat ramp.

Lindon Boat Harbor, on the northeast side of the lake, has two boat ramps, picnic tables, water, and a portable toilet. To reach Lindon, take I–15 exit 276 (Lindon, North Orem) west to Geneva Road. Turn right and go under the freeway to railroad tracks at 200 South. Turn left and go to the end, then turn left at 2000 West. The road makes a sharp turn to the right and will take you straight to the harbor.

One of the most popular places to fish from shore is known as Lincoln Beach, on the south side of the lake. To reach the beach, take exit 256 on I–15 and head west to Highway 115, then head north on Highway 147, then west on 6400 South. Lincoln Beach is on the north point of West Mountain. Anglers with boats usually head for Bird Island about 2 miles directly north of Lincoln Beach. The island is a good place to start for walleye, white bass, and catfish.

The state announced a warning for the level of PCBs in carp at Utah Lake in the spring of 2006. Expect the other species, ones people are a lot more fond of eating, to make the consumption advisory in the future. It's not that the fish are suddenly becoming toxic, only that they haven't been tested.

Fishing Index: The most commonly caught fish at Utah Lake is white bass. There is a large population of these aggressively feeding fish. The best times to fish for them are in the spring when they are spawning and in the fall when they gather in large schools. Anglers do well from shore at these times with spinners, small Rapalas, 2- to 4-inch plastic or feather jigs, and cut bait or night crawlers. Chartreuse, white, yellow, red, and perch are the best color choices. Fish near stream inlets and rock structures, such as the harbors and Lincoln Beach. The white bass at Utah Lake commonly reach 15 inches.

Another great time to fish for white bass is as soon as the lake freezes. Fishing is best in the boat harbors. The fish are schooled, so fishing can be fast, once you've caught one. Morning and evening are the best times. Spoons like Heddon Sonar, Swedish Pimple, and Kastmasters in silver, chartreuse, white, and glow-in-the-dark are solid choices. Jigging aggressively is a must for getting the school's attention. Ice flies tipped with bait will help on slow days.

In the summer, fish scatter throughout the lake and are hard to locate. Most white bass are caught in the summer by anglers going after catfish with bait.

Channel and bullhead catfish anglers spend many hours seeking big fish off Lincoln Beach, the Lindon Boat Harbor, and near the Spanish Fork river inlet. Fish up to 30 pounds are caught with night crawlers, cut bait, frozen minnows, and stink bait fished on the bottom. If you are only catching bullheads, suspend the bait about

12 inches off the bottom to increase your odds of hooking a channel cat. Late spring and early summer are the best times to pursue catfish at Utah Lake. Rock structure is the place to find channel cats during the spawn in June.

Walleye anglers crowd the water at Utah Lake in early spring, hoping to land trophy fish. Fishing is best during consistent weather. Shore anglers have access to concentrations of fish as the walleye group to spawn near river inlets and on rock structures in the lake. Rapalas, Storm thin fins, Cordell Wally divers, and 3- to 5-inch plastic and feather jigs are the lures of choice for most anglers. The best lure colors are chartreuse, white, orange, purple, and perch.

Summer walleye fishing is best in a boat because the fish are spread out. Trolling bottom bouncers with spinners tipped with a worm and diving crankbaits is effective. Bird Island, Lincoln Beach, and the flats near the Geneva Bubble-up are good places to try.

Big largemouth bass are caught at Utah Lake on a regular basis. Fish up to 10 pounds are not unheard of. Fishing from a boat gets anglers on the best side of flooded vegetation and allows them to cover more water as they search for fish. Spring fishing means spinnerbaits, jig-n-pig, plastic worms/lizards, and night crawlers. Largemouth can be found near stream inlets, in springs, and in areas with deep water nearby. Try using lures in chartreuse, black, purple, and brown.

In the summer, largemouth are more spread out and are best caught by covering a lot of water with lures. Spinnerbaits, topwater lures, and crankbaits are the ticket. Look for the bass to be around deeper brush edges and shaded cover. The largemouth sometimes come into the shallows to chase baitfish.

Perch numbers are increasing at Utah Lake. Catfish anglers frequently catch them while using night crawlers on the bottom. Ice anglers also catch these tasty panfish while trying for white bass.

The bluegill and crappie can be found near harbors and springs. They are best caught on 1- to 3-inch plastic and feather jigs or night crawlers suspended 3 to 6 feet below a bobber close to flooded brush edges. The best time to fish for them is in the late spring when they group to spawn.

14 Hobble Creek

Key Species: Brown trout and rainbow trout.

Best Way to Fish: Bait and flies.

Best Time of Year to Fish: Summer and fall.

Special Regulations: Closed east from Utah Lake to Interstate 15 March 1 to 6:00 a.m. May 1.

Description: This small stream is accessible just south of Springville on Forest Road 058 (Hobble Creek Canyon Road). There are two campgrounds you can reach by car in Hobble Creek Canyon, and you can hike to another on Trail 003, about a mile from the road. Forest Road 132 runs along the Left Fork of Hobble Creek.

Hobble Creek is a short drive and a pleasant respite from the city of Provo. Special regulations protect the population of brown trout. Photo by Larry Mathis

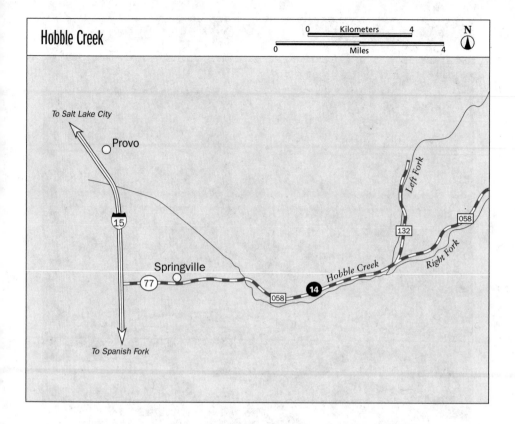

Fishing Index: A large population of wild brown trout makes Hobble Creek a fun fishery. The DWR plants some rainbows, primarily in the catch basin, in the spring. However, in the future a reduced number of rainbows will be planted, as the browns have shown an ability to provide a wild fishery. Royal Wulff and terrestrial patterns are a good choice for fly fishers. Small Rapalas and spinners produce some fish as well.

15 Diamond Fork Creek

Key Species: Brown trout, cutthroat trout, and rainbow trout.

Best Way to Fish: Flies, lures, and bait.

Best Time of Year to Fish: Summer and fall.

Special Regulations: None

Description: In Spanish Fork Canyon, take U.S. Highway 6 to Forest Road 29, about 7 miles. A paved road parallels most of the creek. It turns to dirt near the upper stretches. The USDA Forest Service runs an 11-site campground with restrooms called Palmyra, which is 5 miles up the Diamond Fork Road. The Diamond Campground has 32 sites and restrooms, and is 6 miles beyond Palmyra.

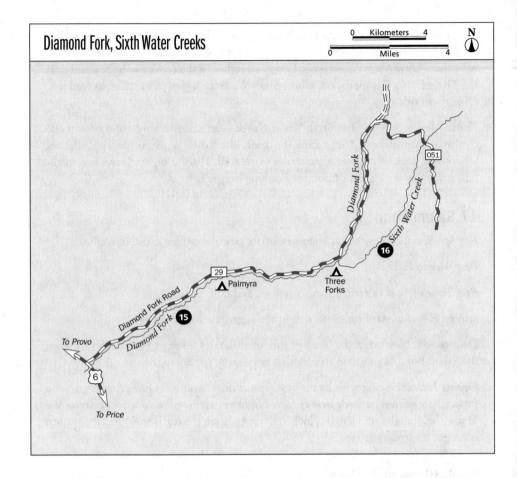

0   Kilometers   4

0   Miles   4

N

Diamond Fork

Sixth Water Creek

051

16

29

▲ Palmyra

Diamond Fork Road

15

To Provo

Diamond Fork

▲ Three Forks

6

To Price

Fishing Index: Diamond Fork serves as a main irrigation provider via the Strawberry Tunnel. Fishing in the summer is difficult due to high water. In the fall, Diamond Fork is one of the state's best brown trout fisheries. Fishing with bead-head nymphs is good when the water is high. Attractor patterns are the norm when it comes to dries. Terrestrials also work well. Night crawlers are always a good bet.

16 Sixth Water Creek

Key Species: Brown trout and cutthroat trout.

Best Way to Fish: Flies.

Best Time of Year to Fish: Summer and fall.

Special Regulations: Closed to the possession of cutthroat trout and trout with cutthroat markings.

Description: Sixth Water Creek is created by the Strawberry Tunnel. Officials have obtained a regulated flow, securing a year-round home for fish. From U.S. Highway

6, turn north on the Diamond Fork Road. Follow the road for about 15 miles, then turn east on Forest Road 051, which crosses Sixth Water Creek and ends up on the west side of Strawberry Reservoir. Lower stretches of the creek can be reached near the Three Forks Campground, where Sixth Water and First Water Creeks feed into Diamond Fork.

Fishing Index: For its size, Sixth Water Creek is an unbelievably good brown and cutthroat trout fishery. Large attractor dries, like Royal Wulff, trudes, stimulators, Chernobyl ants, and other terrestrials, work well. During higher flows and in the fall, streamers are a great option for hooking bigger fish.

17 Salem Pond

Key Species: Rainbow trout, channel catfish, largemouth bass, and bluegill.

Best Way to Fish: Bait.

Best Time of Year to Fish: Spring, summer, and fall.

Special Regulations: Limit four fish in the aggregate for all species.

Description: Nestled in the heart of this small Utah County town south of Provo, the Salem Pond is an urban fishery that sees heavy use by locals.

Fishing Index: Fishing with bait is best. Traditional trout baits like salmon eggs and Power Bait should be your first choice. Night crawlers will also work. Fish on the bottom with night crawlers or chicken livers to hook the catfish. A rare largemouth is caught by trout anglers.

18 Settlement Canyon

Key Species: Rainbow trout, brook trout, and brown trout.

Best Way to Fish: Bait from shore.

Best Time of Year to Fish: Summer.

Special Regulations: Fishing from boats and float tubes is prohibited.

Description: This is the only fishable water in the Oquirrh Mountains west of Salt Lake City. Located east of Tooele in a pretty wooded setting, there are few facilities here. Though a few Salt Lake residents wander over to fish Settlement Canyon, it is primarily a local fishery utilized by anglers in Tooele. From downtown Tooele, go south on Main Street. At the south end of town the road meets the Oquirrh Mountains and bends toward the west. Where the residential area ends, there is a white, windowless Masonic lodge. Turn left at the lodge and go up the canyon for about 0.5 mile to Settlement Reservoir. Fishing is the only recreational use permitted on the reservoir.

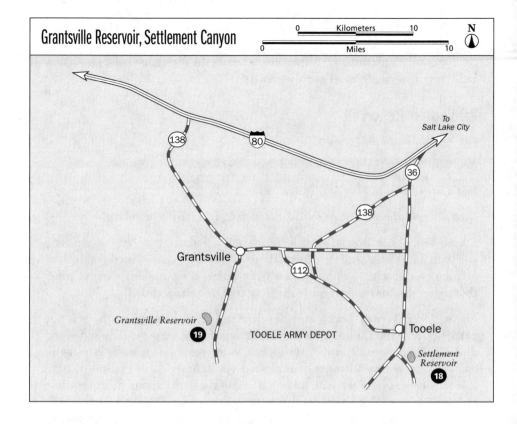

Fishing Index: From Memorial Day to Labor Day, and sometimes earlier in the season, Settlement Canyon receives healthy doses of catchable rainbow trout. Shore fishing with salmon eggs and night crawlers is the norm. There are few surprises here, but it is a good place for parents to take their children after work or for a quick Saturday fishing outing.

19 Grantsville Reservoir

Key Species: Brown trout and rainbow trout.

Best Way to Fish: Bait, flies, and lures.

Best Time of Year to Fish: Spring, summer, and fall.

Special Regulations: Boats with gas motors prohibited.

Description: This reservoir is about 30 minutes from Salt Lake via Interstate 80 and the Tooele/Stansbury Park exit (99). Drive through Grantsville; 2 miles outside of town, turn right on the first paved road. Twenty-three picnic tables with grills and 24 RV pads are the only facilities. Small boat launching is possible from shore.

Fishing Index: Fish the edges with spoons, spinners, jigs, and flies. The best color options are black, purple, pink, and orange. The stream inlet on the west end is a good spot for large rainbows. Bait fishing is best in the spring and fall. Salmon eggs and Power Bait are the most popular choices.

20 Vernon Reservoir

Key Species: Rainbow trout.

Best Way to Fish: Bait from shore and float tubes.

Best Time of Year to Fish: Spring, summer, and fall.

Special Regulations: Fishing from a boat with a gas engine is prohibited.

Description: About 35 miles south of Tooele, this is a surprisingly large desert reservoir with only a little shade and few facilities. There is a small, isolated Forest Service campground with vault toilets nearby. But there is no drinking water at either the campground or the reservoir, so anglers need to come prepared.

Fishing Index: Vernon Reservoir's main claim to Utah fishing fame is that it is one of the first reservoirs near the Wasatch Front to be free of ice in the early spring and thus is one of the first to be planted with fish. Vernon tends to get warm in late summer as irrigators take water out, so it gets most of its heavy quota of planted catchable rainbows early in the year, making it one of the better spring fisheries within an hour's drive of Salt Lake City. It can get heavy pressure. Most folks fish from shore with bait, but it is large enough for small fishing boats to try some trolling or for those in canoes to get out and do some paddling.

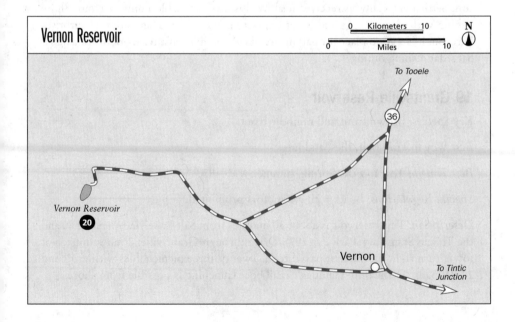

21 Strawberry Reservoir

Key Species: Cutthroat trout, rainbow trout, and kokanee salmon.

Best Way to Fish: From a boat or from shore.

Best Time of Year to Fish: Year-round.

Special Regulations: Limit of four trout or kokanee salmon in the aggregate; no more than two may be cutthroat trout under 15 inches and only one may be a cutthroat trout over 22 inches. All cutthroat trout between 15 and 22 inches must be released; any trout with cutthroat markings is considered a cutthroat trout. Anglers are encouraged to release all cutthroat trout.

Description: Strawberry is Utah's premier trout fishery. No reservoir is as consistently productive. Strawberry was at one time two reservoirs separated by a dike. The reservoir now has three major areas: the original Strawberry portion, the Soldier Creek side, and the Narrows, which links the two. At 17,000 acre-feet, Strawberry is the fifth-largest body of freshwater in the state.

The reservoir is located just off U.S. Highway 40 between Heber City and Duchesne, about 90 minutes from Salt Lake City via Interstate 80. Strawberry Bay Marina on the west side of the reservoir is the site of numerous facilities. Five miles

Eleven-year-old Kialee Johnson caught this cutthroat trout by herself fishing from shore on a trip to Strawberry Reservoir with dad, Dane. They caught six that day and let them all go, including the lunker.

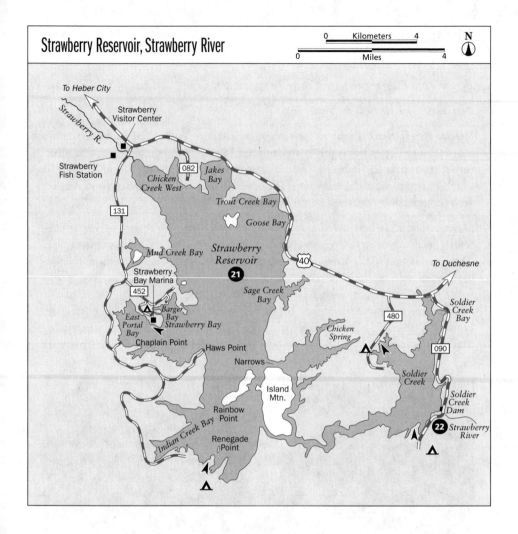

Strawberry Reservoir, Strawberry River

from Daniel's Summit on US 40, take well-marked Forest Road 131, 5 miles to Forest Road 452. A fee station is located at the entrance to the marina area. The Forest Service has 372 family units spread out in the marina area, so it is rare to launch a boat without a wait.

Strawberry Bay Marina is a private concessionaire. The marina provides a cafe, store with tackle, boat rentals, guide service, and a lodge. The road to the marina is plowed when conditions allow during the winter, making Strawberry Bay a popular ice-fishing destination.

Another large Forest Service campground has 166 units on the Soldier Creek side. It is reached by taking Forest Road 480 about 9 miles past the Strawberry Marina turnoff on US 40. Facilities include a boat ramp, restrooms, and picnic areas.

The Aspen Grove campground across the reservoir from the Soldier Creek site provides more of a camping feeling. It is nestled in a forested canyon, while the other campgrounds sit on exposed sagebrush flats. Aspen Grove is reached via Forest Road 090 just over 1 mile from the Soldier Creek campground turnoff. There are 52 units, a boat launch, and restrooms.

The least-used launch is Renegade, on the southwest end of the reservoir. Take Forest Road 131 past Strawberry Marina and continue for about 7.5 miles, following signs to Renegade. There are 62 campsites here, plus a ramp and restrooms.

Day-use areas are a great place to access Strawberry for shore fishing. Chicken Creek West is about 1.3 miles past the turnoff to the marina on Forest Road 082. Chicken Creek East is another mile along US 40. These are also good areas for float tubers to launch.

The Ladders area is one of the most popular day-use areas, especially in the winter. It is 4 miles south of the marina turnoff on US 40.

On the west shore, Mud Creek along the road to the marina is also a popular place for float tubers. Chaplain Point and Haws Point are great places to access the shore for fishing.

The Strawberry Visitor Center, about 0.5 mile on Forest Road 131 from the Strawberry Junction, is a good place to take children to learn about the wildlife in the Strawberry Valley. This is also a great place to watch spawning kokanee salmon in the fall.

Fishing Index: Chemically treated in the fall of 1990 to remove a predominate population of nongame fish, Strawberry was then planted with Bear Lake cutthroat and kokanee salmon in hopes they would help control chub and sucker numbers. Now, anglers are enjoying some of the best fishing ever at the Berry.

Fishing is traditionally best at Strawberry when the weather is at its worst. Cloudy, windy days usually offer the best fishing. The weather changes quickly in the Strawberry Valley, so be prepared for anything.

Strawberry is Utah's premier trout fishery and arguably the most important because it reduces pressure on other waters. Fish grow fast in this fertile reservoir, making it a natural draw for anglers from all over the West.

Countless boats and float tubes dot the water while anglers line the shore. Still, Strawberry continues to produce incredible catch rates of healthy fish.

Fishing from shore is best in the spring and fall, when trout move into the shallows. It is also easier to fish because vegetation isn't as thick.

Shore anglers more commonly catch rainbows, especially with bait. Power Bait and worms tipped with marshmallows are the most popular. Look for weed edges or channels in the weeds and stream inlets, as rainbows cruise these areas looking for insects. Rainbows up to 10 pounds are often caught from shore. Some of the best places to find rainbows are Chicken Creek West, Indian Creek Bay, East Portal Bay, and the shallow bays on the Soldier Creek side.

As the summer progresses, weed growth inhibits fishing from shore in some places. Use a boat or float tube to fish the outside edge of weed beds with bait. Trollers rarely catch rainbows because they don't usually get close enough to the weed beds where the fish are hiding.

Fly fishing can also be productive for rainbows. Try stripping damselfly nymphs, scuds (gray and olive), mayfly nymphs, and leech patterns around weed edges with sink tip or slow-sinking lines. Olive, brown, black, and purple are the best leech colors. Float tubers generally fish in this fashion. In the early summer, rainbows can be caught on dry flies during mayfly and midge hatches. You will see more rising fish on cloudy days or during low-light conditions.

Perhaps the best time of year to catch big trout is as the ice melts away from the shore. The fish concentrate in the warmer, exposed water. They're also drawn by increased insect activity. Cast small plastic and feather jigs in black, purple, white, and chartreuse. Fly fishing with dark-colored leech patterns can also be effective. Stream inlets will melt the ice away first. Areas with shallow water will go next.

Ice fishing is good for rainbows. Fish in shallow water (5 to 20 feet), along weed edges, or on points, with small plastic or feather jigs and ice flies tipped with Power Bait, a night crawler, or a wax worm. Fish away from crowds; heavy activity on the ice can spook fish away from the shallow water. Chartreuse, glow-in-the-dark, black, smoke, and purple are good color choices.

Because cutthroat are more aggressive and more of an open-water fish than rainbows, trolling is the best way to catch them in the summer. The Bear Lake cutthroat in Strawberry readily hit lures up to 8 inches long. Try Rapalas, flatfish, large needlefish, and Triple Teazers down to 50 feet. Pop gear and a worm also work. In sunny conditions, use subtle colors like rainbow, perch, frog, and silver. Under cloud cover, try white, chartreuse, black, purple, and gold. Trolling is most effective in the summer and early fall because the cutts tend to be grouped in open water.

Cutthroat can be caught from shore in the early spring and late fall. In the late fall, as the water cools, cutthroat move closer to the surface and can be caught on monofilament, rather than on weighted lines. When the fish are in the shallows, bait fishing with a night crawler or frozen minnow works well. Casting spoons and spinners in flashy colors can also be effective at this time.

Fly fishing with leech patterns in black, red, brown, and chartreuse work well, as do streamer patterns in white, tan, and gray. Those without fly rods can fish with flies by using a casting bubble and trailing the fly about 4 to 6 feet behind.

Like rainbows, cutthroat will concentrate in the shallows during the ice-off period. This is perhaps the best time of year to fish for them, especially from shore. Fishing 2- to 3-inch feather or plastic jigs, Rapalas, spinners, and bait below a bobber are common methods as the ice recedes.

As the water cools in the fall, cutthroat suspend close to the surface and are caught with minnow-imitating lures like Rapalas, jerkbaits, tube jigs, and bait below a bobber. Smoke, pearl, black, white, and chartreuse are good colors.

In the winter, the cutthroat are caught in 10 to 50 feet of water through the ice. Jig small spoons, 1- to 3-inch plastic or feather jigs, and large ice flies tipped with night crawler, cut bait, or wax worm. Access to Strawberry can be difficult in the winter, which can cause numerous people to fish the same areas. If you can get away from the crowd, fishing will improve. Look for points and drop-offs near the shore. The fish sometimes suspend over deeper water. Cutthroat are more aggressive than rainbows and frequently hit a lure as it falls. Jigging increases your chances.

Kokanee are best caught from a boat because they are usually found in deeper water than trout. Trolling with downriggers or leaded line is the best way to reach them. Fish at 40 to 60 feet with bright-colored lures like needlefish, Super Dupers, Krocodiles, Triple Teazers, and Kokanee Kings. Troll at faster speeds for kokanee than you would for trout. Some good areas include the Soldier Creek side between the dam and the Narrows and in the middle part of the main lake around Sage Hen Knoll. Because they group in larger schools, kokanee can often be recognized on fish finders. For that reason, once a fish is caught, mark the spot mentally and make repeated passes until the school moves. In the fall, salmon move toward stream inlets when preparing to spawn. Sometimes anglers from shore catch them with bright-colored lures, flies, and Power Bait.

22 Strawberry River

Key Species: Brown trout and cutthroat trout.

Best Way to Fish: Flies and lures.

Best Time of Year to Fish: Summer and fall.

Special Regulations: Artificial flies and lures only from Soldier Creek Dam downstream to the confluence of Red Creek (near the Pinnacles).

Description: The Strawberry River below the reservoir is more of a fishery than the one coming into the reservoir. Access is at the Soldier Creek Dam from U.S. Highway 40 on Forest Road 090. The first mile of the river below the dam is artificial flies and lures only. Bait is allowed below that, but fishing with flies is still the best method.

An angler taking a break to re-rig on the Strawberry River.

Most anglers fish the river near the Pinnacles. That portion of the Strawberry is accessed about 3 miles south of Fruitland on US 40. The road runs along Red Creek until it reaches the Strawberry. Head west; the road follows the river. There is no camping allowed on DWR land.

Fishing Index: This is a beautiful stream that provides quality fishing for brown and cutthroat trout. High water can make fishing difficult and heavy pressure does affect success. Many anglers fish with a large stimulator or terrestrial on top and a bead-head dropper. Streamers are also a good choice, especially when the water is high or murky. There can be a good blue-winged olive hatch on overcast days. There are few open areas along the road, but the river is lined with trees and brush, which makes casting and reaching the river difficult in most places. Wading is the best method.

23 Thistle Creek

Key Species: Brown trout.

Best Way to Fish: Bait, spinners, and flies.

Best Time of Year to Fish: Summer and fall.

Special Regulations: None.

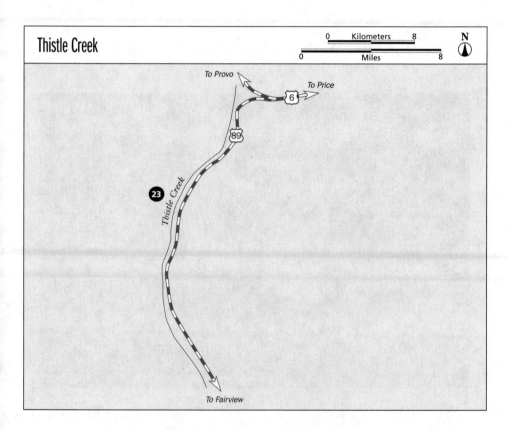

Description: Most of this stream is posted as private property. Some landowners allow access. There are some access points along U.S. Highway 89 between Fairview and the junction of U.S. Highway 6.

Fishing Index: A healthy population of browns means the DWR has discontinued planting rainbows in Thistle Creek. High water means poor fishing; wait until spring runoff has dissipated. Night crawlers are a solid bait choice. Rooster tail spinners also work well. Some dry fly fishing is possible, but streamers are especially effective in the fall.

24 Mill Hollow Reservoir

Key Species: Rainbow trout and brook trout.

Best Way to Fish: Bait, spinners, and flies.

Best Time of Year to Fish: Summer and fall.

Special Regulations: None.

Description: Mill Hollow is reached via Highway 35 about 11 miles southeast of Woodland. From Highway 35 take the well-marked gravel road (Forest Road 054) 3.5 miles to the reservoir. Mill Hollow rests on Uinta National Forest land and

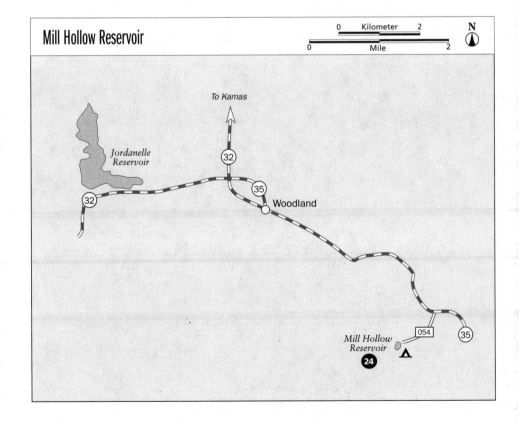

public access is unrestricted. A 46-unit campground is located at the lake. This is a popular weekend camping destination, but it is rarely crowded during the week.

Fishing Index: Since the reservoir has been secured as a fishery by the DWR, success has remained constant for planted rainbows. Fish Power Bait or salmon eggs on the bottom for the best results. Dry flies trailed behind a casting bubble can be especially effective in the evening. Small spoons and spinners work well in the midmorning and midafternoon.

25 Payson Lakes

Key Species: Rainbow trout and brook trout.

Best Way to Fish: Bait from shore.

Best Time of Year to Fish: Summer.

Special Regulations: None.

Description: As the name implies, there are a series of small lakes just east of the town of Payson in Payson Canyon on the Nebo Loop (also known as Forest Road 015). Payson Lake, McClellan Lake, Box Lake, and Maple Lake are all reached on the Nebo

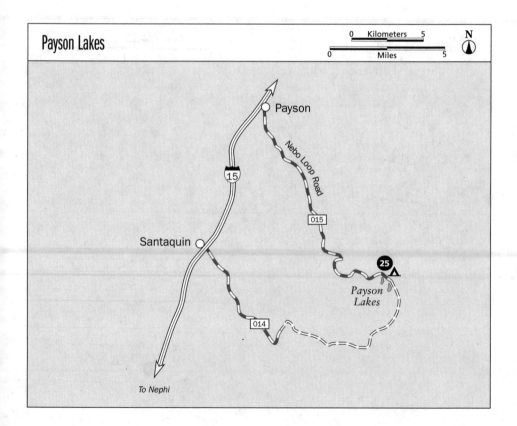

Loop. There are some nice developed facilities, especially at Payson Lake, which features access for the disabled, a paved trail, some nice grassy areas, and a highly developed Forest Service campground. This is a nice place to take the family for a day picnic or an afternoon of fishing. The canyon offers cool temperatures in the summer. Parents appreciate the paved trail and grassy picnic areas, largely because it helps keep their children clean. The Nebo Loop is an especially nice place for a fall drive. If the fishing is not up to par at Payson Lake, which receives the heaviest pressure due to its fine facilities, the other three lakes are nearby, giving families several choices.

Fishing Index: These lakes are heavily fished. Hatchery trucks from nearby Springville make regular stops on the mountain during the busy summer months. Planted rainbows and brookies provide anglers with variety. Some try a fly-and-bubble, especially early in the day or late in the evening when the fish are feeding on the surface, but most folks opt to use traditional trout baits. Nice facilities and beautiful scenery make a day of fishing at the Payson Lakes well worth the drive.

26 Burraston Ponds

Key Species: Rainbow trout.

Best Way to Fish: Bait from shore.

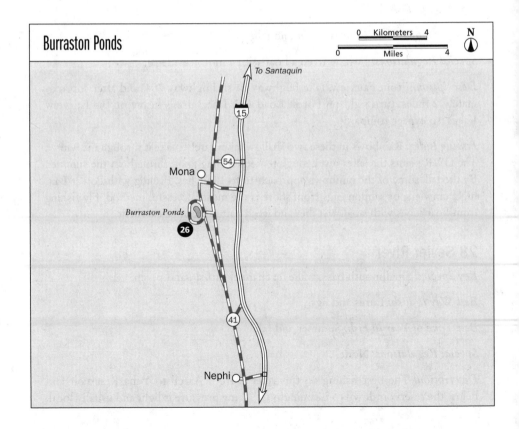

Best Time of Year to Fish: Year-round.

Special Regulations: Boats with motors are prohibited.

Description: An urban fishery located between Nephi and Santaquin, these small ponds are the kind of place parents love to take their kids. They are fairly close to the Wasatch Front but not well known, so they're rarely crowded. Facilities are limited here. The ponds are reached via Interstate 15, exit 236, west 1 mile to Highway 41, then 2 miles south to a dirt road on the west side. The road stretches for 0.5 mile to the ponds.

Fishing Index: This is a classic put-and-take fishing situation. Hatchery trucks visit this area on a regular basis, even during the winter months, providing a ready source of catchable rainbow trout year-round. Occasionally, hatcheries dump some large, trophy-size brook stock in the pond, offering a kid the chance to catch a surprisingly large fish. No boats are needed at these small ponds. Most anglers use a variety of baits, but spinners and flies will also work.

27 Fairview Lakes

Key Species: Rainbow trout.

Best Way to Fish: Bait.

Best Time of Year to Fish: Summer and fall.

Special Regulations: Fishing from a boat with a motor is illegal.

Description: From Fairview, take Highway 31 to Highway 264, and after approximately 2 miles, turn right on Forest Road 187. Local use is heavy on the Fairview Lakes, so expect company.

Fishing Index: Rainbows in these two shallow lakes rarely make it through the winter. The DWR plants the lakes just enough to keep fishing good throughout the summer. By the fall, some of the rainbows approach 16 to 18 inches. Fishing with Power Bait, night crawlers, or salmon eggs from shore is the most successful method. Fly fishing from float tubes with small wet flies and leech patterns can be excellent.

28 Sevier River

Key Species: Smallmouth bass, walleye, channel catfish, and perch.

Best Way to Fish: Lures and jigs.

Best Time of Year to Fish: Summer and fall.

Special Regulations: None.

Description: The best fishing on this river is from Axtell to Yuba Reservoir and below the reservoir down to Leamington. Fishing pressure is light and usually local.

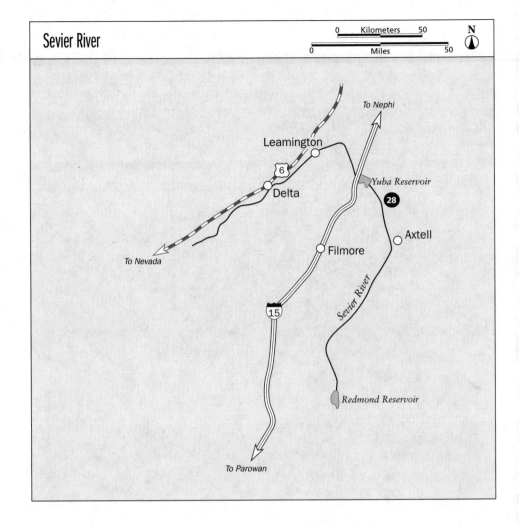

Sevier River

Leamington

Delta

To Nevada

Yuba Reservoir

Axtell

Filmore

Sevier River

To Nephi

Redmond Reservoir

To Parowan

Private property is common along the river (respect the NO TRESPASSING signs). Access is limited to county roads that cross the river.

Fishing Index: Fishing below the dam at Yuba is good for smallmouth bass, walleye, and perch. Night crawlers fished on the bottom could produce walleye, catfish, or perch. The perch are often suspended, so look for them in any possible water, and try night crawler pieces fished below a bobber. Channel catfish are the only species common below Leamington. The smallmouth will hit minnow-imitating lures. Above Yuba, there are walleye, pike, and channel catfish.

29 Yuba Reservoir

Key Species: Walleye, perch, northern pike, rainbow trout, and channel catfish.

Best Way to Fish: Trolling.

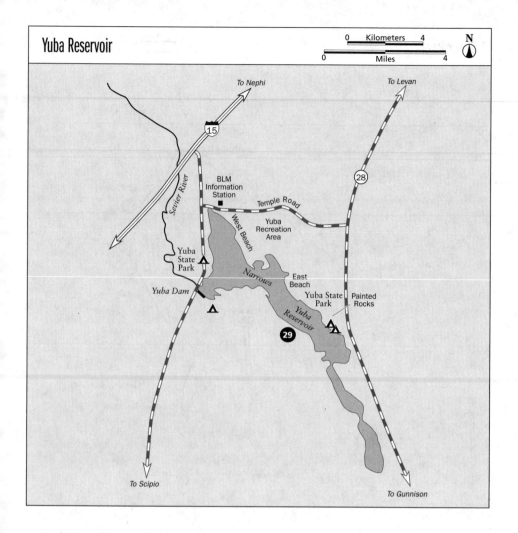

Yuba Reservoir

Best Time of Year to Fish: Spring, summer, and fall.

Special Regulations: Yellow perch limit is 10. All yellow perch caught from January 1 to April 30 must be kept.

Description: This 20-mile-long, 2-mile-wide reservoir is serviced by Yuba State Park, 30 miles south of Nephi off of Interstate 15. Facilities include a 27-unit campground, modern restrooms, hot showers, drinking water, a sewage disposal station, group-use pavilion, and boat-launching ramp. An additional boat-launching ramp and a primitive campground are located on the east side of the reservoir at Painted Rocks, 15 miles south of Levan just off Highway 28. Called Yuba Reservoir by most people, it shows up as Sevier Bridge Reservoir on some maps.

Fishing Index: Anglers once considered Yuba lost to rough fish, but the reservoir rebounded in the mid-1990s and provides some great fishing opportunities, especially for walleye and perch. Most walleye anglers head for Yuba in early May. Walleye fishing peaks in mid-June. Troll at 5 to 30 feet along brush or weed edges, near rocky points, and on flats with bottom bouncers trailing a spinner harness tipped with worm. Diving crankbaits are also a popular choice. The best colors are chartreuse, gold, orange, silver, and perch patterns. Fishing with the wind is better than avoiding it.

Anglers sometimes catch perch in shallow water when fishing for walleye, but larger perch are usually deeper, down to 50 feet. In these depths, fish with heavy spoons or jigs tipped with perch meat. If you are looking for fast perch action, seek weed edges of about 10 to 20 feet and use small spoons or plastic jigs tipped with night crawler or perch meat.

Some trout can be caught while trolling for walleye. If you want to target trout, troll suspended with flatfish, Rapalas, or pop gear and a worm. Early spring is the best time to catch trout from shore. Try salmon eggs, Power Bait, or night crawlers.

Yuba is one of the few places anglers can catch northern pike in Utah. There is a limited number in the reservoir. Most are caught while anglers fish for walleye. If looking for pike, the best technique is to troll large perch and fire tiger-colored spoons and diving crankbaits. Look for weed flats in the spring and deeper points during summer and early fall.

The few channel catfish in Yuba are big and rarely caught. Try fishing at night with frozen minnows, carp cut bait, and night crawlers.

Yuba Reservoir was drained for dam repairs in 2003, and all the fish populations were impacted. Perch numbers were augmented by transplants from Jordanelle Reservoir and a shipment of fish from Minnesota in the fall of 2003. Rock structures and artificial structures were created throughout the empty reservoir to help forage fish carry a better survival rate in Yuba. Rainbow trout were also planted in the fall of 2003, and they always provide fast action for anglers at Yuba.

It will only be a matter of time before the productive reservoir produces trophy perch and walleye. Northern pike and catfish will also return from the Sevier River. Watch for the regulations to change at Yuba as the fishery continues to recover from being drained.

Northern Utah

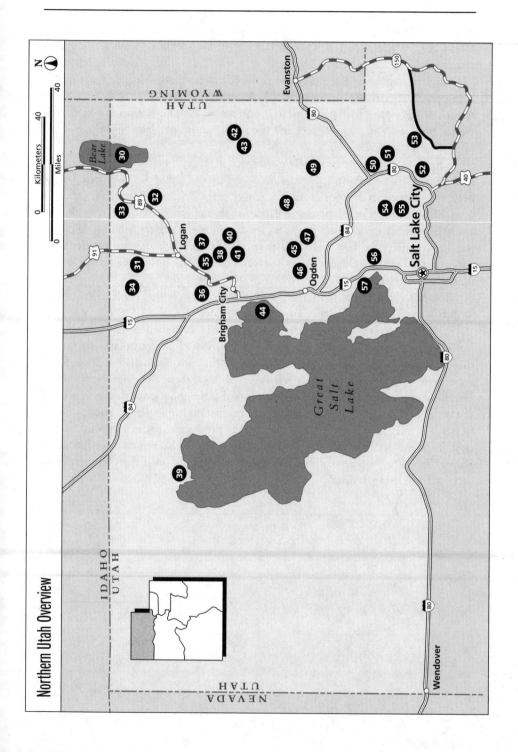

Northern Utah Overview

30 Bear Lake

Key Species: Cutthroat trout, lake trout, Bonneville cisco, and whitefish.

Best Way to Fish: Trolling and jigging.

Best Time of Year to Fish: Spring and fall.

Special Regulations: Trout limit two. Trout with cutthroat markings and with all fins intact must be released. Only cutthroat with one or more healed clipped fins can be kept. Cisco limit 30. Cisco may be taken with a handheld net. Net openings may not exceed 18 inches in any dimension. When dip-netting through the ice, the size of the hole is unrestricted. When ice fishing for fish other than cisco, the size of the hole may not exceed 18 inches. The holder of a valid Utah or Idaho or combination fishing license may fish within both the Utah and Idaho boundaries of Bear Lake. Only one bag limit may be taken and held in possession, even if licensed in both states.

Description: Bear Lake is a natural body of water straddling the Utah-Idaho border in the northeastern corner of the state. As Utah's second-largest freshwater lake at 20 miles long and 8 miles wide, there is plenty of room for waterskiing, swimming, scuba diving, and sailing on or below its breathtakingly blue surface.

Three state-owned facilities provide boating, camping, and picnicking. Bear Lake Marina is on U.S. Highway 89, 2 miles north of Garden City. The marina provides a sheltered harbor; an 80-foot-wide, five-lane, concrete launching ramp; 355 boat slips; marina sanitary disposal station; a group pavilion; restrooms; hot showers; and a visitor center. A concessionaire provides boat rentals, gasoline, fishing/boating supplies, and a fast-food grill.

Bear Lake Rendezvous Beach is on the south shore near Laketown on Highway 30. It extends for 1.3 miles and offers 138 campsites, modern restrooms, hot showers, and utility hookups. A wide, sandy beach provides excellent camping, picnicking, and small watercraft activity. Rendezvous Beach is a popular area for groups and family reunions, and it is the site of an annual Mountain Man Rendezvous each September. A local concessionaire provides small boat rentals.

Eastside Bear Lake is 10 miles north of Laketown. The area around Bear Lake is famous for producing some of the best raspberries in the world. They are available in August; several drive-ins offer perhaps the best raspberry shakes in the world. Bear Lake is best reached via US 89 through scenic Logan Canyon.

Fishing Index: Fishing is for cutthroat, lake trout, and whitefish. In the winter, snowmobilers and ice anglers are drawn to the area. However, the lake doesn't always freeze. Bear Lake is famous for its annual January cisco run.

Bear Lake cutthroat are quite predacious, so biologists have stocked them in lakes and reservoirs across the state hoping they will help control nongame fish. Cutthroat are caught spring, summer, and fall while trolling primarily along the east shoreline with Rapalas, spoons, and flatfish. When water temperatures are cool in the spring and fall, troll at faster speeds.

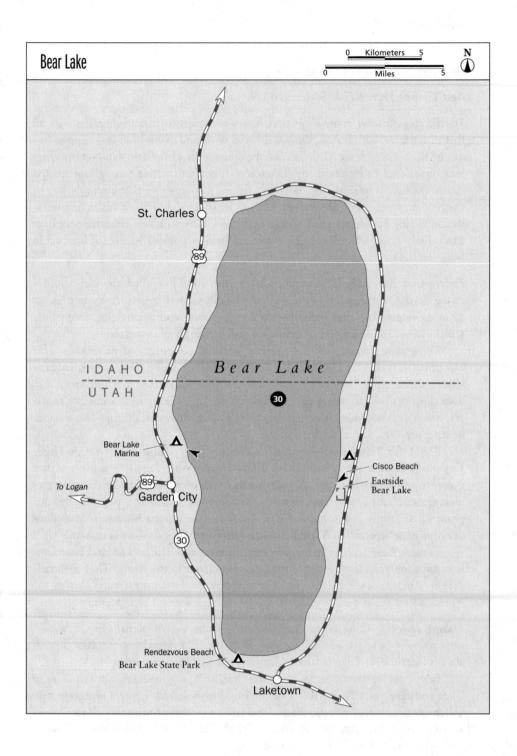

Bear Lake

To help stimulate natural reproduction, the Division of Wildlife Resources (DWR) has implemented catch-and-release on the wild cutthroat. Cutthroat with clipped fins can be kept, but those with all fins intact must be released.

Lake trout are caught using downriggers between 50 and 100 feet with large spoons and Rapalas near Cisco Beach and Rainbow Cove. Some anglers jig for lake trout using bright-colored lures and plastic tube jigs at 60 to 100 feet. Tip the lures and jigs with cisco or sucker meat. Fall is one of the best times to jig for lake trout. By late September, the mackinaw are starting to spawn. Fishing is best near the rock pile located on the southwest side of the lake. In late 2005 DWR officials created four new rock piles measuring approximately 30 by 30 feet about 200 yards apart near the marina.

Cisco are such an integral part of Bear Lake that a beach on the east side of the lake has been named after the species. The sardinelike 6- to 9-inch fish are found nowhere else in the world. Anglers from around the West gather each January when the cisco run starts, usually on January 15, but as late as January 25.

Fishing for cisco is done with dip nets either through the ice or while wading in the shallow waters of the lake. On years when the lake does not freeze, anglers jig for the fish from boats along the beach. The run usually lasts about ten days. Morning is the best time to seek cisco.

Some people like to deep-fry their cisco, but most anglers keep the fish and use pieces throughout the year as bait at Bear Lake to catch cutthroat and lake trout.

31 Bear River

Key Species: Channel catfish, bullhead catfish, walleye, crappie, and largemouth bass.

Best Way to Fish: Canoe and shore.

Best Time of Year to Fish: Late spring and early summer.

Special Regulations: Setlines are okay with a permit; two poles are allowed with an additional permit.

Description: When the Bear River enters Utah at the Idaho state line, it is a far different water than it was at its start in the Uinta Mountains. By the time it passes near Cornish, the Bear is murky, warm, and slow-moving. Fishing is for warm-water species, primarily channel and bullhead catfish. Because much of the land surrounding the river is private property, the best way to fish the river is by canoe. There are some access points for shore anglers at bridges. A ramp is located on the Bear near Amalga where Highway 218 crosses the river. A popular place to launch is below Cutler Reservoir Dam. Other possible entries can be found in Riverside and Corrine. Eventually, the river dumps into the Bear River Migratory Bird Refuge. The DWR plants fingerling channel catfish below the Cutler Marsh.

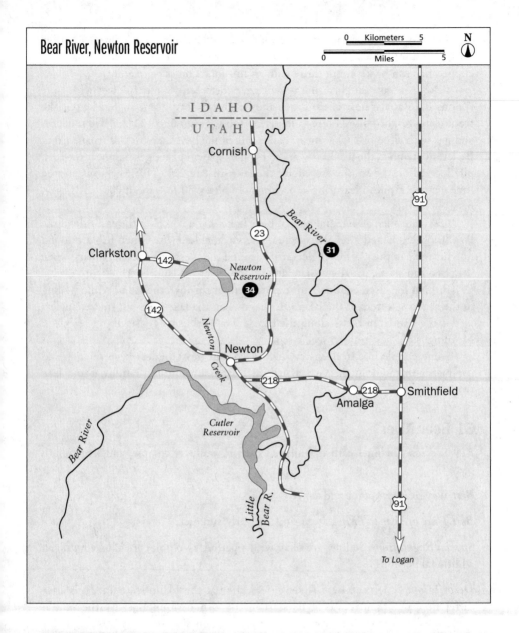

Bear River, Newton Reservoir

Fishing Index: Most anglers fish in the late spring and early summer, although fishing is usually good throughout the year. Trophy-size channel catfish are what most anglers are after. Reports of catfish up to 30 pounds have been heard, but most of the larger fish run 8 to 12 pounds. Anglers use anything that smells strong to catch catfish. The most common baits are carp meat and chicken liver. Night crawlers are also popular, and they increase your chances of catching walleye and largemouth bass. During the hottest stretch of summer, fishing at night is more productive.

32 Logan River

Key Species: Rainbow trout, brown trout, cutthroat trout, brook trout, and whitefish.

Best Way to Fish: Bait, flies, and lures.

Best Time of Year to Fish: Year-round.

Special Regulations: Artificial flies and lures only and a trout and whitefish combination limit of two from Card Canyon Bridge upstream to the highway bridge at Red Banks Campground and all tributaries in between. Closed January 1 to the second Saturday in July from the highway bridge at Red Banks Campground upstream to the Idaho state line, including all tributaries.

Description: The Logan offers anglers three different kinds of fishing opportunities. Three reservoir-like impoundments near the city of Logan are stocked regularly with rainbow trout and provide good family fishing from shore with bait. The river between the impoundments has large populations of rainbow, albino, and brown trout. The Logan from the upper dam upstream to Card Canyon Bridge, roughly 3.5 miles, is more heavily fished than the upper stretches because of easier access. Brown trout, whitefish, and an occassional cutthroat are the primary catches is this

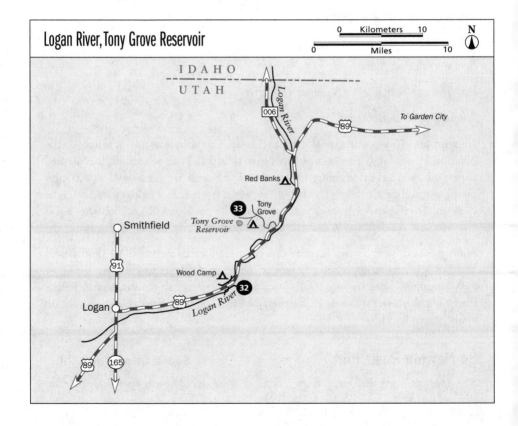

stretch. The portion from Card Canyon to Red Banks Campground is a quality mountain fishing experience. Cutthroat are more common in this part of the river. Upstream from Red Banks to the Idaho state line, the Logan is a small river with thick vegetation guarding the banks with few clear areas. Brook trout are the predominant fish on the upper stretches of the Logan.

Fishing Index: Expect company when fishing the river and impoundments near Logan. Bait is the best option for the planted rainbow and albino trout. Large browns lurk in the lower stretches of the river, but few anglers fish with the minnow-imitating lures and flies needed to tempt them.

The artificial-only section of the river is hard to fish during runoff but can be productive in the spring with San Juan worms, stone fly nymphs, and beadhead nymphs. As the water clears, stimulators, stone flies, and attractor dry flies work best. As summer progresses, good caddis and mayfly hatches occur. Terrestrial patterns are also a good choice. Spin fishers have success with spinners, small Rapalas, and feather jigs.

Once the top portion of the river opens to fishing in mid-July, fly fishers use stimulators, terrestrials, mayflies, caddises, and attractor dry flies. Fishing the Logan in the winter can be good. Look for deep holes and send nymphs through them. More whitefish are caught in the winter months than other times of the year.

33 Tony Grove Reservoir

Key Species: Rainbow trout.

Best Way to Fish: Bait.

Best Time of Year to Fish: Summer and fall.

Special Regulations: Trout limit four.

Description: This small glacial lake in Logan Canyon rests on Wasatch-Cache National Forest land. The 25-acre fishery isn't deep and can winterkill. It is planted with rainbow trout throughout the summer. The Forest Service maintains a 37-unit campground near the lake. The lake is accessed from U.S. Highway 89 in Logan Canyon, 22 miles from Logan. Signs point out Forest Road 003, which after an 8-mile scenic drive deposits you at the campground.

Fishing Index: Tony Grove is more of a camping locale than a fishing destination. The DWR plants trout as soon as trucks can reach the lake, usually late spring or early summer. There are rarely holdovers from one year to the next, so fish longer than 14 inches are rare. Bait is the preferred method, but fish are also caught on small spoons and flies.

34 Newton Reservoir See map on page 74.

Key Species: Tiger muskie, yellow perch, crappie, largemouth bass, bluegill, and channel catfish.

Best Way to Fish: Lures and bait.

Best Time of Year to Fish: Year-round.

Special Regulations: Bass limit six, only one over 12 inches; tiger muskie limit one, and all tiger muskies less than 40 inches must be released. It is illegal to use whole fish or amphibians, including water dogs, for bait, and cut bait must not be larger than 1 inch in any dimension and no more than one piece per hook.

Description: Just north of the Cache Valley town of the same name, Newton Reservoir resembles a large farm pond. It is out in the open with limited facilities, although it is possible to launch a boat here. Thick brush and trees line the shore of Newton, making shore angling difficult. Fishing from a boat or a float tube is the best way to go here.

Fishing Index: If you are looking for diversity in a single fishery, Newton is your place. The reservoir at one time produced some fairly nice-size trout; it has reverted to a warm-water fishery offering anglers a variety of choices. The introduction of tiger muskie should help keep panfish such as crappie, perch, and bluegill from becoming too numerous. The tigers are caught in the shallows with spinnerbaits, jerkbaits, and topwater lures. Trolling minnow-imitating crankbaits along brush edges and points will produce tiger muskies in the early spring and fall.

There is a nice population of largemouth bass, but most are under the legal size. Because of the large number of flooded trees and brush, try fishing with spinnerbaits, weedless plastic baits, and topwater lures.

Panfish are most commonly found near flooded brush. For the perch, try fishing on the bottom with night crawlers or jigs tipped with perch meat. Crappie fishing is best in the spring around outer brush edges with small jigs suspended 3 to 6 feet below a bobber. Bluegill can be found in shallow bays in the spring and can provide fast action for anglers using spinning or fly tackle.

Newton is one of the first reservoirs in the state to freeze and usually provides excellent fishing through the ice. For the panfish, use similar lures as those used in the summer, tipping them with a wax worm or colored larvae. Occasionally, a tiger muskie is hooked while fishing for panfish at Newton.

35 Hyrum Reservoir

Key Species: Brown trout, rainbow trout, bluegill, yellow perch, and largemouth bass.

Best Way to Fish: Trolling and bait from shore.

Best Time of Year to Fish: Spring, fall, and winter.

Special Regulations: Bass limit two.

Description: Part of Hyrum State Park, this 450-acre reservoir is fed by the Little Bear River and lies within the city limits of Hyrum. It is heavily used, with the

Hyrum Reservoir is a popular recreation site and a diverse fisher. Brown or rainbow trout, bluegill, perch, or largemouth bass could come on any cast.

emphasis on boating, waterskiing, swimming, and fishing. From U.S. Highway 89 south of Logan, take Highway 101 to Hyrum. Follow the signs to the state park. It is a 15-minute drive from Logan. The state park has 51 campsites with picnic tables and restrooms.

Fishing Index: Locals seek trout from shore in the spring and fall using Power Bait, worm and marshmallow, or casting spoons. Trollers have the best success in the summer, but usually give up after competing with water-skiers for space.

Hyrum usually freezes around the first of the year. Trout anglers will find the fish suspended between 10 and 25 feet. Try chartreuse and glow-in-the-dark jigs and ice flies tipped with wax worms or Power Bait.

Bass fishing is best in spring and early summer. The best area is on the east end in the shallow flats. In early spring, the fish are located near flooded trees and brush close to deep water. Jig-n-pigs, spinnerbaits, jerkbaits, and plastic baits 4 to 10 inches are good choices. As the water warms, the fish move to the flats for spawning.

Hyrum is a great place to fish for perch, especially in the winter. Search for perch on the bottom in the 20- to 50-foot range. Use spoons, jigs, and ice flies tipped with wax worm or perch meat. In the summer and fall, the perch can be found near weeds and flooded brush. Use night crawlers or small jigs close to the bottom.

The best time to fish for bluegill is in the spring during the spawn. Look for shallow flats with vegetation. The east half of the reservoir is a good place to start. Fish small plastic or feather jigs, spinners, and night crawlers around the spawning areas. Fly fishing is good for bluegill with small poppers and dry flies with rubber legs.

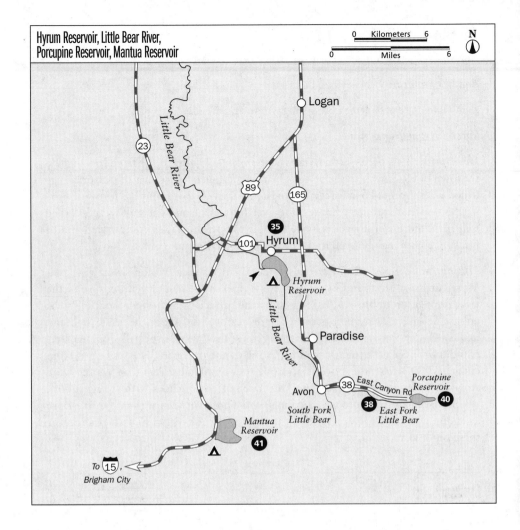

36 Wellsville Reservoir

Key Species: Rainbow trout.

Best Way to Fish: Bait.

Best Time of Year to Fish: Summer and fall.

Special Regulations: Closed January 1 to the Saturday before Memorial Day.

Description: This small reservoir in the Logan Valley is stocked with catchable and fingerling rainbows. Concerns about the safety of ice fishing by the city of Wellsville keep the reservoir closed in the winter months.

Fishing Index: Bait is the most common method for taking the planted trout. Try Power Bait, salmon eggs, or night crawlers fished on the bottom.

37 Blacksmith Fork

Key Species: Brown trout, cutthroat trout, and brook trout.

Best Way to Fish: Wet flies and bait.

Best Time of Year to Fish: Late spring, summer, and fall.

Special Regulations: None.

Description: This pretty little river is accessible via Highway 101 from just outside the town of Hyrum up to the DWR's Hardware Ranch. Once an artificial-only regulated water, stunted fish forced biologists to open the river to other forms of fishing. Some private property borders the river, but most landowners allow access. The Left Hand Fork of the river is more suitable to fly fishing. A significant amount of pressure comes mainly from locals or anglers from Logan.

Fishing Index: Brown trout are the predominant species. Whitefish rank second. More cutthroat are found in the Left Fork than in the main river. Because of the large population of browns, fishing under the surface is the best method. Fly fishers use a variety of nymph patterns: hare's ear, caddis pupae, pheasant tail, and midge. Under the right conditions, dry flies also work, especially on the Left Hand Fork. Small attractor, caddis, mayfly, and terrestrial patterns are solid choices. The Blacksmith Fork is also one of a few Utah rivers that has the large stone fly known as the salmon fly. This hatch often coincides with spring runoff, which makes it difficult to take advantage of. Those who know the river pay close attention and hope for years when the river will clear in time for the fish to see these big insects.

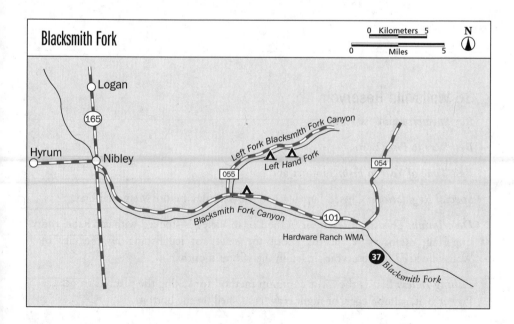

38 Little Bear River

See map on page 79.

Key Species: Rainbow trout, cutthroat trout, and brown trout.

Best Way to Fish: Flies.

Best Time of Year to Fish: Spring, summer, and fall.

Special Regulations: East Fork Little Bear River and its tributaries upstream from Porcupine Reservoir closed mid-August to late September. East Fork Little Bear River from Porcupine Reservoir downstream to the Avon/Paradise Road Highway 165, second stream crossing below reservoir, artificial flies and lures only with a trout and salmon limit of two.

Description: The Little Bear River starts at the confluence of the South Fork Little Bear and East Fork Little Bear near the town of Avon. The artificial-only section between Porcupine Reservoir and Avon is the most heavily fished. The portion of the river from Avon to Hyrum Reservoir is mostly private property. The river is accessed via Highway 165 south out of Hyrum. Just south of Avon, a road runs along the river to Porcupine Reservoir.

Fishing Index: During low water, royal coachmans, renegades, and other attractor patterns work well. Some caddis hatches can provide fast fishing. The area below the dam offers good fishing during the runoff period with bead-head nymphs and San Juan worms. During the summer, terrestrial patterns like grasshoppers, ants, and beetles are a good choice.

39 Locomotive Springs

Key Species: Rainbow trout, bluegill, and largemouth bass.

Best Way to Fish: Bait.

Best Time of Year to Fish: Spring, summer, and fall.

Special Regulations: None.

Description: Situated on the north shore of the Great Salt Lake, Locomotive Springs Wildlife Management Area has a handful of freshwater springs. There are two ways to reach Locomotive. The easiest is to take Interstate 84 north to Snowville and then a gravel road for 18 miles. The other way is to take the Corinne exit on Interstate 15 and head west on Highway 83 toward the Golden Spike National Historic Site. At Lampo Junction, go west toward Golden Spike for roughly 6.5 miles to where the blacktop road turns south to the historic site. Continue heading west, leaving the pavement and away from the historic site, in favor of the gravel road. In another 20 or so miles you will be at Locomotive. Take mosquito repellent in the summer months or you will pay the price.

Fishing Index: Although quite far from civilization, anglers know the stocking schedule at Locomotive well. Rainbows are planted on a regular basis in Teal, Baker,

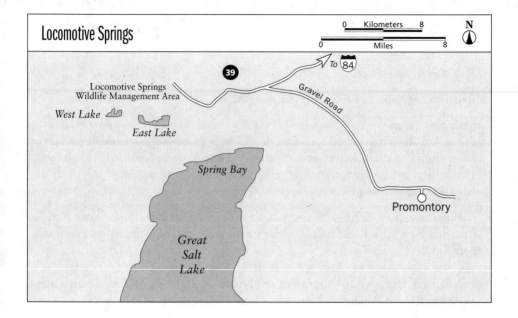

Locomotive Springs Wildlife Management Area

West Lake

East Lake

Spring Bay

Gravel Road

To 84

Promontory

Great Salt Lake

0   Kilometers   8

0   Miles   8

N

and the Bar-M Springs. A popular activity at Locomotive is sight-casting flies to large carp in the crystal clear springs. Sparks Spring has some bass and bluegill, but weed growth makes it difficult to fish for them.

40 Porcupine Reservoir

See map on page 79.

Key Species: Kokanee salmon, brown trout, cutthroat trout, and rainbow trout.

Best Way to Fish: Trolling.

Best Time of Year to Fish: Early summer.

Special Regulations: Closed to the possession of kokanee salmon with any red color from mid-August to late September. Trout and salmon limit 12; no more than four may be rainbow, cutthroat, or brown trout. To take 12 fish, eight must be salmon.

Description: Situated in a remote part of Cache County on the East Fork of the Little Bear River, facilities at Porcupine are limited. While it is possible to launch a small boat or canoe, the steep shoreline can make it difficult. Watching kokanee salmon spawn in the river above the reservoir in September is a popular fall activity. From Paradise, go south through Avon until you cross the East Fork of the Little Bear River. Turn east on a well-traveled road up the canyon. The road turns to gravel, but the reservoir is only about 2 miles away.

Fishing Index: There was a time when Porcupine was Utah's premier kokanee salmon water. Angling pressure and poor natural reproduction hurt the kokanee.

The situation was made worse when whirling disease was found at Porcupine. The future for kokanee at Porcupine is unsettled, but officials hope it will rebound.

The reservoir is known for producing some good-size brown trout. They are caught on Rapalas and large minnow-imitating lures. Porcupine does not freeze often, and when it does it provides a dangerous environment. It's probably best to avoid ice fishing at Porcupine.

41 Mantua Reservoir See map on page 79.

Key Species: Rainbow trout, cutthroat trout, bluegill, largemouth bass, and yellow perch.

Best Way to Fish: Flies and lures.

Best Time of Year to Fish: Spring, summer, and fall.

Special Regulations: Trout limit two; yellow perch limit 50; bass limit six, but only one over 12 inches.

Description: Set at the top of Box Elder Canyon, Mantua Reservoir is accessible via U.S. Highway 89 between Brigham City and Logan. The shoreline of the 544-acre fishery is publicly owned and administered by Brigham City, which has built a small, paved launching ramp and restrooms.

Personal watercraft such as pontoon boats and float tubes are an effective and enjoyable way to fish many of Utah's lakes and reservoirs. Photo by Byron Gunderson

Fishing Index: Mantua is probably best fished with a float tube or boat because the reservoir is usually choked with vegetation by midsummer. Bear Lake cutthroat are aggressive. Catch them by throwing minnow-imitating jigs or lures, especially in the spring and late fall. Fly fishers catch the most fish with streamer, Crystal Killer, and woolly bugger patterns.

Topwater lures, spinnerbaits, plastic grubs, and tubes are good bets for the bass. Look for the largemouth along weed edges, near logs and stumps, and in the few rock structures found in the reservoir.

Rainbows are easiest to catch in the spring before the weeds grow thick. Fish near stream inlets and along the dam for greater success. Use small jigs, wet flies, spoons, and spinners. Ice fishing is good for trout, bluegill, and perch with jigs and flies fished near weed edges or suspended in open water.

Spring and summer are the best times to fish for bluegill. Look for the fish to concentrate in shallow flats for the spawn. Fish with small spinners and jigs in water usually less than 10 feet deep. Ice fishing can also be a good time to catch bluegill. Use small spoons and ice flies in deep areas of the reservoir.

42 Birch Creek Reservoir

Key Species: Tiger trout and cutthroat trout.

Best Way to Fish: Bait.

Best Time of Year to Fish: Spring and fall.

Special Regulations: None.

Description: Nestled in Rich County just west of Woodruff off Highway 39, this is just far enough away from the big Wasatch Front population centers to be relatively uncrowded. There are some picnic tables and a pit toilet here as well as a couple of ponds right below the dam that dry up toward the end of hot summers. Primitive camping is allowed on the Bureau of Land Management (BLM) ground around the lake.

Fishing Index: Birch Creek receives a plant of fingerling tiger trout each year. Anglers may also catch a few native cutthroat trout. The reservoir tends to be best early in the season before it is drawn down. Most anglers simply cast bait from shore, though some cast hardware or even flies in the evening. The nature of the reservoir does not lend itself to boats, though it would probably be possible to launch a small canoe or float tube here.

43 Woodruff Reservoir

Key Species: Cutthroat trout.

Best Way to Fish: Bait and lures.

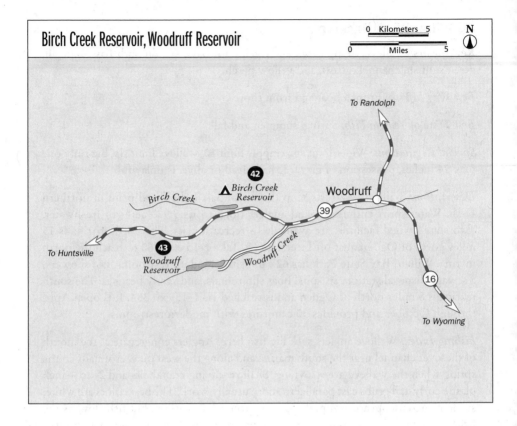

0 Kilometers 5

0 Miles 5

N

To Randolph

42

Birch Creek

Birch Creek Reservoir

Woodruff

39

To Huntsville

43

Woodruff Reservoir

Woodruff Creek

16

To Wyoming

Best Time of Year to Fish: Spring and summer.

Special Regulations: Artificial lures and flies only; 2 trout limit.

Description: Facilities are limited at this remote little Rich County reservoir. Expect drawdowns in the late summer to impact the fishing. While there is no boat ramp, it is possible to launch small boats or canoes. The reservoir is about 38 miles east of Huntsville, exactly 2 miles east of the Birch Creek Reservoir turnoff, and 6 miles west of Woodruff. Turn south and follow this gravel road to the southwest up Woodruff Creek for about 4 miles to the reservoir. The turnoff is poorly marked, but the road is not hard to find.

Fishing Index: The DWR is currently managing the reservoir as a self-sustaining cutthroat trout fishery. During the spring, use bright-colored spinners or wet flies near the stream inlets. In the summer, cast Jake's Spin-a-lure or Maisie spoons in open water. Come fall, the cutthroat become more aggressive and will often be found chasing minnows in shallow water. Try small Rapalas, marabou jigs, and streamer fly patterns in bright colors. This is a good time to use a float tube at Woodruff.

44 Willard Bay Reservoir

Key Species: Walleye, crappie, wiper, largemouth bass, smallmouth bass, bluegill, green sunfish, channel catfish, and yellow perch.

Best Way to Fish: From a boat and from shore.

Best Time of Year to Fish: Spring, summer, and fall.

Special Regulations: Wiper limit six; crappie limit 10; walleye limit six, but only one over 24 inches; possession of gizzard shad, dead or alive, is unlawful.

Description: Willard Bay rests atop the Great Salt Lake flood plain in northern Utah. Water-sport enthusiasts and anglers flock to its 9,900 acres of freshwater. Two state-owned facilities are available to recreationists. The north marina is 15 miles north of Ogden, just off Interstate 15. Take I–15 exit 360 to reach the north marina. Willard Bay State Park has 62 campsites, modern restrooms, hot showers, a sewage disposal station, seasonal boat slip rentals, and sandy beaches. The south marina is 8 miles north of Ogden and is reached via I–15 exit 354. It is open April through October and provides 30 campsites with modern restrooms.

Fishing Index: Walleye anglers seek big fish here. Anglers congregate at the mouth of the river channel near the south marina and along the west dike, especially in the spring when the walleye are spawning. Shallow-diving crankbaits and 2- to 4-inch plastic curly-tail grubs cast parallel to shore usually work. The best colors are white, silver, chartreuse, pearl, and pink. Try to cover a lot of water, but fish slow, as the fish are sluggish in the cool water. Early morning, late evening, and night are the best times to find active fish.

After the spawn, as the water warms, walleye start feeding more aggressively. Trolling is a good option at this time. Use 0.5- to 1-ounce bottom bouncers and worm harnesses as shallow as 5 feet. Some fish are also caught trolling or casting diving crankbaits or plastic jigs. The walleye will hold on ledges and near the bottom of the dikes. Submerged islands are also a good place to find them. Fishing will slow in mid-July as shad fry become more prevalent in Willard Bay.

Wipers, a white bass–striped bass hybrid, are most often fished for during boils in the summer and fall, but can be caught in early spring when they concentrate in the river channel until it closes March 1. In the current, use heavy spoons or 2- to 3-inch plastic grubs on ¼- or ⅜-ounce jig heads. After the closure, troll at 10 to 15 feet on the main lake with crankbaits, jigs, and spoons in shad-imitating colors. In the late spring, a good area to hit is near the outlet on the north end. Fish in the evening with crankbaits, spinners, and 2- to 4-inch plastic grubs.

Wiper boils begin in July and run through the fall. They occur when schools of wipers chase groups of gizzard shad. The boils typically happen at first and last light on the east half of the reservoir. Occasionally, in cloudy situations, the boils may happen at midday. Look for birds focusing on the water. Troll for wipers a

Heather Wilson caught this nice wiper—a white bass and striped bass hybrid—while fishing with her neighbor Ralph Naylor. Photo by Ralph Naylor

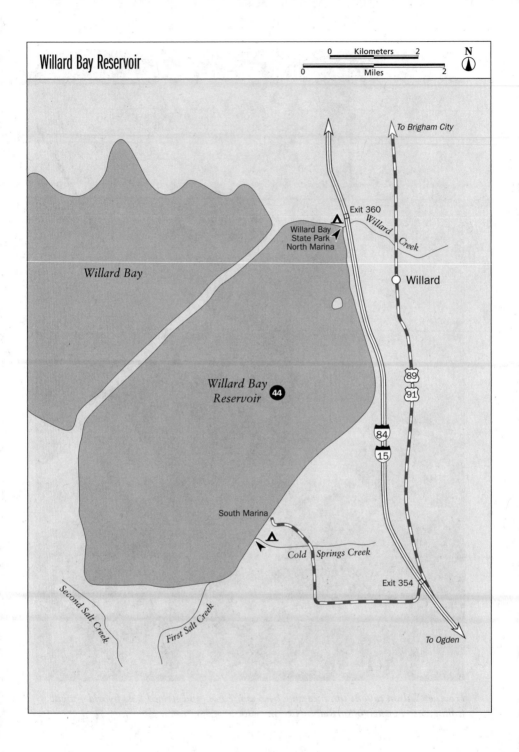

Willard Bay Reservoir

Kilometers 0 2
Miles 0 2
N

Willard Bay

To Brigham City

Exit 360
Willard Creek

Willard Bay
State Park
North Marina

Willard

Willard Bay
Reservoir 44

89
91

84
15

South Marina

Cold Springs Creek

Exit 354

Second Salt Creek

First Salt Creek

To Ogden

little faster than the typical 3- to 5-mph speed. Shad-colored plastic grubs, crankbaits, spoons, spinners, and topwater lures can all work during boils. Fishing the edge of a boil often produces bigger fish and prevents spooking the school. In the late fall, when the boils have decreased, trolling in deeper water is the best method.

Catfish numbers have increased since the introduction of the gizzard shad. Anglers experience fast action for fish up to 16 inches and the occasional fish over 10 pounds. In the spring, fish in and around the river inlet at the south marina on the bottom with night crawler, cut bait, or stink bait. As the water warms, fish along the rock dikes and suspend baits like night crawler, frozen minnow, and carp meat 4 to 6 feet below a bobber. Sometimes, the catfish can be caught on lures like Rapalas, jigs, and flies, especially while they are spawning on the rocks in June.

Crappie numbers have recovered due to a better forage base and a more restrictive limit. Fishing is best in the early spring, after the first warm spell, when the fish group along gravel shorelines and shallow bays near spawning areas. In cold water, the crappie are not as aggressive. Fish slowly and be prepared for very light hits; a bobber helps. Use small 1- to 2-inch plastic grubs or ice flies either tipped with bait or scented. Black, red, yellow, white, chartreuse, and combinations of these colors are best. As the water warms, the fish group near flooded brush, boat docks, and in select locations off the dikes for the spawn.

Smallmouth bass are the newest species in the reservoir. The bass are growing rapidly with an abundance of food. Fishing is best in the spring and fall. In the spring, use diving crankbaits, spinnerbaits, and plastic jigs around gravel flats and near the river inlet. As the water cools in the fall, the smallmouth start feeding aggressively and can be caught with small shad-colored crankbaits, spinners, and plastic jigs fished along rock dikes. Topwater lures work in low-light conditions. Sometimes, smallmouth are mixed in with the wipers on shad boils.

Largemouth bass are less numerous than smallies. Fish for them near flooded brush with spinnerbaits, weedless plastic baits, and topwater lures. Unlike the smallmouth, largemouth remain active throughout the year and are easier to catch in the colder months.

Perch are most commonly caught when fishing through the ice. Small spoons, ice flies, and jigs tipped with perch meat, colored larvae, or wax worm work well. The north and south marinas usually freeze first and provide good spots to ice fish. Some perch are caught in the summer by anglers fishing for catfish on the bottom.

Bluegill and sunfish are caught in the summer and fall in shaded areas. Night crawlers and 1- to 2-inch plastic and feather jigs work best. Fish for them with a bobber or cast parallel to the shore. Some large bluegill are caught on spinner harnesses by anglers seeking walleye.

45 Pineview Reservoir

Key Species: Tiger muskie, yellow perch, crappie, bluegill, bullhead catfish, largemouth bass, smallmouth bass, and an occasional trout.

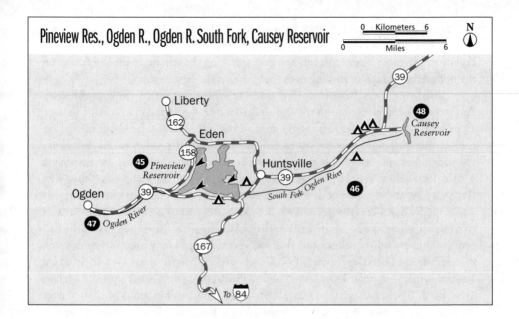

Pineview Res., Ogden R., Ogden R. South Fork, Causey Reservoir

Best Way to Fish: From a boat and from shore.

Best Time of Year to Fish: Year-round.

Special Regulations: Bass limit six, only one over 12 inches; tiger muskie limit one, all tiger muskies less than 40 inches must be released; black crappie limit 20; yellow perch limit 50. Closed inside buoys by spillway near the dam. Unlawful to use whole fish or amphibians, including water dogs, for bait. Cut bait must not be larger than 1 inch in diameter and no more than one piece per hook.

Description: At the top of Ogden Canyon, approximately 10 miles from Ogden, Pineview receives pressure from all forms of water recreationists. It is best accessed on Highway 39 from Interstate 15 or Highway 167 from Interstate 84. Two Forest Service campgrounds are located at the reservoir. Jefferson, on the southeast end of the reservoir, has 29 sites. Anderson Cove, on the south side of the reservoir, provides 96. The Port Ramp launching area is found on the west side, just north of the dam. Another ramp can be reached by taking a well-marked road from Huntsville to Cemetery Point on the lake's east side. Anderson Cove also has a boat ramp.

Fishing Index: Originally introduced to Pineview in 1989 to help control panfish, tiger muskies have become a huge draw at this reservoir. The toothy cross between a northern pike and muskellunge feeds on the perch, crappie, and trout in Pineview. The long, predacious hybrid may be the fish of a thousand casts, but the thrill they provide is worth the effort and anglers have found ways to reduce that number.

The best times to fish for tigers are late spring and fall. In the spring, look for them to follow the perch and crappie to the shallows as the panfish prepare to

Ice fishing is known for surprises. A Pineview Reservoir angler holds the tiger muskie he caught while angling for perch. Photo by Jim Gunderson

spawn. A boat is helpful to cover water because muskies don't roam the reservoir once they have found a feeding area. Use large (4- to 8-inch) spinnerbaits, bucktail spinners, and jointed Rapalas in perch, fire tiger, chartreuse, white, and black. Occasionally, the tigers can be caught on topwater lures. Steel leaders or heavy line can help ensure landing a hooked tiger.

In the fall, when the water level drops and cools, the tiger muskies leave the shallow water and hold on points, ledges, and drop-offs. Trolling is a good choice when the fish head deep. Look for them in 10 to 25 feet of water and try medium to large diving crankbaits or leaded line with shallow-running lures. Once an area with tiger muskie is located, mark it in your mind. Even if the fish aren't aggressive at that time, they may be later in the day.

Since the tigers were introduced, the perch can understandably be found hiding in the weeds and flooded brush. The tasty panfish lucky enough to avoid being eaten have doubled in size thanks to population control by the predators. In the spring and summer, perch are found near deep brush edges and along the bottom. Small plastic jigs, spoons, or night crawlers work best. In the fall, the perch leave the shallows and head for depths of 20 to 50 feet and hold there throughout the winter.

The best perch fishing is through the ice. Once a school is found, fishing for perch in the winter is fast. If you haven't had any luck within 20 minutes, move to different depths. Anglers tend to congregate near Cemetery Point, in the dam arm, and off of Browning Point. Spoons, ice flies, and small jigs tipped with perch meat, wax worms, or colored larvae are effective. Chartreuse, glow-in-the-dark, orange, and perch are the best colors. Tiger muskies are often hooked by surprised anglers fishing for perch in the winter.

Crappie are more commonly fished for in the spring and summer. In early spring and late summer, look for the panfish to hold on drop-offs just out from spawning areas at 5 to 15 feet. As the water warms in midspring and the reservoir fills, crappie move into the flooded brush to spawn. May and June are the best months to seek crappie at Pineview. Catch them with small (1- to 2-inch) plastic or feather jigs and spinners in chartreuse, white, yellow, green, red, black, and combinations of these colors. Fly fishing can also be productive with bead-head nymphs in bright colors. Because the fish are suspended in the brush, fishing a lure below a bobber can make it easier to avoid snags.

Most anglers avoid fishing for crappie in the winter because they are more difficult to locate. They tend to suspend 15 to 30 feet in deep water and can be found near the dam. Fish with ice flies and small jigs tipped with wax worm or colored larvae. Fishing for crappie can be better at night, as they are often attracted to light.

Bluegill are rarely caught in the spring and summer because they do not frequent the same areas as perch and crappie. Large concentrations of bluegill are found near the dam in the warm months. They tend to hold near broken rock in about 5 to 20 feet of water. Small jigs and night crawlers are effective. In the winter, bluegill move deeper (usually 30 to 60 feet). Use small spoons and ice flies tipped with night crawler, wax worm, or colored larvae. Bluegill seem to prefer darker-colored lures than the perch and crappie.

Spring and fall are the best times to seek largemouth bass, some of which reach 6 pounds at Pineview. They are found near stream inlets, along brush edges, and in weed lines in the spring. Spinnerbaits, weedless plastic baits, jerkbaits, and crankbaits work well at this time. In the fall, largemouth can be hard to find. They tend to group up at this time, so once you have found them spend some time in the area. Topwater baits in low-light conditions can be fun and effective. Diving crankbaits and small plastic baits can also work.

Although smallmouth are easier to catch in the summer than largemouth, the best time to fish for them is spring and fall. In the spring, they gather on gravel flats to spawn. Crankbaits, spinnerbaits, and plastic grubs/tubes in chartreuse, smoke, watermelon, and pumpkin work best. During the summer and into the fall, smallies concentrate on deep points and ledges, especially near the dam. Topwater lures fished in the early morning and late evening work well. Diving crankbaits are another good choice. Plastic grubs and tubes work when the fish are holding deeper, down to 30 feet.

Most anglers come to Pineview for its warm-water species, but there are a few trout in the reservoir. To target the trout, troll pop gear and small spoons in open water.

46 Ogden River   *See map on page 90.*

Key Species: Brown trout.

Best Way to Fish: Bait and spinners.

Best Time of Year to Fish: Spring, summer, and fall.

Special Regulations: From Pineview Dam downstream to the first bridge, approximately 0.5 mile closed to fishing.

Description: The river parallels Highway 39 from Pineview Reservoir down Ogden Canyon to the city of Ogden. Fishing is best when the river is clear. High flows can be a problem with irrigation demands. Private property also presents a problem to anglers wishing to fish the Ogden River.

Fishing Index: The river is loaded with brown trout. Bait anglers do best with night crawlers. Frozen minnows can increase the odds of catching larger fish. Minnow-imitating lures, spinners, and jigs are also good options. Fly fishers stick with bead-head nymphs and San Juan worms in the spring and during high water. Attractor patterns, stone flies, caddis flies, midges, and terrestrials work when the water is clear. State fisheries officials encourage harvest of brown trout on the Ogden to promote a more healthy fishery.

47 South Fork Ogden River   *See map on page 90.*

Key Species: Cutthroat trout, brown trout, rainbow trout, and whitefish.

Best Way to Fish: Wet flies and bait.

Best Time of Year to Fish: Fall and winter.

Special Regulations: None.

Description: The South Fork of the Ogden River is east of Pineview Reservoir and accessed on Highway 39 east from Huntsville. An abundance of USDA Forest Service campgrounds make this a popular summer destination for Wasatch Front residents. That can hurt fishing at times, largely because many recreationists like to float on inner tubes down the river in the summer months. There is a good paved trail, and there are some wheelchair-accessible fishing docks near the Perception Park campground. This is a good place to take a novice fly fisher looking to gain some confidence. In the winter, when the crowds are gone, look for bald eagles roosting in the trees above the river.

Fishing Index: Though impacted by whirling disease, trout fishing can be good on this stretch of the Ogden. Fishing is especially good for mountain whitefish, which tend to congregate in large numbers in the deep holes during the winter and are vulnerable to fishing with nymphs. Anglers also like the variety of fish that can be caught on either bait or flies. Bead-head and caddis nymphs produce well for trout when fly fishing. This is primarily a wild fish area, though some rainbow trout are planted in the summer near the campgrounds.

48 Causey Reservoir

See map on page 90.

Key Species: Splake, kokanee salmon, brown trout, cutthroat trout, and tiger trout.

Best Way to Fish: Bait, from a canoe or float tube.

Best Time of Year to Fish: Winter and spring.

Special Regulations: Closed to the possession of kokanee salmon with any red color from mid-August to the end of September (check proclamation for dates). The Wheat Grass Creek tributary to Causey Reservoir (including Dry Bread and Bear Hollow) is closed January 1 to 6:00 a.m. the second Saturday of July and is closed again mid-August to late September. The right and left forks of the South Fork Ogden River are artificial flies and lures only, with a trout and salmon limit of two, and are closed mid-August to late September. Operating a boat above a wakeless speed is prohibited.

Description: Settled in a scenic area near the top of the South Fork of Ogden Canyon, Causey has long been popular with Ogden-area anglers. Camping facilities are located down the canyon. Canoe enthusiasts like exploring the small arms of this reservoir. The reservoir is reached by heading up Highway 39 through Ogden Canyon to Huntsville. Continue for 8 more miles to a well-marked turnoff that may indicate a Boy Scout camp on the right. Follow the road for 2 miles to the reservoir. Primitive camping is allowed in the area. Deep drawdowns in late summer can restrict use at Causey.

Fishing Index: This reservoir was once managed as a rainbow trout fishery, but the increasing spread of whirling disease in this part of Utah has forced biologists to make changes. The primary species now are splake and kokanee salmon, though Causey seems to yield at least one or two trophy-size brown trout each year. There are also a few wild cutthroat in the reservoir. Most fishing is from canoes and float tubes. Bank fishing is difficult due to steep shorelines and limited access. Fishing with Power Bait near the inlets can be good in the spring and fall. This is not a bad place to try winter fishing for splake and kokanee through the ice. Fish with bright-colored spoons and jigs tipped with sucker meat down to 30 feet.

49 Lost Creek Reservoir

Key Species: Rainbow trout and cutthroat trout.

Best Way to Fish: Trolling, bait, and ice fishing.

Best Time of Year to Fish: Year-round.

Special Regulations: Closed from 10:00 p.m. to 6:00 a.m. daily. Operating a boat above a wakeless speed is prohibited.

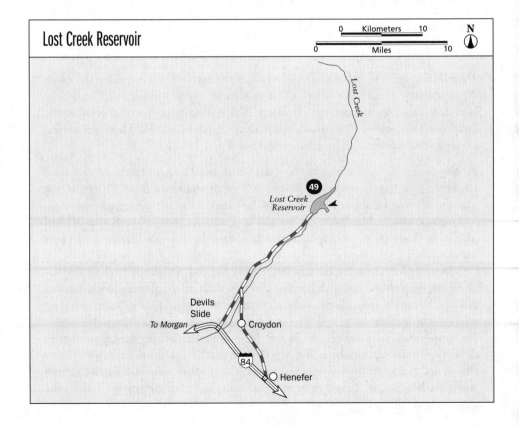

Description: Lost Creek is a 365-surface-acre reservoir perfect for boating, fishing, and water sports. It is fished primarily by anglers from the Ogden Valley. Take Interstate 84 to exit 111 in Weber Canyon and head north. Lost Creek State Park is 10 miles northeast of Croydon on a well-marked road. Facilities at the nonimproved state park include a boat-launching ramp, primitive camping, pit privies, and trash removal. Check road conditions before visiting the park in winter.

Fishing Index: Rainbow trout and Bear Lake cutthroat fishing is good throughout the year. In the spring, trout baits such as salmon eggs, night crawlers, and Power Bait work well around the inlet. Casting Rapalas, spinners, and spoons in the spring and fall when the fish are not too deep can provide fast fishing. Trolling with Rapalas, flatfish, and spoons is best in the summer months.

Ice fishing is most productive soon after the reservoir freezes. Jig for cutthroat with spoons and plastic baits tipped with wax worm or night crawler. Rainbows prefer ice flies or small jigs tipped with Power Bait or salmon eggs, but both species can be caught with either method.

50 Echo Reservoir

Key Species: Rainbow trout, brown trout, channel catfish, smallmouth bass, and perch.

Best Way to Fish: Trolling and from shore.

Best Time of Year to Fish: Year-round.

Special Regulations: Bass limit six, with only one over 12 inches.

Description: Echo is one of Utah's most visible reservoirs, as it lies along Interstate 80 for about 3 miles. Water-skiers are more common here than anglers. The fishery is underutilized for the diversity it offers. There is no state-run boat ramp at the reservoir. The owners of a private ramp charge a fee to launch. There are several places on the southeast shore where small boats may launch.

Fishing Index: Because of the heavy water-sport use, Echo is best fished early and late in the year. Early spring is the best time to go after rainbow trout. Fishing is best near the inlets and along gravel shorelines. Bait anglers use salmon eggs, Power Bait, and night crawlers. Hardware anglers use large casting spoons like Krocodile and Maisie. In the summer, trolling with pop gear, flatfish, or Triple Teazers works best for rainbows.

Some anglers chase big browns in the early fall and at night by trolling shallow along the deep shorelines with Rapalas and other minnow-imitating lures. Browns can also be caught from shore as the ice recedes, with plastic jigs or lures imitating minnows or leeches.

Smallmouth bass anglers fish in the shallows near spawning flats. Bass anglers do well with diving crankbaits and 3- to 5-inch plastic jigs in smoke, brown, chartreuse, and black. As the summer progresses, the smallies move to steep shorelines and main lake points. Topwater lures, crankbaits, and plastic jigs work best in the summer and fall.

Echo also has a good population of channel catfish. Fishing for the whisker fish is traditionally best when the reservoir is at its lowest, at the start of runoff (usually mid-May) and again in the fall. The flats on the south end of Echo are a good spot to look for catfish. Fish with night crawlers, frozen minnows, or stink baits. When the water is high, fish the flooded brush near the inlet.

51 Weber River

Key Species: Brown trout, cutthroat trout, brook trout, rainbow trout, whitefish.

Best Way to Fish: Flies, lures, and bait.

Best Time of Year to Fish: Summer, fall, and winter.

Special Regulations: Artificial flies and lures only from the first Interstate 80 bridge

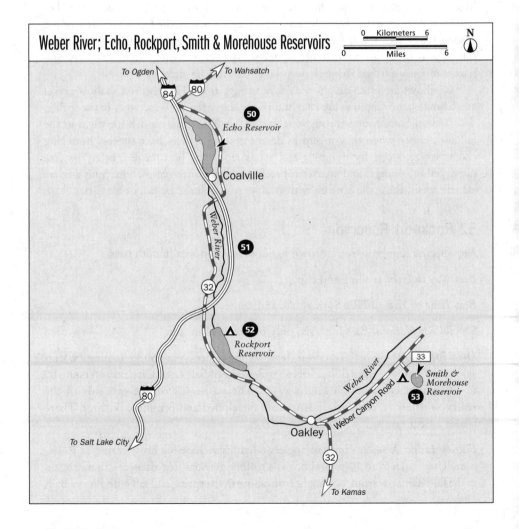

upstream from Echo Reservoir (near exit 164) to the I–80 bridge near Wanship (exit 156). Trout limit of two.

Description: This river starts in the Weber drainage of the Uinta Mountains. It then heads north to Rockport Reservoir and then Echo Reservoir. From there, it flows down Weber Canyon running along Interstate 84. Access along the river is provided at several parking areas. The most popular stretch of the river is between Rockport and Echo Reservoirs. The DWR has secured a considerable amount of access along private lands. Look for well-marked fence crossings, and respect posted private land.

Fishing Index: Brown trout and whitefish are the predominant species in the Weber, but rainbows are stocked at access points. Brook and cutthroat trout are found mostly above the town of Oakley. Water levels and clarity vary due to irrigation demands.

Most fly fishers fish nymphs on the Weber. Bead-head pheasant tail, prince, and hare's ear nymphs are solid choices. Occasional caddis, mayfly, and midge hatches keep dry fly enthusiasts busy. Streamer fishing is good in the fall when browns are getting ready to spawn. Rapalas, spinners, and jigs in gold, copper, white, chartreuse, and black are consistent producers for the browns. Night crawlers and frozen minnows fished through deep holes can also be effective.

Rainbows are often caught with salmon eggs around bridges and shallow gravel areas. Some large rainbows are caught directly above the two reservoirs in the spring.

Whitefish are found throughout the Weber. Most anglers fish for them in the fall and winter when they group in deep runs. Fly fishers have success bouncing caddis larvae, stone fly nymphs, and scuds along the bottom. Bright colors like pink, yellow, orange, and chartreuse seem to be the most consistent. Spin anglers also do well fishing the bottom with wax worms, colored larvae, or ice flies.

52 Rockport Reservoir

Key Species: Rainbow trout, brown trout, perch, and smallmouth bass.

Best Way to Fish: Trolling and bait.

Best Time of Year to Fish: Spring, fall, and winter.

Special Regulations: Bass limit six, only one over 12 inches.

Description: Rockport Reservoir features first-rate year-round fishing, waterskiing, swimming, and sailing. It is 45 miles east of Salt Lake City on Interstate 80 to Wanship then south on Highway 32. The state park on the east side of the reservoir offers 86 campgrounds in both developed and primitive settings. There is also a boat ramp.

Fishing Index: A select group of anglers religiously chase big brown trout at Rockport. They catch 5- to 10-pound browns trolling Rapalas just after ice-out and again in the fall. Rainbow trout are caught from shore in the spring and fall with Power Bait, night crawlers, and salmon eggs. Casting spoons and wet flies can also be productive at this time. In the summer, troll with flatfish, pop gear, or Triple Teazers. Chartreuse, frog, perch, and black are good color options. If seeking rainbows through the ice, suspend lures in less than 20 feet of water. Small plastic or feather jigs, ice flies, and small spoons tipped with wax worm, Power Bait, or salmon eggs work best.

Fishing for perch through the ice can be fantastic. The perch at Rockport are healthy, and fishing can be fast once the panfish are located. Search for the perch on the bottom in 30 to 60 feet of water. Small spoons and jigs tipped with wax worms or perch meat work best.

Smallmouth fishing can be sporadic; spring and fall are the best times to fish for them. In the spring, the bass will be in shallow areas with flat rock or gravel. Anglers do well with crayfish and minnow-colored crankbaits and plastic grubs or tubes. In the summer, fish steep shorelines or main lake points with topwater lures in low-light conditions. Crankbaits and plastic baits are also effective. Smallmouth will move to depths of 20 to 40 feet when the water cools in the late fall.

53 Smith & Morehouse Reservoir

Key Species: Rainbow trout and cutthroat trout.

Best Way to Fish: Bait, flies, and lures.

Best Time of Year to Fish: Summer and fall.

Special Regulations: None.

Description: Near the top of Weber Canyon above the town of Oakley, this pretty little pine-shrouded spot is popular with campers. Smith & Morehouse is reached via Highway 32 to Weber Canyon. Head east up the canyon on the paved road about 10 miles to Forest Road 33 leading to the reservoir. Two large Forest Service campgrounds are located near the reservoir. There is a small boat launch, but on this small reservoir it is more appropriate to use rafts, float tubes, and canoes.

Fishing Index: Smith & Morehouse has a good population of catchable rainbow trout. A few cutthroat sometimes enter from the inlet to the reservoir. Traditional baits work well, though casting a flashy-colored spoon can yield surprising success. Fishing near the inlet from a float tube can be exceptional with wet flies and spinners. The big draw at Smith & Morehouse is the scenery, with fishing serving as a bonus. The reservoir is stocked often from Memorial Day to Labor Day.

54 East Canyon Reservoir

Key Species: Rainbow trout, cutthroat trout, brown trout, and smallmouth bass.

Best Way to Fish: Trolling and bait.

Best Time of Year to Fish: Spring, fall, and winter.

This brilliantly spotted cutthroat trout fell for a large dry fly.

Special Regulations: None.

Description: East Canyon is a 680-acre reservoir northeast of Salt Lake City. It is best reached by taking Highway 65 from Interstate 80. (Highway 65 from I–80 is closed during the winter.) East Canyon can also be accessed from Highway 66 off Interstate 84 near Morgan. A dirt road through East Canyon near Jeremy Ranch can be used when the weather is cooperative. A state park on the north end of the reservoir, near the dam, provides a concrete launching ramp, paved parking area, modern restrooms, showers, fish-cleaning stations, and a 33-unit campground. Two spacious, covered pavilions with electricity are available for groups. A concessionaire provides boat rentals and a refreshment stand.

Fishing Index: Avoid midsummer fishing, when the water is warm and watersport enthusiasts are out in force. Rainbows are planted at the reservoir. East Canyon is underfished for as close as it is to Salt Lake. The best time to fish from shore is in the spring as the ice recedes. Try salmon eggs, night crawlers, and Power Bait near shallow gravel areas and stream inlets. Casting Maisie, Jake's Spin-a-lure, and Krocodile spoons can produce fish in cold water.

In the summer and fall, trolling is usually the best method. Flatfish, needlefish, and pop gear work. When East Canyon gets warm in the summer, the fish are suspended in cool thermoclines. During the warm months, the fish develop scars caused by anchor worms, but they are safe to eat.

Ice fishing can also be productive. Use ice flies, small spoons, and jigs tipped with wax worms, night crawlers, or Power Bait in less than 30 feet of water. Move around often to find schools of fish.

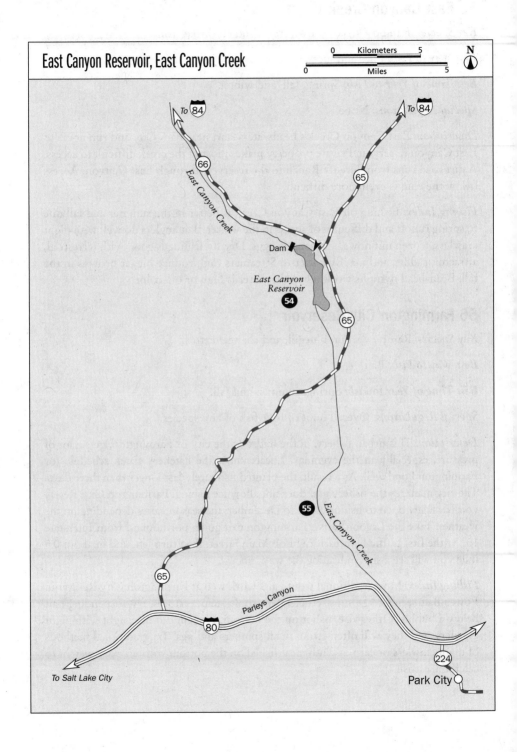

East Canyon Reservoir, East Canyon Creek

0 Kilometers 5

0 Miles 5

N

To 84

To 84

66

65

East Canyon Creek

Dam

East Canyon Reservoir

54

65

65

55

East Canyon Creek

65

Parleys Canyon

80

To Salt Lake City

224

Park City

55 East Canyon Creek

Key Species: Rainbow trout, brown trout, and cutthroat trout.

Best Way to Fish: Flies and lures.

Best Time of Year to Fish: Spring, fall, and winter.

Special Regulations: None.

Description: East Canyon Creek's headwaters start near Park City and run north to East Canyon Reservoir. Private property makes most of the creek difficult to access. A dirt road runs from Jeremy Ranch to the reservoir through East Canyon. Access below the dam is even more difficult.

Fishing Index: Fishing on East Canyon Creek is better in the summer and fall due to spring runoff and difficulty of access in the winter. Bait anglers do well with night crawlers, frozen minnows, and salmon eggs. Dry fly fishing is good with terrestrial, attractor, caddis, and mayfly patterns. Streamers can produce bigger browns in the fall. Bead-head nymphs work when the water is high or off-color.

56 Farmington City Reservoir

Key Species: Rainbow trout, bluegill, and channel catfish.

Best Way to Fish: Bait.

Best Time of Year to Fish: Spring, summer, and fall.

Special Regulations: Overall limit of four fish of any species.

Description: This urban fishery, in the midst of the city of Farmington, gets a lot of pressure, especially in the evenings. Locals know the hatchery truck schedule for Farmington Pond well. As a result, the planted fish rarely last longer than three days. The city manages the fishery and does not allow ice fishing. Farmington City Reservoir is usually open to fishing April to December; the season varies depending on the weather. Take the Lagoon Drive/Farmington exit going northbound from Interstate 15. At the first traffic light turn right on Main Street, then turn left, and in about 0.5 mile you will see a sign indicating the way.

Fishing Index: Most traditional trout baits work well at Farmington City Reservoir. Power Bait seems to be most efficient. In cooler temperatures, try suspending bait below a bubble. Otherwise, fish it on the bottom. Bluegill can be caught with night crawlers, and they will often strike small spinners and jigs. Try traditional methods of night crawlers or carp or chub meat fished on the bottom with no extra weight to catch the catfish.

57 Kaysville Pond

Key Species: Rainbow trout, channel catfish, bluegill, green sunfish, and large-mouth bass.

Best Way to Fish: Bait and lures.

Best Time of Year to Fish: Spring, summer, and fall.

Special Regulations: Overall limit of four fish of any species.

Description: As with other urban fisheries across the state, locals know the hatchery truck schedule for the Kaysville Pond. There are not many bluegill or bass here, but officials sure hear about it when anglers catch warm-water species. The pond, set on the edge of a Kaysville subdivision, can be seen from Interstate 15.

Fishing Index: Bait is the best method for trout. Salmon eggs and Power Bait are especially effective. Catfish will hit night crawlers and other smelly baits. Bass are commonly caught with night crawlers, but are more apt to hit spinnerbaits, topwater lures, and plastic baits. The bluegill and sunfish like small jigs or night crawlers fished 3 to 6 feet below a bobber.

Northeastern Utah

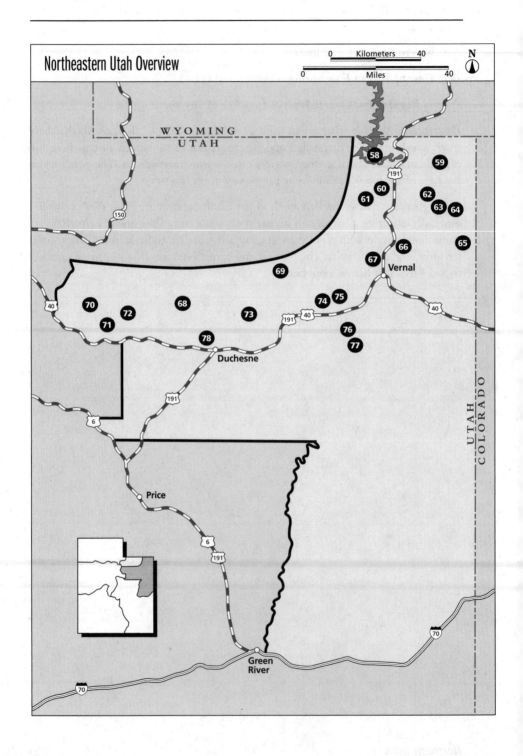

58 Flaming Gorge

Key Species: Lake trout, brown trout, rainbow trout, kokanee salmon, smallmouth bass, and channel catfish.

Best Way to Fish: From a boat and from shore.

Best Time of Year to Fish: Year-round.

Special Regulations: Any person possessing a valid Wyoming fishing license and a Utah reciprocal fishing permit for Flaming Gorge is permitted to fish within the Utah waters of Flaming Gorge. Utah residents with a valid Utah fishing license must purchase a reciprocal fishing permit from Wyoming to fish the portion of the reservoir in that state. Limit four trout (excluding lake trout) or kokanee salmon in the aggregate, no more than three may be kokanee; limit on lake trout/mackinaw is eight, but only one may exceed 28 inches; all kokanee caught September 10 through November 30 must be released. West of the line from the easternmost point of the south shore of Linwood Bay (mouth of canyon) to easternmost point of the north shore of Linwood Bay (Lucerne Point) is closed between 6:00 p.m. and 7:00 a.m. October 15 through December 15. Catfish limit six; smallmouth and largemouth bass

Jeff Mount, Ty Pettigrew, and Jay Koyle (left to right) and Steve Davis took a trip to Flaming Gorge Reservoir and came away with four dandy lake trout.
Photo by Steve Davis

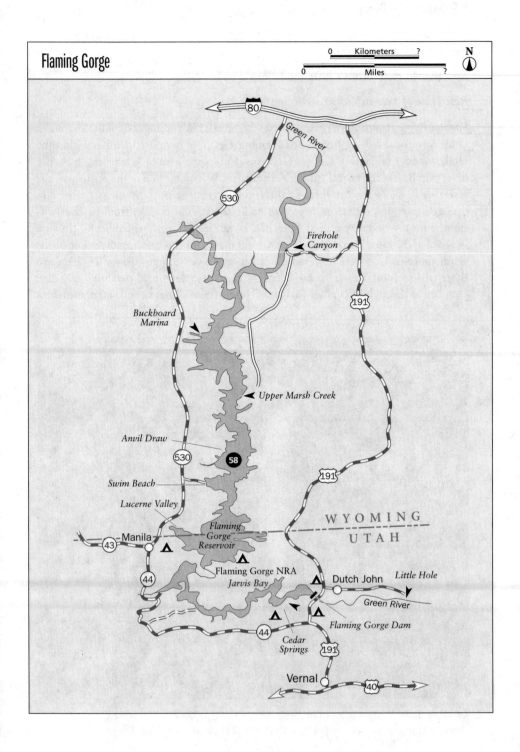

Flaming Gorge

Kilometers

Miles

N

Green River

80

530

Firehole
Canyon

191

Buckboard
Marina

Upper Marsh Creek

Anvil Draw

530

58

Swim Beach

Lucerne Valley

Manila

43

44

Flaming
Gorge
Reservoir

WYOMING
UTAH

Flaming Gorge NRA
Jarvis Bay

Dutch John   Little Hole

Green River

Flaming Gorge Dam

Cedar
Springs

44

191

Vernal

40

limit of 10 in aggregate; burbot limit 25, anglers may not release any burbot they catch. No line may have more than three baited hooks or artificial flies in a series or more than three lures; possession of a gaff while fishing is unlawful. When ice fishing, the hole size may not exceed 18 inches; mandatory catch and kill on burbot.

Description: When the Flaming Gorge Dam was completed in 1963, the only fish in the new reservoir were channel catfish and Utah chub. Eventually, some brown and rainbow trout drifted in from the Green River. But the biggest surprise was the appearance of the lake trout. The big fish, also known as mackinaw, migrated down the Green from its headwaters, the Finger Lakes of the Wind River Mountains in Wyoming.

Division of Wildlife Resources (DWR) biologists introduced smallmouth and largemouth bass in the late 1960s to help control the Utah chub. The smallmouth are now so prolific that DWR employees catch the fish en masse and transplant them to other reservoirs. The largemouth failed to thrive because the water was too cold, and as it turned out, the smallmouth were not needed because lake trout were busy chasing the chubs. Now smallmouth and brown trout dine on chub fry in the shallows, while the 50-pound-plus lake trout eat the largest chubs they can find but end up eating stocked rainbows and kokanee salmon.

The peak of Flaming Gorge fishing came in the late 1970s, when anglers pulled monster after monster from the reservoir. In 1977 Robert Bringhurst caught the current state record brown trout of 33 pounds, 10 ounces. In 1979 Del Canty landed a record rainbow weighing 26 pounds, 2 ounces. The grand champion of Utah records was set in 1988, when Curt Bilbey somehow got a 51-pound, 8-ounce lake trout into the boat.

Eventually, chub numbers diminished and the predacious lake trout turned to other fish, namely kokanee and rainbows. That led to a battle between the Utah DWR and its counterpart, Wyoming Game and Fish. Wyoming officials and anglers wanted the reservoir to be managed primarily for trophy-size lake trout. Utah biologists wanted to protect diversity and the family-friendly atmosphere of Flaming Gorge. DWR officials believed both objectives could be met by increasing the harvest on the lake trout to improve feeding conditions for the remaining fish.

In many areas of Flaming Gorge, an angler can land kokanee salmon or rainbow trout while trolling along canyon edges. Drop a jig in the same spot and pull out a lake trout. Head for the rocky outcroppings near shore and hook a smallmouth bass.

In the extreme northeast corner of Utah and southwest Wyoming, the reservoir is 91 miles long and covers 42,000 acres. Flaming Gorge is reached quickest from Salt Lake via Interstate 80 by taking the Fort Bridger exit to Manila on Wyoming Highway 414 to Utah Highway 44, which runs from Manila through the Ashley National Forest to its junction with U.S. Highway 191. Out of Vernal, take US 191 north; it runs across the 502-foot Flaming Gorge Dam and leads to Dutch John.

Visitors to the Flaming Gorge National Recreation Area are required to obtain a "Use Pass." Single-day Use Passes are $2.00, 16-day passes cost $5.00, and annual passes cost $20.00. Facilities within the Flaming Gorge National Recreation Area include 18 Forest Service campgrounds (four boat campgrounds), nine paved boat ramps, and three full-service marinas.

Mustang Ridge is located on the southeast corner of the reservoir and is accessed from US 191 via Forest Road 184. Mustang has 73 campsites with water and a boat ramp.

Arch Dam, on the south end near the dam, has four group sites and is by reservation only.

Cedar Springs has a ramp, a marina, and 23 sites. It is on the south end of the reservoir and is reached from US 191; go southwest on Forest Road 183 for approximately 2 miles. Deer Run, with 19 sites, is up the road from Cedar Springs.

Firefighters Memorial is situated high on US 191 away from the reservoir. Nestled among ponderosa pines, it has 94 sites.

Greendale is located off US 191 near Flaming Gorge Lodge. It has four sites. Skull Creek, also away from the reservoir, is adjacent to UT 44. It has 17 sites. Green's Lake is situated next to a rainbow trout fishery on Forest Service lands. It has 19 sites and is reached from UT 44 and Forest Road 95. Just down the road from Green's is the 18-site Canyon Rim Campground.

The Antelope boat ramp and 121-site campground is on the east side of the Gorge and is reached by heading north toward Wyoming on US 191 and then turning right on Forest Road 145 and driving for approximately 5 miles.

For Lucerne Valley, go 8 miles north of Manila on Utah Highway 43 then, right on Forest Road 146; it serves as the main facility at the Gorge with 161 sites, a boat ramp, marina, boat rentals, grocery store, and picnic areas.

The four boat-only campgrounds are in the eight-site Jarvies Canyon on the south end of the reservoir north of Cedar Springs. Gooseneck, near Red Canyon has six sites; Hideout Canyon near Sheep Creek Bay has 18 sites; and Kingfisher Island, northeast of Sheep Creek, eight sites.

A boat ramp is located at Sheep Creek Bay, about 7 miles south of Manila on UT 44. There is no campground here.

Visitor centers are located at the dam and at Red Canyon.

The Flaming Gorge Lodge provides motel rooms and condominiums, a store, cafe, raft rentals, boat storage, and guide service. Red Canyon Lodge has cabins and a restaurant.

Fishing Index: Since impoundment, rainbow trout have been stocked in Flaming Gorge every year, and they provide the bulk of the harvest. Kokanee salmon and smallmouth bass were stocked during the mid-1960s and have developed naturally reproducing fisheries. After rainbow trout, kokanee are typically second in harvest and popularity with anglers.

The lake trout, which drifted into the Gorge from the upper Green River drainage, have established a wild population. Flaming Gorge is known as one of the premiere trophy lake trout waters in the country. Fish over 50 pounds have been caught on both sides of the state line. Lake trout are difficult to catch, and the average angler can expect to put in many hours between fish. According to surveys in the early 1990s, the catch rate was about 0.04 fish an hour, or one lake trout caught for every 25 hours of fishing. However, anglers willing to spend that kind of time are usually rewarded with a fish over 25 pounds.

During the early spring and late fall, lake trout can be found in shallow water. Anglers without special equipment use long-line No. 13 to No. 18 Rapalas in popular colors such as perch-scale, frog, white, chartreuse, and black/silver or black/gold combinations.

During the summer months and generally under the ice, lake trout can be found in depths between 70 and 120 feet. They look for structures, like points, river channels, humps, or drop-offs.

A popular summer technique is dragging the bottom with steel line using a flatfish or Kwikfish. This requires saltwater-size rods and high-capacity reels. Much of the fun of fishing is lost using this method because it requires heavy gear and takes away much of the fight.

Downrigger fishermen do well with lures trailing 50 to 100 feet behind the weight, with the depth adjusted to keep the lure off the bottom. A popular downrigger method is to use a plastic squid, large fly, or frozen minnow 18 inches behind a large dodger or flasher. A depth finder is important, as it helps you locate fish and keep the weight from snagging bottom.

Good areas to try for lake trout include Mustang Ridge, Jarvies Canyon, Hideout, Linwood Bay, Antelope Flats, Stateline, Anvil Draw, and Buckboard.

Vertical jigging is also productive. It works from a boat or through the ice. Large ¼- to 1½-ounce jigs with marabou, bucktail, or plastic skirts, such as Mac Attacks or Gitzit tubes, are popular. The jig is often tipped with a minnow or sucker meat, which is especially effective during winter. Large spoons, BuzzBombs, and Kastmasters can work, but keep the lure bouncing right on the bottom.

Jigging through the ice is effective and doesn't require specialized equipment. Ice forms at the confluence area by early January, and hot fishing often results from following the formation of ice to the south as winter progresses.

During winter, there is a movement of lake trout as far north as the confluence, while late summer finds most fish south of Anvil Draw. Because of this migration, Currant Creek and Big Bend provide good fishing early in the spring, while Linwood Bay continues to get better as the summer progresses.

Rainbows are found throughout Flaming Gorge and usually become active during April as ice recedes and water temperatures warm. In the spring, rainbows are readily caught from shore using salmon eggs or Power Bait. Casting medium-size spinners, spoons, or Rapalas, or marabou jigs in black, brown, orange, chartreuse, and gold can also be effective.

Fly fishers do well with woolly bugger, scud, or renegade patterns fished with a sinking tip, sinking fly lines, or trailed behind a casting bubble when using spinning gear.

Good places to fish for rainbows are the Flaming Gorge Visitor Center, Mustang Ridge, Sheep Creek, Linwood Bay, Antelope Flats, Anvil Draw, South Buckboard, Breeze Hill, Sage Creek, and the confluence.

Boat anglers do equally well during the spring, trolling along the shoreline in these areas. F6 flatfish, No. 5 or No. 7 Rapalas, Super Dupers, Jake's, and other medium-size spoons and lures can be deadly. Large Rapalas, spoons, and flatfish in rainbow trout, silver, chartreuse, and white also work well. Most Gorge anglers use monofilament line rather than leaded line in the spring.

Warm water temperatures force rainbows into deeper water during summer months, making shore fishing less productive. Boat anglers catch rainbows using lead-core line, downriggers, or extra weight on their monofilament line with pop gear and lures.

Fishing picks up again in the fall when the rainbows move back into the shallows. Jarvies Canyon, Carter Creek, Sheep Creek, Linwood Bay, Squaw Hollow, Big Bend, Halfway Hollow, and Firehole provide the best rainbow fishing each fall.

When Flaming Gorge freezes—though the main lake near Lucerne may not always freeze—rainbow fishing is usually good at around 10 to 15 feet. Try small jigs, spoons, or ice flies tipped with a salmon egg or a piece of worm.

Kokanee salmon spend their four-year lifetime feeding on zooplankton that average 1 millimeter in length. They don't strike a lure because it resembles food but rather for its action and color. Effective kokanee lures at Flaming Gorge are up to 4 inches in length in fluorescent orange, chartreuse, pink, silver, gold, or white. Popular styles include needlefish, Super Dupers, Krocodiles, Triple Teazers, Kokanee Kings, and Apex.

The most popular method is to troll these lures using a downrigger. If the kokanee are aggressive, fish the lure behind a small flasher or dodger. If the fish seem finicky, trail the lure farther behind the downrigger weight without an attractor. Either way, kokanee at Flaming Gorge like fast-traveling lures, so keep boat speed at 2 to 3 mph. Another technique that works is vertical jigging with Kastmasters, BuzzBombs, or Crippled Herrings.

The main thing in catching kokanee is to locate schools and fish at the proper depth. By May or early June, kokanee action picks up with fish suspended at 25 to 30 feet over deep, open water. As the summer progresses, kokanee move deeper, and by August they may be from 60 to 70 feet deep.

A depth finder is invaluable for locating fish; then, either a lead-core line or a downrigger is necessary for trolling lures through the schools you find. Without a depth finder, work deeper intervals until you locate fish. Kokanee hold for long periods of time, so if you catch one, it pays to make several more passes through the same area.

Kokanee concentrate in different specific locations every year, but consistent producers include Cedar Springs, Jarvies Canyon, Hideout, Red Cliffs, Horse Shoe Canyon, Pipeline, Wildhorse, Squaw Hollow, Lowe Canyon, and Big Bend. As the fall spawning season approaches, mature kokanee concentrate or "stage" adjacent to spawning areas, which include Sheep Creek, Wildhorse, Squaw Hollow, and Anvil Draw.

Channel catfish are found in the north end of Flaming Gorge, generally upstream of the confluence in the Blacks Fork and Green River arms. Most catfish are caught on whole dead minnows or cut bait fished on the bottom. Trout anglers occasionally hook a catfish when fishing with night crawlers. Some catfish are also caught with lures around rock structure during the spawn. Catfish are typically more active in the warmer months and are most often caught at night.

Smallmouth bass are found throughout Flaming Gorge Reservoir. A dense population dominated by smaller fish exists from the dam north to Linwood Bay. From Antelope Flats north, fewer bass are found, but growth rates are greater. Therefore, biologists encourage harvest of smallmouth on the south end of the reservoir to help curtail stunting.

The smallmouth in Flaming Gorge are aggressive. Lures imitating crayfish or chub minnows are especially effective. Crankbaits, spinners, plastic baits, and top-water lures are consistent producers. Fly fishers do well for smallies by stripping leech or streamer patterns from shore or in float tubes.

Smallmouth spawn from late May through early July. During this period mature fish move into shallow water where they are easily reached with lures. Try crankbaits, plastic grubs and tubes, and spinnerbaits near shallow points and flats. As summer progresses, bass move deeper and are best reached by retrieving a jig slowly along the bottom.

59 Green River

Key Species: Brown trout, rainbow trout, and cutthroat trout.

Best Way to Fish: Flies and lures.

Best Time of Year to Fish: Year-round.

Special Regulations: From the Colorado state line in Brown's Park upstream to Flaming Gorge Dam, including Gorge Creek (a tributary entering the Green River at Little Hole), artificial flies and lures only, with a trout limit of three (two under 13 inches and one over 22 inches). Closed to fishing from a boat with a motor between the Colorado state line and Flaming Gorge Dam. Catch and kill on all smallmouth bass.

Description: The blue-ribbon section of the Green River flows from Flaming Gorge Dam to the Colorado state line, some 30 miles. The river is broken into three recognized sections. The A Section runs from the put-in ramp below the dam 7.5 miles to the three take-out ramps at Little Hole. The approximate 9 miles of river from Little Hole to Brown's Park is called the B Section, and the last 15 miles to the state line (Swallow's Canyon take-out) is the C Section.

First-time anglers on the Green should consider taking a guided float trip. Knowledgeable fly fishers can do well wading the river, but spending eight hours up front with a guide can make every trip thereafter more productive. Wade anglers have access to the entire A Section and parts of the B Section via a riverside trail. Raft rentals are available at Trout Creek and Green River Outfitters.

The put-in below the dam is accessed via U.S. Highway 191 at the dam. Little Hole is reached from US 191 just north of the town of Dutch John on Forest Road

The Green River's fishing is matched only by its scenic grandeur of canyon walls, clear water, and abundant wildlife.

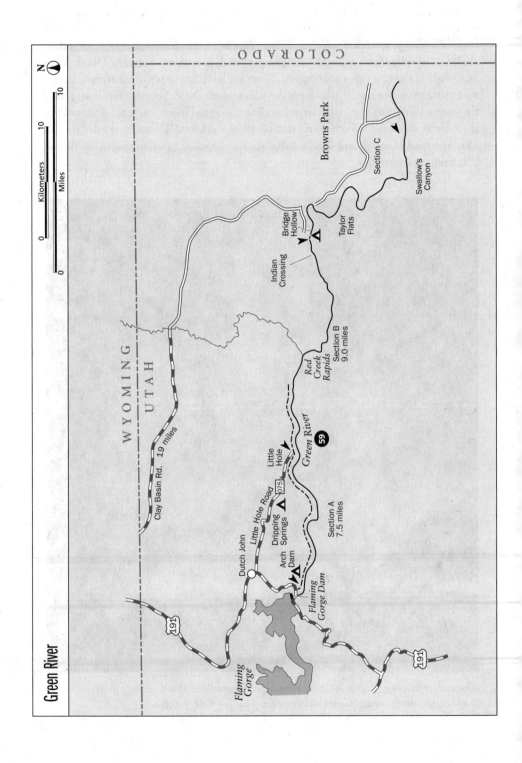

Green River

075. Most anglers using their own boats unload gear at the spillway, then drive to the Little Hole and leave the car there. Shuttle service is available in Dutch John and from Flaming Gorge Lodge, but many people make arrangements with other anglers. Dripping Springs, a 21-unit campground, is halfway between Dutch John and Little Hole. It is open year-round. Most anglers camp here when staying in the area more than one day. Camping is not allowed on the A Section, but first-come, first-served sites dot the lower stretches. Ramps on the lower river are accessed via the Clay Basin Road, which starts just north of the Utah-Wyoming border on US 191. The road is rough and can be dangerous to travel in poor weather conditions. Flat tires are common.

The author with a 9-pound brown trout caught by wildlife officials during an electroshocking survey on the Green River below Flaming Gorge Dam.
Photo by Michael Doyle

Catch-and-release and special regulations help keep the Green a blue-ribbon fishery despite heavy fishing pressure.

Fishing Index: Any questions about the reputation of the Green as one of the best fly-fishing destinations in North America are usually answered by one amazing number—biologists have figured that some stretches of the A Section hold more than 20,000 trout per square mile. Fishing the Green can be frustrating because the fish are so visible. Some guides call the upper stretches of the river the Aquarium. Too often, anglers get so caught up in fishing they fail to take time to enjoy the incredible red canyon and the wildlife in it.

While there are plenty of fish, the number of people using the river is growing at an alarming rate. The Green sees about 80,000 visitors a year—90 percent of them on the A Section. Part of that incredible number comes from recreational raft use. Weekdays are the best time to avoid the rafts and the crowds. Temperatures may not cooperate, but fishing in the winter provides a sense of solitude summer anglers rarely experience.

Brown trout are the most common catch. These hardy types make up about 60 to 70 percent of the trout below the dam and 85 percent of the fish near Little Hole. Browns are naturally self-sustaining. Rainbows are found primarily in the few miles below the dam. Cutthroat are diminishing along the river and were last planted in 1998. The DWR plants 7-inch rainbows each year.

Wind is a swear word on any fly-fishing trip. Expect afternoon canyon winds on the A Section. Some days, it will turn boats around. The weather is fickle on the Green. Make sure you have rain gear and sunscreen.

The riffles on the Green River hold many large trout. Drifting a nymph through the faster water can reap rewards.

A guided trip is a great way to learn the subtleties of fishing the Green and to exercise your fish-fighting arm.

The river record is a 29-pound, 12-ounce monster brown caught just below the dam with a minnow-imitating lure in December 1996. Officials call the fish caught by Don Brown an anomaly that likely grew to that size by feeding on fish ground up by the dam turbines and on pellets fed to fish just below the dam by tourists. The average fish caught in the Green is 15 to 17 inches. However, a 23-pound rainbow was landed in 1985 and an 18-pound brown was caught in 1993.

Fish stack up in eddies and along riverbanks. Many anglers make the mistake of fishing the middle of the river—they probably scared a dozen fish just getting in the water. Dry-fly fishers in boats almost always fish right along the shore, especially with terrestrials.

Blue-winged olive and pale morning dun hatches can be thick on overcast days. Also watch for mayfly and caddis hatches. Fishing with a size 18 to 22 Griffith's gnat, grizzly midge, and midge cluster patterns can be effective on warm winter days. The best dry fly fishing is May to September.

Knowing anglers eagerly await the cicada hatch, usually early May to June. Fishing cicada patterns can be phenomenal. As summer progresses, other terrestrials like ants, beetles, and hoppers come into play. The large Chernobyl ant pattern was created on the Green. Fish often find it too much of a morsel to pass up. Fishing a bead-head nymph dropper below a big dry fly is an effective way to fish this large river.

While most fly fishers use dries on the Green, nymphing is most productive. The primary food source of the trout, especially in the spring, is the scud. The most common color patterns are orange, tan, pink, and olive. Other popular nymph patterns include pheasant tail, RS-2, WD-40, serendipity, San Juan worm, Glo-Bugs, and emergers in sizes down to 22. In the late summer and fall, streamers and Zonkers bring in some big browns, especially in the lower sections

Lure anglers can do well on the Green. Rapalas work well in the shallows, especially at night. Diving Rapalas can be effective in the deep stretches above Little Hole. Marabou or plastic jigs in green, brown, olive, black, and white turn up nice trout. Large spoons and spinners in gold, silver, and white can also be productive.

60 East Park Reservoir

Key Species: Rainbow trout.

Best Way to Fish: Bait from shore.

Best Time of Year to Fish: Summer and fall.

Special Regulations: None.

Description: Just west of U.S. Highway 191 north of Vernal on a scenic road known as the Red Cloud Loop, this pretty little reservoir has a campground. The reservoir receives moderate pressure, particularly on three-day holiday weekends. While there is no boat ramp here, it is possible to launch small boats from the southwest corner of the reservoir, unless rain creates wet and muddy conditions.

Fishing Index: Expect to catch mostly small rainbows in this reservoir. Fishing can, and usually does, hold up here through much of the summer. Bright-colored lures and standard trout baits are the most popular methods. Fishing from a float tube or canoe can add to the experience and the success. Nearby streams can also produce some good fishing.

61 Oaks Park Reservoir

Key Species: Rainbow trout.

Best Way to Fish: Bait and wet flies.

Best Time of Year to Fish: Summer and fall.

Special Regulations: None.

Description: This is a small alpine lake surrounded by forest located on the Red Cloud Loop Road north and west of Vernal. Though not as scenic as East Park Reservoir, it nevertheless features a quiet Forest Service campground. Boat launching is difficult here, though it would be a good place for a canoe, rubber raft, or float tube.

Fishing Index: Fishing pressure tends to be lighter here than in other Uintah Basin locations, but it can receive moderate pressure on some of the busy holiday weekends. Fish tend to be small but plentiful. This is a good place to beat the crowds and take the kids for some fast action. Standard trout baits are always a good choice from shore. Fly fishers do well with dark woolly buggers and some streamers. Maisie and Jake's spoons are another option.

62 Matt Warner Reservoir

Key Species: Rainbow trout.

Best Way to Fish: Bait and wet flies.

Best Time of Year to Fish: Summer and fall.

Special Regulations: None.

Description: Named after a famous local outlaw, Matt Warner Reservoir is the largest of the three Diamond Mountain reservoirs and usually offers the best fishing. Facilities are limited to a boat ramp and a toilet. Though some snowmobilers try to make the trip in during the winter, it is primarily a summer fishery. The Diamond Mountain reservoirs are accessible from US 191 between Dutch John and Vernal. A road heading east is found 10.5 miles south of Highway 44 and US 191 when coming from the north and 4 miles north of the Red Cloud Loop turnoff (west) when coming from the south. Signs should be in place to help you find the reservoir, but a detailed map will ensure you get there in a timely manner. Another route is on the Jones Hole Road from Vernal. Travel west on 500 North in Vernal as it goes out of town and winds up Diamond Mountain. Twenty-two miles from Vernal, turn left on a gravel road marked Highway 44.

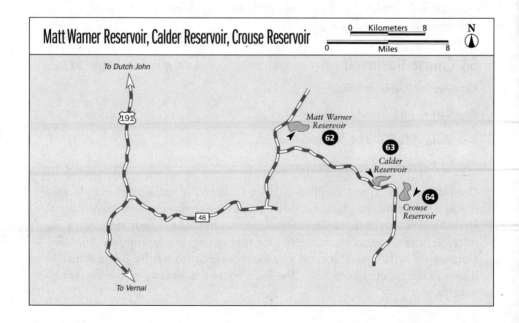

Fishing Index: Expect heavy pressure here. The trout fishing holds up through much of the summer, and anglers from nearby Vernal know it. That's the reason the limit is half the statewide normal limit. In the spring and fall, fish will be shallow and can be caught from shore. Bait fishing is good with Power Bait, salmon eggs, or a night crawler with a marshmallow. Casting bright-colored lures and spoons should also work. Fishing with flies is good with dark-colored wet flies and nymphs. In the summer, the fish will hold in deeper water. Trolling with pop gear, Triple Teazers, and flatfish will produce more fish at this time.

63 Calder Reservoir

See map on page 119.

Key Species: Rainbow trout.

Best Way to Fish: Flies.

Best Time of Year to Fish: Summer and fall.

Special Regulations: Artificial flies and lures only; only 1 trout over 22 inches.

Description: Facilities at this spot on scenic Diamond Mountain northeast of Vernal are limited to a small boat ramp mainly used to launch car toppers. There is also a toilet. This popular area hosts many local anglers throughout the summer. Because it is close to Crouse and Matt Warner Reservoirs, anglers have the option of trying different bodies of water without driving too far.

Fishing Index: The low trout limit tells much about this popular little reservoir. It receives heavy plants of rainbow trout that nevertheless seem to grow fat and feisty. The lower limit was set to prevent Calder from being fished out too quickly. Good shoreline access makes it popular with bait anglers. Spinners, spoons, and flies work well from shore or float tubes.

64 Crouse Reservoir

See map on page 119.

Key Species: Rainbow trout.

Best Way to Fish: Bait from shore.

Best Time of Year to Fish: Summer and fall.

Special Regulations: Trout limit four.

Description: This is one of three popular Diamond Mountain fisheries located northeast of Vernal on Diamond Mountain in the extreme northeastern corner of Utah. The smallest of the three, facilities here are limited to a boat ramp. Since the reservoir is small, small boats, canoes, or rubber rafts are appropriate. Shoreline access is good. If fishing is slow, you can always go to nearby Jarvie Ranch at Browns Park on the Green River and learn about the outlaws who once roamed the area.

Fishing Index: This reservoir has a reduced limit due to high fishing pressure. Traditional baits such as salmon eggs, night crawlers, or Power Bait work well here. Fishing with flies can also be productive on occasion.

65 Jones Hole Creek

Key Species: Rainbow trout and brown trout.

Best Way to Fish: Flies.

Best Time of Year to Fish: Spring, summer, and fall.

Special Regulations: Trout limit two, only one brown larger than 15 inches; artificial flies and lures only.

Description: About an hour's drive from Vernal, this creek runs from the Jones Hole National Hatchery to the Green River. The U.S. Fish and Wildlife Service hatchery is 40 miles northeast of Vernal near the Colorado border. It is reached by heading east on 500 North in Vernal, marked as the Jones Hole Road on some maps. Driving the road can be dangerous in the winter. Underground springs provide up

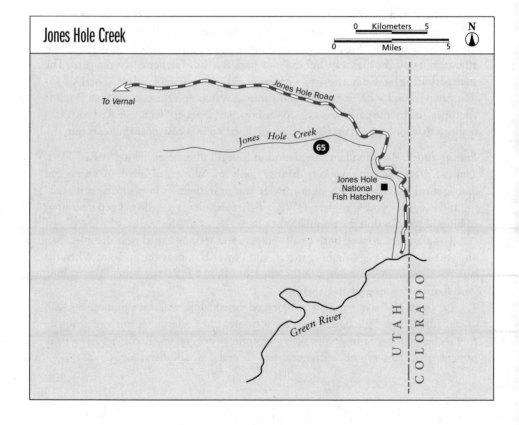

to 15,000 gallons of water per minute at the trout-loving temperature of 54 degrees. Picnic tables, a visitor center, tours, and restrooms are available at the hatchery. A trail leads from the hatchery 4 miles down to the Green River.

Fishing Index: Heavy cover on the banks makes fishing difficult, especially with flies. On top of that, the water in the small creek is clear and the fish are spooky. Large groups of escaped rainbows stack up below the hatchery, but it is hard to get their attention. Most anglers wait until late spring and then fly fish with big terrestrials and stone flies along the banks. Bead-head nymphs work well when the fish are not looking up. Some big browns can be caught where the creek dumps into the Green River.

66 Red Fleet Reservoir

Key Species: Bluegill, largemouth bass, and rainbow trout.

Best Way to Fish: From a boat and bait from shore

Best Time of Year to Fish: Spring, summer, and fall.

Special Regulations: Bass limit six, only one larger than 15 inches.

Description: Red Fleet Reservoir is reached via U.S. Highway 191 north from Vernal, toward Flaming Gorge. A marked road about 9 miles north of Vernal leads to the reservoir and Red Fleet State Park. A boat launch is located on a dirt road soon after turning off the highway, but the state park is a little farther down the road. The state park has a large day-use area with grass and covered picnic tables. There's a 35-unit campground with restrooms and running water. A large cement boat ramp is also operated by the park. It is easy to see how Red Fleet got its name. Red rock formations that look like giant battleships are lined up in a row near the reservoir.

Fishing Index: An abundant population of bluegill offers fast fishing at Red Fleet. This is a great place to take kids fishing. Look for submerged brush or weeds and dangle small jigs tipped with night crawler near or in them. A bobber makes it exciting and easier for young anglers. DWR officials encourage people to keep their limit of bluegill to help thin the population.

Trout anglers do well with small spinners and spoons fished near the inlet. Bait anglers use salmon eggs, night crawlers, and Power Bait near the bottom. When the water warms in the summer months, the trout head for deeper water. Try trolling with flatfish or pop gear and a worm.

Largemouth bass hang in submerged brush and will hit spinnerbaits and crankbaits. In low-light conditions, try topwater lures. Plastic worms and grubs up to 4 inches work well in deeper water as summer progresses. Red Fleet has a large population of largemouth, with occasional 2- and 3-pound fish caught.

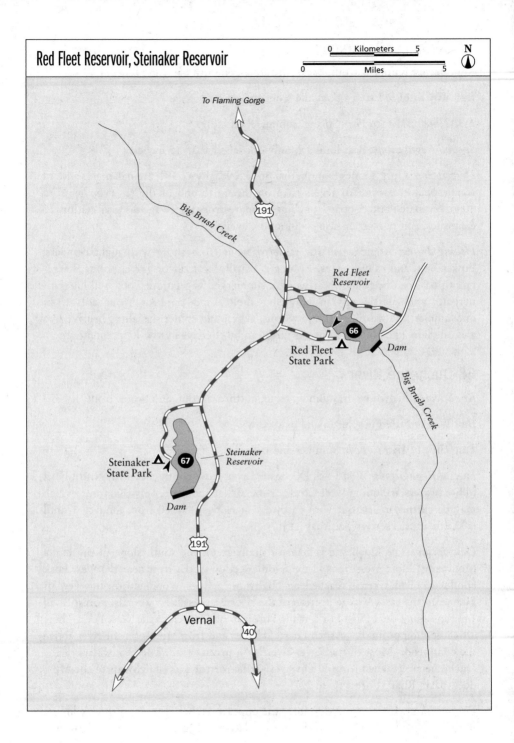

Red Fleet Reservoir, Steinaker Reservoir

0 Kilometers 5
0 Miles 5

N

To Flaming Gorge

Big Brush Creek

191

Red Fleet
Reservoir

66

Red Fleet
State Park

Dam

Big Brush Creek

Steinaker
State Park

67

Steinaker
Reservoir

Dam

191

Vernal

40

67 Steinaker Reservoir

Key Species: Rainbow trout, brown trout, largemouth bass, and bluegill.

Best Way to Fish: From a boat and from shore.

Best Time of Year to Fish: Spring, summer, and fall.

Special Regulations: Bass limit six, only one larger than 15 inches.

Description: Only 4 miles from Vernal on U.S. Highway 191, Steinaker gets a lot of recreational pressure. An access road on the north end of the reservoir leads to Steinaker State Park. A boat-launching ramp, restrooms, sewage disposal station, 31 campsites, and two group-use pavilions are available.

Fishing Index: Anglers fish for rainbow trout from shore with night crawlers, Power Bait, and salmon eggs. Fishing is usually best off of gravel points. Largemouth bass can be found in areas with submerged vegetation. They will hit spinnerbaits and plastic jigs in crayfish, smoke, and rainbow trout colors. In midsummer, use weedless plastic worms, tubes, and spider jigs along brush edges and on main lake points. Topwater lures can be effective in low-light conditions.

68 Duchesne River

Key Species: Brown trout, rainbow trout, cutthroat trout, and brook trout.

Best Way to Fish: Flies, lures, and bait.

Best Time of Year to Fish: Summer and fall.

Special Regulations: West Fork Duchesne River, from confluence with North Fork to headwaters, including Wolf Creek: artificial flies and lures, only two trout (which may be cutthroat or trout with cutthroat markings), closed from January 1 until 6:00 a.m. on the second Saturday of July.

Description: The Duchesne is a major drainage on the south slope of the Uinta Mountains. Most pressure is in the middle section of the river near the West Fork confluence. The river is reached on Highway 35 from Woodland on the west or Hanna on the east. A large portion of the river is accessible via roads. Forest Road 144 runs along the North Fork, while Forest Road 050 serves the West Fork. There are three campgrounds—Aspen Grove, Hades, and Iron Mine—on the river above the confluence. Most of the lower river is on private land. The headwaters of the Duchesne are reached from Highway 150, the Mirror Lake Highway, to the Murdock Basin Road (Forest Road 027).

Fishing Index: Brook trout dominate the upper stretches. There is a short window of time to fish the headwaters—high water lasts until July, and by late August it is

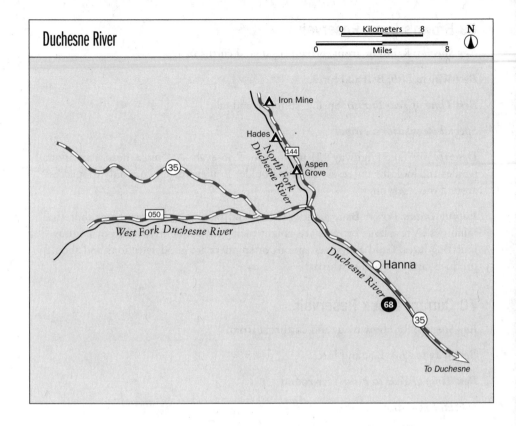

often too low to make it worth a visit. Attractor and terrestrial patterns work for the brookies.

Due to heavy pressure, the river near campgrounds is frequently stocked with catchable rainbows. Baits like salmon eggs and night crawlers are effective here. Flies and lures also work.

A large population of cutthroat trout inhabits the West Fork. A spring closure and the two-fish limit protect the cutthroat. The fish here are generally larger than those on the North Fork. Fly fishing is best with dry flies like parachute Adams, elk hair caddis, and terrestrials later in the summer. A few browns are caught in the West Fork; look for them near the confluence, particularly in the fall.

Browns rule the lower river. This is the best chance for a large fish on the Duchesne. Private property is a major obstacle. Fishing for browns is best in the fall as they prepare to spawn and become aggressive. Rapalas and spinners are good in gold, white, chartreuse, and black. Look for browns to be grouped near areas with gravel. When fly fishing, use large and bright-colored streamers during low-light conditions.

69 Brown's Draw Reservoir

Key Species: Rainbow trout, brown trout, and cutthroat trout.

Best Way to Fish: Bait and lures.

Best Time of Year to Fish: Spring, summer, and fall.

Special Regulations: None.

Description: Take Highway 121 north from Roosevelt. At Neola, head west about 6 miles and look for the reservoir near Boulder Boulevard. There is only foot access around the reservoir.

Fishing Index: Power Bait, night crawlers, and salmon eggs work from shore for rainbows. A few large browns are caught each year on night crawlers or minnow-imitating lures. Gold and silver spoons or spinners are good selections and should produce rainbows and cutthroat.

70 Currant Creek Reservoir

Key Species: Rainbow trout and cutthroat trout.

Best Way to Fish: Bait and lures.

Best Time of Year to Fish: Year-round.

Special Regulations: None.

The crisp, clear water of Currant Creek is well known for fly fishing for native cutthroat trout and husky brown trout. Photo by Marta Savage-Stott

Description: It is reached from U.S. Highway 40 between Strawberry Reservoir and Fruitland. When coming from Strawberry, look for the Currant Creek Cafe, which is located next to Forest Road 083. The road runs along most of the length of Currant Creek for 14 miles to the reservoir. Some call this "Mini-Strawberry." The road is kept open in the winter when conditions allow. The USDA Forest Service runs a 99-site campground at the reservoir. The ramp and campground are located on the west side.

Fishing Index: Because it is so close to Strawberry, pressure is relatively light at Currant Creek Reservoir. Fishing is usually fair to excellent for Bear Lake cutthroat and stocked rainbows. Fish up to 5 pounds are not uncommon. In cooler weather, the fish are near the surface and can be caught with brightly colored lures. Stripping dark woolly buggers from a float tube is usually most productive when the weather cools. In warmer temperatures, trolling is best, but bait fishing with Power Bait, night crawlers, or frozen minnows can also bring some nibbles.

71 Currant Creek

Key Species: Brown trout, cutthroat trout, and rainbow trout.

Best Way to Fish: Flies and lures.

Best Time of Year to Fish: Spring, summer, and fall.

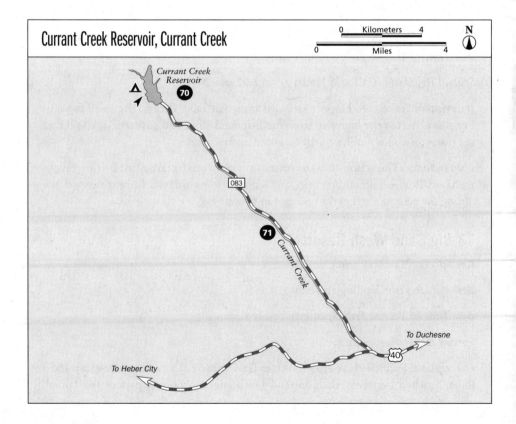

Special Regulations: From Water Hollow Creek upstream to headwaters, trout limit two; artificial flies and lures only.

Description: The most commonly fished section flows out of Currant Creek Reservoir. It is reached from U.S. Highway 40 between Strawberry Reservoir and Fruitland. When coming from Strawberry, look for the Currant Creek Cafe, which is located next to Forest Road 083. The road runs along most of the length of the creek for the 14 miles to the reservoir. The road is kept open in the winter when conditions allow.

Fishing Index: This is a popular fly-fishing destination. Big browns and an abundance of cutthroat trout provide plenty of excitement. In the cooler months, beadhead nymphs and streamers are the best bet. In warmer conditions, try pale morning dun and blue-winged olive patterns. As the summer progresses, look for terrestrials to be effective, especially grasshoppers. Spin anglers do well with Rapalas and spinners. Some anglers use jigs in the deep holes. Bait is allowed below Water Hollow Creek. Drift salmon eggs and night crawlers through riffles and pools for rainbows.

72 Red Creek Reservoir

Key Species: Rainbow trout.

Best Way to Fish: Bait and spinners.

Best Time of Year to Fish: Summer and fall.

Special Regulations: Closed January 1 to 6:00 a.m. May 1.

Description: Take U.S. Highway 40 east from Salt Lake City to the small town of Fruitland. Across the highway from the Fruitland store and gas station, you'll find the reservoir about 7 miles north on an unmarked road.

Fishing Index: The action after the reservoir is open can be fast. Most fish are caught with bait. Power Bait, salmon eggs, and night crawlers are best. Fishing slows down during the summer, but picks up again in the late fall.

73 Big Sand Wash Reservoir

Key Species: Rainbow trout.

Best Way to Fish: Trolling and bait.

Best Time of Year to Fish: Spring and early summer.

Special Regulations: None.

Description: Facilities here are primitive. They consist of a cement boat ramp and a toilet. Situated between Altamont and Duchesne in a remote part of the Uintah

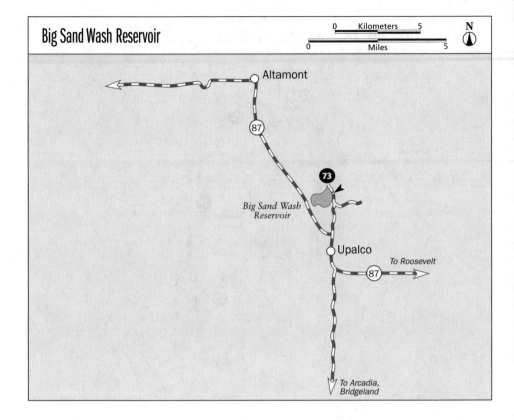

Altamont

87

73

Big Sand Wash
Reservoir

Upalco

To Roosevelt

87

To Arcadia,
Bridgeland

Basin, the main reason to come here is to fish. This is not a large enough reservoir to enjoy powerboating, there are no camping facilities, and it is not particularly scenic. Therefore, it is seldom crowded, though the good fishing can mean moderate weekend crowds. The best time to visit is in spring and summer. Later in the year it gets drawn down by irrigation. That can make boat access a problem.

Fishing Index: Fishing can be reasonably good for small rainbow trout, but every now and then anglers are surprised by a big holdover. There have been reports of fish up to 10 pounds. Power Bait, salmon eggs, and night crawlers are the baits of choice. This is a good place to troll slowly with lures in open water.

74 Bullock Reservoir

Key Species: Smallmouth bass, tiger muskie, and rainbow trout.

Best Way to Fish: Bait and lures.

Best Time of Year to Fish: Spring, summer, and fall.

Special Regulations: Tiger muskie limit one; all tiger muskies less than 40 inches must be released. It is unlawful to use whole fish or amphibians, including water

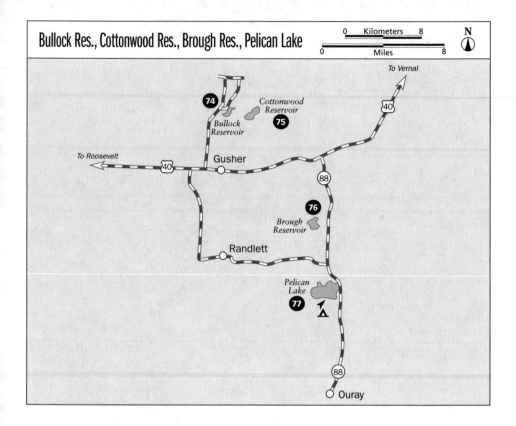

dogs, for bait. Cut bait must not be larger than 1 inch in any dimension and no more than one piece per hook.

Description: Situated 5 miles north of Gusher off U.S. Highway 40, this reservoir has no boat ramp, but small boats can be launched in the southwest corner near the dam.

Fishing Index: Trout fishing is slow, but best with bait or bright lures. Bass fishing is good in the spring with 3- to 5-inch curly-tail grubs in crayfish, smoke, and rainbow trout colors. The DWR is considering discontinuing the rainbow plants here.

75 Cottonwood Reservoir

Key Species: Smallmouth bass, tiger muskie, and rainbow trout.

Best Way to Fish: Lures and plastic baits.

Best Time of Year to Fish: Spring, summer, and fall.

Special Regulations: Bass limit six, only one over 15 inches; tiger muskie limit one, all tiger muskies less than 40 inches must be released. It is unlawful to use whole fish or amphibians, including water dogs, for bait. Cut bait must not be larger than 1 inch in any dimension and no more than one piece per hook.

Description: This small reservoir about 5 miles north of Gusher and near Bullock Reservoir is reached by a dirt road from Bullock. It receives little pressure. There is no ramp at Cottonwood, but boats can be launched in the northwest corner. It's an ideal reservoir for float-tubing.

Fishing Index: Cottonwood can provide some good fishing for smallmouth bass. Most are less than a pound, but fish up to 4 pounds are often caught. Use diving crankbaits and plastic grubs in crayfish and natural colors. Look for points or areas with rock for the best success.

76 Brough Reservoir

Key Species: Smallmouth bass and rainbow trout.

Best Way to Fish: Flies and lures from shore.

Best Time of Year to Fish: Spring, summer, and fall.

Special Regulations: Artificial flies and lures only. Only one trout over 22 inches.

Description: To reach Brough, take Highway 88 (Ouray Road) south from U.S. Highway 40. Turn west at the second dirt road past the high power lines. Follow the road about 0.75 mile, staying to the left at each fork. There is no boat ramp, but small boats can be launched on the north side.

Fishing Index: Fishing with lures and spinners from shore is good for the rainbows in spring and fall when the water is cool. The smallmouth bass fishing can be excellent at times. Plastic worms and grubs up to 4 inches in crayfish colors work best. Most fish are small, but the reservoir does produce a few over 2 pounds. DWR asks anglers to keep bass to help increase the growth of remaining fish.

77 Pelican Lake

Key Species: Bluegill, largemouth bass, green sunfish, and catfish.

Best Way to Fish: Flies, lures, and bait.

Best Time of Year to Fish: Spring, summer, and fall.

Special Regulations: Bluegill and green sunfish limit of 20 in the aggregate; bass limit six, only one larger than 15 inches.

Description: Pelican Lake is accessible from U.S. Highway 40 via Highway 88 (the Ouray Road) 15 miles west of Vernal and 15 miles east of Roosevelt. Access is possible from Highway 88 on the east shore of the lake. Dirt roads provide

Pelican Lake in northeastern Utah is known for producing large bluegill. Photo by Larry Mathis

Pelican Lake also holds plump bass, such as the largemouth this happy angler caught.
Photo by Jim Gunderson

access to other parts of Pelican. A Bureau of Land Management (BLM) camping area with 18 units and a boat ramp is located on the south side. There may be no better bluegill fishing in the state, or even in the entire West. In the 1980s Pelican grew huge, hard-fighting bluegill up to 2 pounds, but consecutive low-water years and heavy pressure took its toll. It has taken a while, but the lake has recovered and the big fish are back. The larger bluegill bulldoze into the reeds and make it tough to get them out with light tackle. Pelican's bluegill are twice the size of bluegill in most waters.

Fishing Index: During the spring, adult bluegill pack the clear, reedy shallows of Pelican and provide outrageous fly fishing with surface poppers and flies. In the right conditions, anglers can sight cast to the panfish. This is a great time to teach beginning fly fishers.

Bluegill are often caught with small spinners, plastic/feather jigs, and night crawlers on light spinning tackle. When the spawn winds down, the fish leave the shallows and head for deeper water. Fishing from boats and float tubes is a good choice. Weed growth can make fishing difficult, but it is worth the hassle.

Pelican Lake is not known as a largemouth bass fishery, but this lake hosts a large population. Although most of the bass are less than 12 inches, there are some 4-pounders.

Largemouth move into the shallow water before the bluegill. They can be caught with spinnerbaits, jig-n-pigs, spider jigs, and large plastic worms or lizards. Dark colors of black, purple, and brown are best. The bass at Pelican are known to take topwater lures more readily than at other waters. Buzzbaits, propbaits, and poppers in bright colors work well cast along weed edges or in pockets for the best success.

78 Starvation Reservoir

Key Species: Walleye, brown trout, rainbow trout, smallmouth bass, and perch.

Best Way to Fish: From a boat.

Best Time of Year to Fish: Summer and fall.

Special Regulations: None.

Description: Access to Starvation Reservoir is on the west end of Duchesne off U.S. Highway 40. Other parts of the shore can be reached on various unpaved roads. Starvation State Park provides a 54-unit campground, modern restrooms, showers, a group-use area, and sewage disposal. Primitive camping is allowed at designated areas around the reservoir.

Fishing Index: Starvation is best known as a walleye fishery, but smallmouth bass fishing is as good here as anywhere in the state, and there is always a chance at a tro-

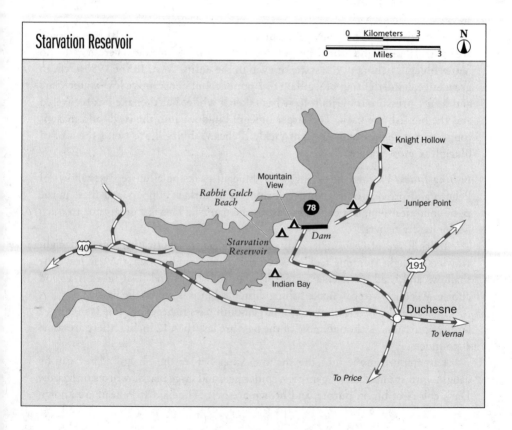

Starvation Reservoir

phy brown trout. Walleye fishing is best in the summer and fall. Rocky points, reefs, and weeded areas tend to hold the most fish. Trolling bottom bouncers trailing a spinner harness tipped with worm at depths down to 40 feet is one of the best ways to find concentrations of fish. When you find them, try jigging with 2- to 3-inch curly-tail grubs or colored jig heads tipped with a night crawler. The walleye at Starvation feed primarily on chub minnows and crayfish. Smoke, blue pearl, chartreuse, orange, and brown are excellent choices.

If you are looking for bigger fish, try fishing at night or at first light. Cast or troll crankbaits parallel to windy shorelines and points. The best places to start early in the summer are south of the US 40 bridge and Saleratus Wash, on the northeast end of the reservoir. Later in the year, walleye head for the main body of the lake.

A large population of smallmouth makes bass fishing at Starvation fun. In the spring, the fish are found on flats preparing for the spawn. In the summer and fall, look for deeper points, ledges, and windy shorelines. Diving crankbaits, in-line spinners, and plastic grubs and tubes in chartreuse, smoke, brown, and watermelon work best in all seasons.

Most brown trout are caught by walleye anglers, but they can be targeted. Perhaps the best times are just as the ice leaves Starvation and again in the fall before it retakes the reservoir. Trolling or casting large minnow-imitating lures or jigs in shallow water at night or on cloudy days should provide some action.

Trout can also be caught while trolling open water with pop gear and worm, flatfish, or Triple Teazers.

Southeastern Utah

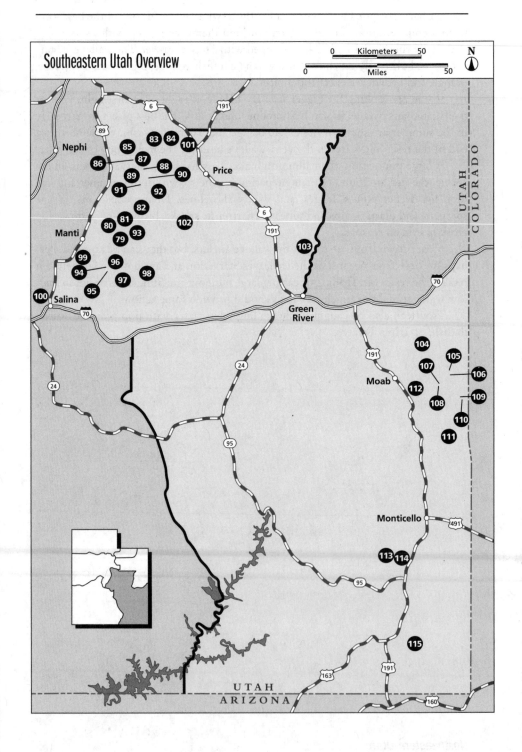

Southeastern Utah Overview

Kilometers 50

Miles 50

N

Nephi

Price

Manti

Salina

Green River

Moab

Monticello

UTAH / COLORADO

UTAH / ARIZONA

79 Mary's Lake

Key Species: Rainbow trout.

Best Way to Fish: Bait, lures, and flies.

Best Time of Year to Fish: Spring and summer.

Special Regulations: None.

Description: Mary's Lake is reached via Forest Road 041 at the south end of Joe's Valley Reservoir. After about 4 miles, the road turns north. Mary's Lake is about 3 miles away.

Fishing Index: Bait is the best method for the lake's planted rainbows. Power Bait, night crawlers, and salmon eggs fished on the bottom are best. Spinners work well in the late morning and early afternoon. Cast small dry flies, such as Adams and

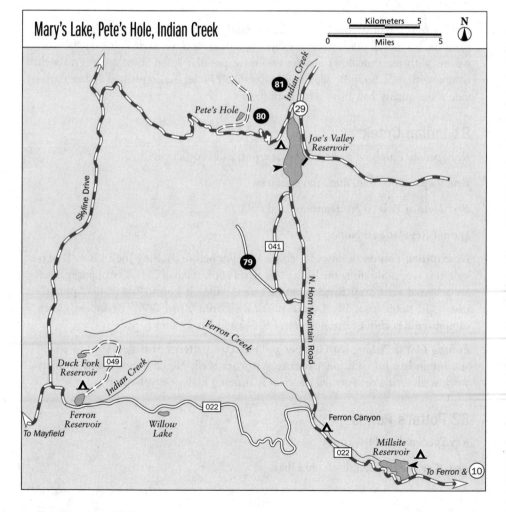

Mary's Lake, Pete's Hole, Indian Creek

mosquitoes, to rising fish in the evening. Lake conditions sometimes become unsuitable for fishing in late summer. Best fishing occurs from mid-May to about the Fourth of July.

80 Pete's Hole

Key Species: Rainbow trout and cutthroat trout.

Best Way to Fish: Bait, lures, and flies.

Best Time of Year to Fish: Summer and fall.

Special Regulations: Pete's Hole tributaries closed January 1 to 6:00 a.m. on the second Saturday of July.

Description: This small but popular fishery is situated between Skyline Drive and Joe's Valley Reservoir. It is accessible from Forest Road 8 and is about 0.75 mile on Forest Road 055.

Fishing Index: Bait fishing for the planted rainbows is fast and furious after a recent planting, but heavy pressure means there will be slow times as well. Power Bait and worms with marshmallows are the two most popular baits. Some anglers do well fishing with flies. Soup Bowl, a pond near Pete's Hole, is also planted and can provide some quality bait fishing for rainbows.

81 Indian Creek

Key Species: Rainbow trout, cutthroat trout, and brook trout.

Best Way to Fish: Bait, flies, and spinners.

Best Time of Year to Fish: Summer and fall.

Special Regulations: None.

Description: This creek flows for about 10 miles before entering Joe's Valley Reservoir. It is accessible along the Miller Flat Road (Forest Road 014). The upper reaches are accessed via Forest Road 8 out of Orangeville on Forest Road 040. Approximately 10 miles from FR 8, head north on Forest Road 017. The Indian Creek campground is about 1.5 miles from FR 040 and has 29 sites.

Fishing Index: Fishing with hopper and attractor patterns provides nonstop action starting in late July. Caddis patterns also work well. Night crawlers and spinners work well during times when the river is running high or is off-color.

82 Potter's Ponds

Key Species: Rainbow trout.

Best Way to Fish: Bait, lures, and flies.

Best Time of Year to Fish: Summer and fall.

Special Regulations: None.

Description: Potter's Ponds are found about halfway between Miller Flat Reservoir and Joe's Valley Reservoir via Forest Road 014. Look for Forest Road 271, a four-wheel-drive road, heading toward Skyline Drive. The ponds are about 0.5 mile off FR 014.

Fishing Index: Planted heavily with rainbows, the ponds are popular for families and Scout groups. Bait is the best bet. Power Bait and salmon eggs fished off the bottom produce the most fish. Look for some fish rising to dry flies in the evening.

83 Scofield Reservoir

Key Species: Rainbow trout, cutthroat trout, and tiger trout.

Best Way to Fish: Trolling and bait.

Best Time of Year to Fish: Year-round.

Special Regulations: Trout limit eight. Tributaries are closed from January 1 to 6:00 a.m. on the second Saturday of July.

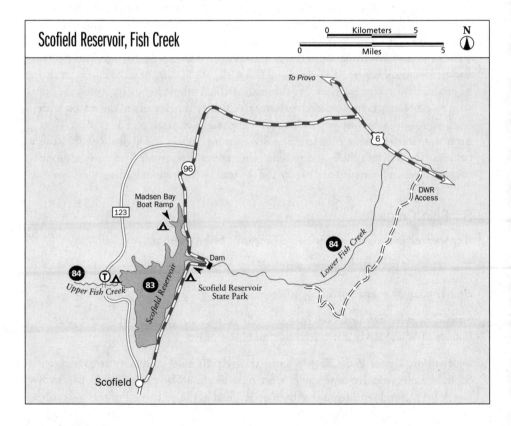

Description: Most objective observers rank Scofield Reservoir as an excellent trout fishery. Though the Division of Wildlife Resources (DWR) has been planting cutthroat trout in Scofield during the past few years, it is primarily a rainbow fishery. It is one of those rare waters that has the right conditions to grow fish rapidly. Bigger fish are not unusual here. It is also a year-round fishery that can be popular with ice anglers. Located near the Wasatch Front, about a 90-minute drive from Salt Lake City, Scofield is surrounded in part by private land with some summer homes and cabins located near its shores. Two state park campgrounds with fish-cleaning stations and launching areas are geared to the large numbers of campers and boaters who enjoy the fishery. This is a relatively large lake that can handle a great deal of pressure. In low-water years, it can be drawn down, and that can create a problem with late-summer fish kills due to a lack of oxygen. Temperatures can be brutally cold in the winter, so go prepared. The reservoir usually ices over in late November or early December and is typically free of ice near the first of May.

Fishing Index: When the fishing is hot, which is on a fairly regular basis, few Utah waters can match Scofield. Perhaps only Strawberry rivals it as a body of water that grows big, fat, hard-fighting fish so fast. That said, it can be spotty, especially at the end of winter and in the middle of the summer. Trolling works well here. Some anglers use the traditional pop gear and worm approach. Others utilize lead-core line and traditional trolling rigs, experimenting with depth until finding the fish. Power Bait and a night crawler tipped with marshmallow are local favorite baits. Shore fishing is best in the spring just after ice-out, or in the fall when the trout begin cruising closer to shore. The island near the south end of the lake provides good structure. Many boat anglers like to anchor near the island and fish with bait. Fishing near the inlets can also be productive for shore anglers. Fly fishing from float tubes can be excellent in the fall with woolly buggers or dark leech patterns. Ice fishing is best early in the season with small jigs and ice flies tipped with salmon egg, night crawler, or Power Bait. Tiger trout were introduced in 2005 to create diversity for anglers and in the hope they can help contain the Utah chubs and redsided shiners in the reservoir. The tigers are fond of small lures and spinners and can be caught readily from shore in the spring.

84 Fish Creek

Key Species: Brown trout, rainbow trout, and cutthroat trout.

Best Way to Fish Bait: Spinners and flies.

Best Time of Year to Fish: Spring summer, and fall.

Special Regulations: From the bridge 1 mile below Scofield Reservoir dam to confluence of White River is artificial flies and lures only.

Description: Upper Fish Creek is approximately 10 miles of quality stream above Scofield Reservoir. Its headwaters start near Skyline Drive. Get to Upper Fish Creek on a gravel road from the town of Scofield at the south end of the reservoir.

The road runs along the southwest shore and eventually turns into Forest Road 123; this leads to the five-site Fish Creek Campground near the creek. There are restrooms. A trail runs the length of Fish Creek.

Lower Fish Creek starts at the Scofield Reservoir Dam. A large parking area grants easy access, and a trail runs along the fishery. The DWR has also provided access via U.S. Highway 6 on a marked four-wheel-drive dirt road that starts just south of the Colton Bridge and accesses the river about halfway between the dam and the highway.

Fishing Index: The lower stretch of Fish Creek has gained a reputation as a quality fishery. Some big browns are caught here. There are also rainbows and cutthroat in the river below the dam. The predominant catch is 12- to 14-inch browns. In the spring when water is high, try San Juan worms and bead-head nymphs. As the water drops and fishing improves, attractor patterns will bring the fish up. As summer progresses, look for terrestrial patterns like grasshoppers, beetles, and ants to turn on. Some anglers fish with a large stimulator or terrestrial pattern and use a bead-head dropper. It is an effective method. Elk hair caddis are a good bet in the fall. The caddis fly hatch is sometimes the best in the state. Rapalas and spinners are good lure choices during low-light periods. Gold, copper, white, chartreuse, and black are the best colors.

Only one thing keeps the 9-mile section of Fish Creek from joining top rivers like the Provo and the Green as a Class I water. The creek is all but de-watered in the late fall and winter when the gates of Scofield Dam are closed to store potable and irrigation water for the summer months. Fish in the first mile are often lost due to a lack of water. Springs downstream from the dam provide just enough of a flow to keep some fish alive throughout the winter.

85 Gooseberry Reservoir

Key Species: Rainbow trout and cutthroat trout.

Best Way to Fish: Bait, lures, and flies.

Best Time of Year to Fish: Summer and fall.

Special Regulations: Gooseberry tributaries closed January 1 to the second Saturday of July.

Description: From Fairview take Highway 31 8.5 miles to Skyline Drive. Turn north at the first left, then head northeast 3 miles on Forest Road 124. The Forest Service runs a campground with 10 sites near the reservoir.

Fishing Index: Cutthroat and rainbow trout range from 10 to 14 inches at Gooseberry. Night crawlers and Power Bait typically produce fast action throughout the summer for planted rainbows. Float tubes work well here, and although there is no ramp, some small boats can be launched. Flashy spoons and spinners work well in the late morning and early afternoon. Dry flies fished behind a casting bubble provide excellent fishing in the evenings. Stripping in dark wet flies is popular with float tubers.

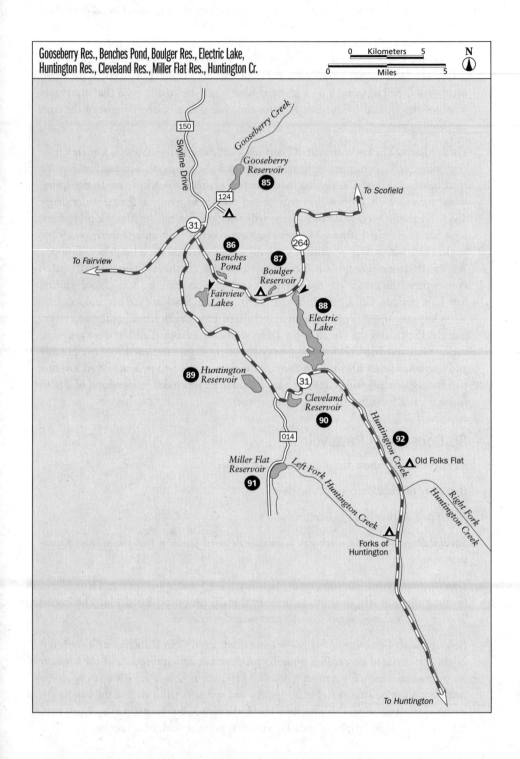

Gooseberry Res., Benches Pond, Boulger Res., Electric Lake, Huntington Res., Cleveland Res., Miller Flat Res., Huntington Cr.

Kilometers 0 5
Miles 0 5

N

150

Skyline Drive

Gooseberry Creek

Gooseberry Reservoir
85

124

31

To Scofield

To Fairview

86
Benches Pond

264

87
Boulger Reservoir

Fairview Lakes

88
Electric Lake

89
Huntington Reservoir

31

Cleveland Reservoir
90

Huntington Creek

92
Old Folks Flat

014

Miller Flat Reservoir
91

Left Fork Huntington Creek

Right Fork Huntington Creek

Forks of Huntington

To Huntington

86 Benches Pond

Key Species: Rainbow trout.

Best Way to Fish: Bait.

Best Time of Year to Fish: Summer and fall.

Special Regulations: Tributaries closed from January 1 to 6:00 a.m. on the second Saturday of July.

Description: Located on the road between Fairview Canyon and Scofield in the Manti–La Sal National Forest, this little body of water is aptly described as a pond. Yet, because of a nice walkway on the south shore, a good parking area, and a nearby restroom, it hosts a number of anglers. Primarily a kids' fishery, Benches Pond is too small for canoes or even float tubes.

Fishing Index: Benches is stocked regularly with catchable rainbow trout throughout the summer. Fishing here is consistently good. Most simply use bait, though a fly and bubble in the evening can work. Small spinners and spoons can also be effective, but bait is best.

87 Boulger Reservoir

Key Species: Rainbow trout.

Best Way to Fish: Bait.

Best Time of Year to Fish: Summer and fall.

With a boardwalk and drive-up access, fishing at Benches Pond is certainly a community affair. Consistent stocking and ease of access make it a great pond for kids.

Special Regulations: Artificial flies and lures only. Closed January 1 to 6:00 a.m. the second Saturday of July. Trout limit two when open.

Description: This little pond, near the Flat Canyon Campground between Fairview and Scofield in the Manti–La Sal National Forest, is popular with families. In fact, there are many times during the summer when it hosts more anglers than Electric Lake, its much larger neighbor to the east. The reservoir itself is in a fairly open meadow, with the nearby campground shaded by trees. The reservoir is small. Even canoes and float tubes are inappropriate and not needed. Shore anglers can cast to almost every corner of this water.

Fishing Index: This is a typical put-and-take Utah trout fishery. Hatchery trucks visit here on a regular basis throughout the summer, dumping in enough rainbow trout to keep most anglers who visit here happy. Do not expect to land any trophies. This is a good place to introduce children to fishing. Baits like salmon eggs, night crawlers, and Power Bait are the popular choices, but do not be afraid to try a dry fly behind a bubble in the evening when the fish rise. This is also an excellent place to teach young or beginning anglers how to catch fish with lures. Fishing at Boulger is usually very good.

88 Electric Lake

Key Species: Cutthroat trout.

Best Way to Fish: Trolling.

Best Time of Year to Fish: Summer and fall.

Special Regulations: None.

Description: High in the Manti–La Sal National Forest in central Utah, this relatively large lake is surrounded by aspen trees, sagebrush, and pines. There are USDA Forest Service campgrounds in the vicinity. Facilities consist of a boat ramp and pit toilet.

Fishing Index: This is a great place to troll in the middle of the summer, using traditional trolling hardware such as needlefish and Triple Teazers or flatfish. Dry-fly surface action can sometimes be enjoyed in the late evening. The area is also popular with float tubers, largely because the lack of pressure gives them a quiet place to enjoy fast fishing. Shore angling can be tough at times. Flies behind casting bubbles or spoons are good choices from shore. The lake has a reputation for being a bit spotty; move around until you find the fish. Fishing on the tributaries in season can be surprisingly good given the fact that anglers can step across most of them with little or no trouble.

89 Huntington Reservoir

Key Species: Tiger trout and cutthroat trout.

Best Way to Fish: Bait, lures, and flies.

Best Time of Year to Fish: Spring, summer, and fall.

Special Regulations: Closed to the possession of cutthroat trout or trout with cutthroat markings.

Description: Located 16 miles east of Fairview and 32 miles north of Huntington on Highway 31, Huntington is a popular fishing destination. During dam reconstruction in 1988, a well-preserved 9,500-old skeleton of a mammoth was discovered. Since then, many have taken to calling it Mammoth Reservoir, but it still shows up on maps as Huntington Reservoir. Some parking is provided along the highway.

Fishing Index: Tiger trout have been the big draw since they were planted here. This mix between a male brown trout and a female brook trout is feisty and likes flashy spinners and lures. Fly fishing from float tubes with dark wet flies is productive. Fishing with night crawlers and Power Bait works in the late morning and early afternoon.

90 Cleveland Reservoir

Key Species: Rainbow trout.

Best Way to Fish: Bait, spinners, and flies.

Best Time of Year to Fish: Summer and fall.

Special Regulations: None.

Description: Cleveland is 19 miles east of Fairview and is accessible via Highway 31. There are no facilities at the reservoir, but it is possible to launch small boats from shore. Cleveland receives heavy fishing pressure, especially on the weekends.

Fishing Index: Cleveland is heavily stocked with catchable and fingerling rainbows. Salmon eggs, Power Bait, and night crawlers work well from shore. Maisie spoons and Jake's Spin-a-lures can be effective. In the late afternoon and evening, try a fly fished behind a casting bubble. Fishing from a float tube or boat with dark leech patterns is usually effective.

91 Miller Flat Reservoir

Key Species: Rainbow trout.

Best Way to Fish: Bait and lures.

Best Time of Year to Fish: Summer and fall.

Special Regulations: None.

Description: Miller Flat is best accessed from Highway 31. Take Forest Road 014 south between Huntington and Cleveland Reservoirs. Miller Flat is about 3.5 miles down the passenger car–friendly road. There is no ramp at the reservoir, but small

Miller Flat Reservoir's reputation for producing lots of fish make it a great place for kids to have a trout-fishing experience.

boats and float tubes can easily be put on the water. Primitive camping is allowed near the reservoir.

Fishing Index: For some reason, bait works nearly twice as well as anything else here. Night crawlers, salmon eggs, and especially Power Bait are effective from shore. Because it almost always provides fast action, Miller Flat is a good place to take children for a fun trout-fishing experience.

92 Huntington Creek

Key Species: Brown trout, cutthroat trout, and brook trout.

Best Way to Fish: Flies, lures, and bait.

Best Time of Year to Fish: Year-round.

Special Regulations: Right Fork (from Flood and Engineers Canyons upstream to Electric Lake Dam), artificial flies only, trout limit two; Left Fork (from top of Forest Service campground, near confluence with Right Fork, to headwaters, including all tributaries—Scad Valley Creek, Rolfson Creek, Lake Creek, Staker Creek, Miller Flat Creek, and Paradise Creek) artificial flies and lures only, trout limit four.

Description: The main arm of Huntington Creek runs along Highway 31 in Huntington Canyon between Skyline Drive and the town of Huntington. Access is easy; therefore, it receives a lot more pressure than out-of-the-way destinations. The road is open in the winter, so this is a good place to hit the river and escape the winter blues. The Old Folks Flat Campground has nine camping sites and is along the highway about 4 miles south of Electric Lake. A six-unit campground called the Forks of Huntington is located where the left fork of the creek joins the main stem. Whirling disease was confirmed in Huntington Creek in 2006. Anglers are encouraged to clean their waders and boots before fishing somewhere after wading in Huntington Creek.

Fishing Index: Huntington is a popular classic fly-fishing stream. Regulations on sections of the creek keep specialized anglers separated. The upper reaches, from Electric Lake down to Engineers Canyon, is flies only. Many anglers are caught each year fishing with lures on this section because they believe the regulation is artificial only, not flies only. The fish—browns and cutthroat—are wary, so approach each hole carefully. The fish are selective. Often a fish will check out each fly only once. Presentation is important: One bad cast can spook all the fish in a run. Pale morning duns and caddis patterns are usually the top producers. Elk hair caddises in sizes 14 to 16 are good in brown, olive, and black. Caddis emergers are also a good choice at times. Midge action can be sensational just below the dam in the colder months. Golden stones are effective late in the spring, and terrestrials work in the later summer. Nymphs and streamers can be a good choice, but most fly fishers stick with dries.

Below Engineers Canyon, anglers can use any legal fishing tackle. Salmon eggs and night crawlers are good bait choices. Small Rapalas and spinners also work.

The Left Fork of Huntington Creek is a walk-in area, and pressure there is not as great. Fishing for brown and cutthroat trout can be exceptional. The Left Fork is artificial flies and lures only. Try flies similar to those recommended for the Right Fork. Terrestrials and attractors usually work better on the Left Fork than in the main creek.

Joe's Valley Area (Sites 93-98)

93 Joe's Valley Reservoir

Key Species: Splake, rainbow trout, tiger trout, and cutthroat trout.

Best Way to Fish: Trolling or bait from shore.

Best Time of Year to Fish: Summer, fall, and winter.

Special Regulations: Trout limit two, only one over 22 inches; all trout 15 to 22 inches must be released. Closed November 1 to 6:00 a.m. the second Saturday of December.

Description: This is a fairly large scenic reservoir located in the Manti–La Sal National Forest west of Orangeville in Emery County. The Forest Service maintains 46 campsites on the west side of the reservoir. A large boat ramp and some

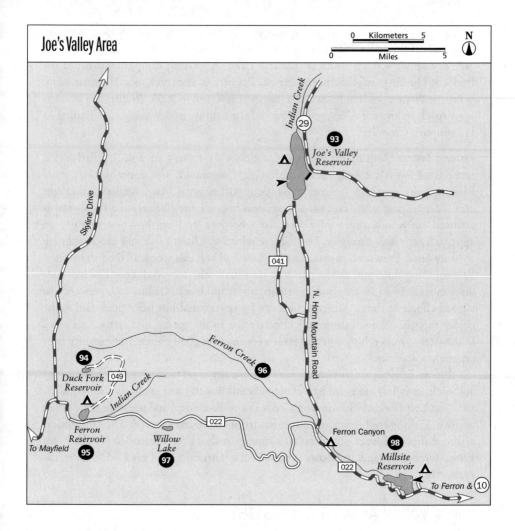

0 Kilometers 5

0 Miles 5

N

Indian Creek

29

93 Joe's Valley Reservoir

Skyline Drive

041

N. Horn Mountain Road

94

049

Duck Fork Reservoir

Indian Creek

Ferron Creek

96

022

Ferron Reservoir

To Mayfield

95

Willow Lake

97

Ferron Canyon

98

Millsite Reservoir

022

To Ferron & 10

commercial rental facilities make it a popular stopover. There is access to Skyline Drive and a number of smaller area ponds and reservoirs.

Fishing Index: The presence of Utah chub, which often competes with rainbow trout for food, has been a problem at Joe's Valley for years. The problem has forced some changes in the way it is managed. Splake, a hybrid between a brook and a lake trout, is one answer because it feeds aggressively on minnow chubs. Some splake can get to trophy size. Anglers fishing for splake troll flashy minnow-imitating lures in deep water. Splake can also be caught through the ice with spoons or jigs tipped with frozen minnow or sucker meat.

94 Duck Fork Reservoir

Key Species: Cutthroat trout and tiger trout.

Best Way to Fish: Flies and lures.

Best Time of Year to Fish: Late spring, summer, and fall.

Special Regulations: Artificial flies and lures only. Closed to the possession of cutthroat trout; tiger trout limit two.

Description: The reservoir is accessible on a dirt road (Forest Road 049) below the dam at Ferron Reservoir. Small boats can be launched from an unimproved ramp on the north side of the dam. The road is usually closed until late June due to snow and four-wheel drive is advised.

Fishing Index: Duck Fork was converted to a native Colorado River cutthroat trout brood lake in 2003. Fishing is usually best in the morning or early evening. Duck Fork is on the state's Blue Ribbon Fisheries list.

95 Ferron Reservoir

Key Species: Rainbow trout, cutthroat trout, and brook trout.

Best Way to Fish: Flies and bait.

Best Time of Year to Fish: Spring, summer, and fall.

Special Regulations: Trout limit four; bonus limit of four brook trout (total limit of trout no more than eight if at least four are brook trout).

Description: Ferron Reservoir is 25 miles west of Ferron and 23 miles east of Mayfield on Forest Road 022. The road is maintained for low-clearance vehicles,

Ferron Reservoir in southeastern Utah is home to stocked rainbow and cutthroat trout.

but weather conditions may force drivers to think twice about taking a passenger car. From Ferron, travel west past Millsite Reservoir and continue on the gravel road as it goes up Ferron Canyon. From Mayfield, you will cross Skyline Drive on the Wasatch Plateau before dropping down to the reservoir. A Forest Service campground at the reservoir has 32 sites with picnic tables, fire pits, privies, and drinking water. Skyhaven Resort, a private enterprise, offers cottage and boat rentals, horse and bicycle rentals, a convenience store, and a cafe. An unimproved boat ramp was constructed on the west end of the dam in 2005 to permit small boat launching.

Fishing Index: Planted rainbows and cutthroat are the catch. While most people fish traditional trout baits from shore, the real action is with flies and lures. Fly fishing with dark leech patterns with sinking line or sunk behind a casting bubble produces trout up to 18 inches. Jake's Spin-a-lure and Maisie spoons also work well.

96 Ferron Creek

Key Species: Cutthroat trout and rainbow trout.

Best Way to Fish: Bait, flies, and spinners.

Best Time of Year to Fish: Summer and fall.

Special Regulations: None.

Description: Ferron Creek starts where George's Creek and Duck Fork Creek meet near Duck Fork Reservoir. Access is via several unimproved roads in Ferron Canyon. There is some posted private property in the canyon. Several camp and picnic sites are maintained in the lower canyon.

Fishing Index: High water makes Ferron Creek difficult to fish until July. When the water drops, try fly fishing with attractor patterns. In late July and early August, look for terrestrial patterns like grasshoppers, ants, and beetles to work. There are also some sporadic caddis and mayfly hatches. Fly fishers do well with bead-head hare's ear, pheasant tail, and prince nymph patterns. When the fish are not taking dries, bait anglers find night crawlers and salmon eggs work best. Small, flashy spinners fished through deep holes should turn up some fish as well.

97 Willow Lake

Key Species: Rainbow trout, brook trout, and tiger trout.

Best Way to Fish: Bait, flies, and lures.

Best Time of Year to Fish: Summer and fall.

Special Regulations: None.

Description: From Ferron, travel west past Millsite Reservoir and continue on the gravel road (Forest Road 022) for about 15 miles up Ferron Canyon. Willow is visible on the south side of the road.

Fishing Index: Willow is planted with rainbows throughout the summer. Bait is the best method, especially Power Bait and night crawlers. Fly fishers do well with wet and dry flies. Spoons like Maisie and Jake's are good lure choices.

98 Millsite Reservoir

Key Species: Brown trout, rainbow trout, and splake.

Best Way to Fish: Bait, lures, and flies.

Best Time of Year to Fish: Spring and fall.

Special Regulations: None.

Description: This secluded 435-acre lake near the mouth of Ferron Canyon is popular for all kinds of water recreation. Millsite State Park amenities include a boat-launching ramp, sandy beach, 20-unit campground, two group-use pavilions, drinking water, modern restrooms, showers, and sanitary disposal station. Millsite State Park is located 4 miles west of Ferron off Highway 10. A nine-hole golf course is adjacent to the park.

Fishing Index: Fishing from shore with bait is productive in the spring and fall when the water is colder. The best success in the summer comes from trolling with pop gear and a worm. Fishing in the summer is typically better in the morning and evening when other enthusiasts are not on the water.

99 Palisade Reservoir

Key Species: Brown trout and rainbow trout.

Best Way to Fish: Bait, flies, and lures.

Best Time of Year to Fish: Spring and fall.

Special Regulations: Boats with motors are prohibited.

Description: Palisade Reservoir is southeast of Manti and is accessible from U.S. Highway 89 north of Sterling via a 1.5-mile access road to Palisade State Park. The reservoir gets a variety of recreational pressure, but because no motors are allowed, the fishery remains fairly quiet. The state park has 53 individual campsites, restrooms with hot showers, a group camping area, and a covered group-use pavilion. Canoe and paddleboat rentals are available.

Fishing Index: Bait fishing is best in the spring and fall when the trout are cruising the shallows. Salmon eggs, Power Bait, and night crawlers are the best choices. Fly fishers in float tubes do well stripping wet flies in dark colors.

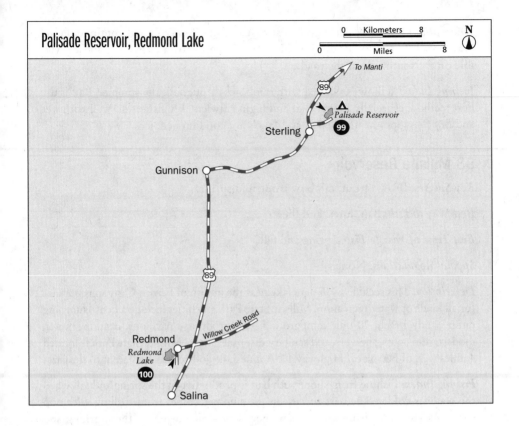

Kilometers

Miles

N

To Manti

89

Palisade Reservoir

Sterling

99

Gunnison

89

Redmond

Willow Creek Road

Redmond Lake

100

Salina

100 Redmond Lake

Key Species: Largemouth bass, northern pike, and catfish.

Best Way to Fish: From a boat or from shore.

Best Time of Year to Fish: Spring, fall, and winter.

Special Regulations: None.

Description: Redmond Lake is 1 mile southwest of the town of Redmond and is reached off U.S. Highway 89. A small ramp serves this low-elevation reservoir.

Fishing Index: Fishing during the warmer months is for catfish and largemouth bass. The catfish are caught with night crawlers, cut bait, and stink bait fished on the bottom. A few largemouth are caught in the spring near the warm springs or the flooded brush with spinnerbaits, jig-n-pigs, and weedless rubber worms or lizards.

Northern pike are caught in the colder months near the warm springs. Use frozen minnows fished below a bobber. Some fish are caught on medium-size spoons, crankbaits, and plastic grubs. It is not uncommon to see a dozen or more people fishing for northerns on nice winter days.

101 Price River

Key Species: Brown trout, cutthroat trout, and rainbow trout.

Best Way to Fish: Bait and lures.

Best Time of Year to Fish: Summer and fall.

Special Regulations: None.

Description: Some people call the river from Scofield Reservoir Dam the Price River; others call it Lower Fish Creek. Still others say the Price River starts where Lower Fish Creek meets the White River near U.S. Highway 6, about 9 miles downstream from the reservoir. Because the river below the White confluence is much different than the special-regulation stream above it, we have distinguished the two.

Fishing Index: The Price is often high and muddy. That, coupled with poor habitat conditions, makes the river one often avoided by anglers. When it isn't high, the Price is often dewatered for irrigation. Access is another problem. There are some places to reach the river from US 6, but most people who fish the Price access it along the Helper Parkway at the end of the canyon. Night crawlers and

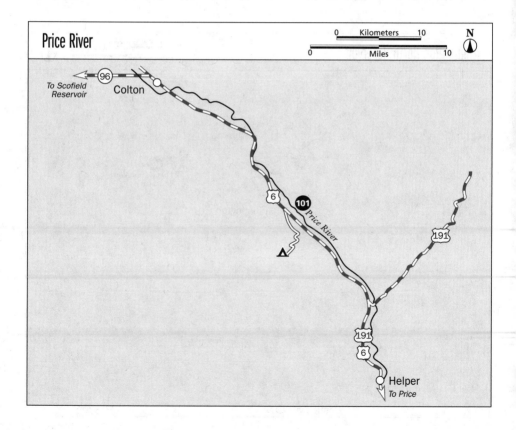

frozen minnows turn up some big browns. Large Rapalas and spinners also work at times. Fishing with salmon eggs near Helper is good for planted rainbows.

102 Huntington North Reservoir

Key Species: Largemouth bass, brown trout, rainbow trout, and bluegill.

Best Way to Fish: From a boat and bait from shore.

Best Time of Year to Fish: Spring and fall.

Special Regulations: Bass limit six, but only one over 12 inches.

Description: Located 2 miles north of Huntington off Highway 10, this reservoir sees a lot of local recreational pressure on its 237 acres. State park facilities include 22 camping units, picnic sites, modern restrooms, showers, sewage disposal station, boat launching, and a large covered group-use pavilion.

Fishing Index: Due to its low elevation and warm water in the summer months, Huntington North is a better bass fishery than trout. Fishing for the bass is best in the spring when the largemouth are staging for the spawn. Look for them near gravel or flat rock and close to flooded brush or trees. Spinnerbaits, jig-n-pigs,

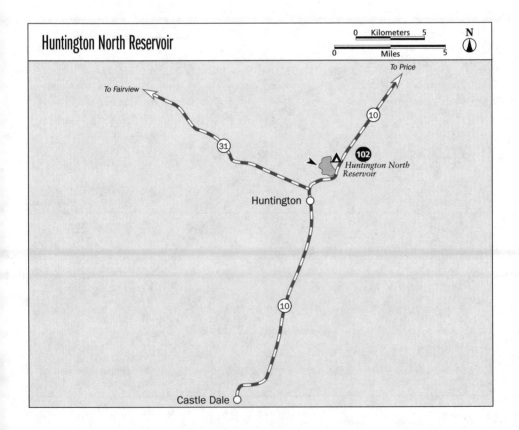

large plastic lizards, spider jigs, and curly-tail grubs are the best bets. After the spawn, look for weed edges and long points. Topwater baits work well in low-light conditions. Diving crankbaits and medium-size plastic baits can also be productive.

The trout are usually caught in the fall by anglers fishing with traditional trout baits from shore. Some large browns can be caught on minnow-imitating lures, especially in the colder months. Fish up to 10 pounds are possible.

Bluegill fishing is best in the spring. Look for these panfish to be schooled on weed flats. Small jigs, spinners, flies, and night crawlers will work from shore or from a boat. A boat makes it easier to find the schools.

103 Green River

Key Species: Channel catfish, northern pike, and smallmouth bass.

Best Way to Fish: Bait.

Best Time of Year to Fish: Year-round.

Special Regulations: Channel catfish limit 24; northern pike limit 12; release endangered species.

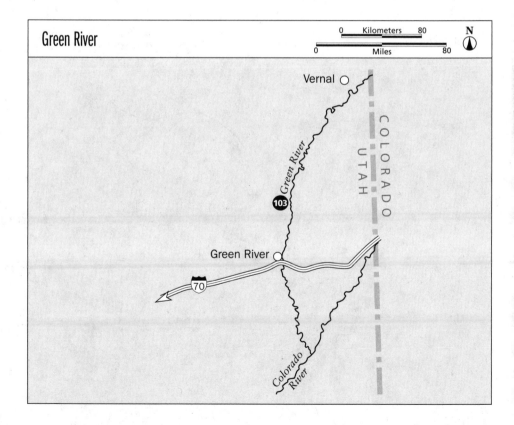

Description: The Green in southeastern Utah is a different river than the one that comes out of Flaming Gorge Reservoir. By the time the Green has come back into Utah from Colorado, it is no longer a river fit for cold-water species like trout. Although there are some big trout in the Green, primarily where tributaries enter the river, catfish rule the lower stretches before it meets with the Colorado in Canyonlands National Park. People floating the river for white-water excitement do most of the Green's fishing.

Fishing Index: Anglers do the best with night crawlers, dead minnows, and cut bait fished on the bottom in deep, slow pools. Anglers are encouraged to keep their limit to help cull the overpopulated catfish.

Fishing for northern pike is more difficult, but a small group of anglers pursue these toothy predators above the town of Green River. Minnow-imitating lures should work on the pike for anglers lucky enough to find them. Bright-colored spinners and sometimes topwater lures will also work.

104 Colorado River

Key Species: Channel catfish and northern pike.

Best Way to Fish: Bait and lures.

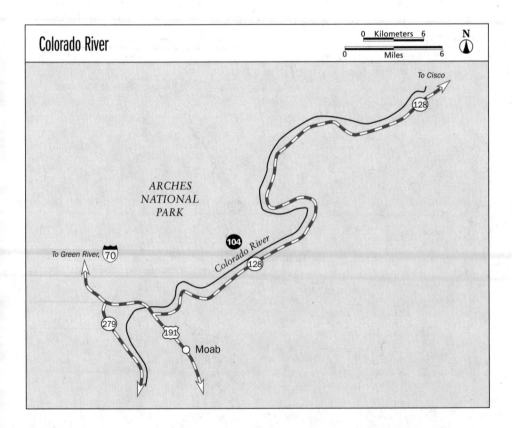

Best Time of Year to Fish: Year-round.

Special Regulations: Channel catfish limit 24; northern pike limit 12; endangered species must be released.

Description: The Utah portion of the Colorado River before it dumps into Lake Powell is more known as a rafting destination than a fishery. However, some people enjoy fishing for channel catfish and northern pike. Highway 128 north of Moab provides the best access for shore anglers.

Fishing Index: Although the mighty Colorado has a multitude of sport fish, channel catfish are the only species found in large enough numbers to target. The whisker fish can be found anywhere in the Colorado from the point where it enters Utah south of Interstate 70 through Moab down to Lake Powell. In fact, there are so many catfish, anglers rarely catch any longer than 12 inches. Night crawlers and stink bait fished on the bottom in side pools is the most productive method here. Keep your limit and enjoy the eating.

Because of the fight they produce, pike is one species anglers will look hard for. These long, toothy predators are worth the effort. They can be hard to locate on such a huge river, but some anglers have locked into them. The most likely place to find northerns is near the Colorado border. Look for back eddies and sloughs when fishing for pike in a river. DWR raised the limit on pike because they feed on endangered species in the river, but few anglers will be able to reach the 12-fish limit. Rapalas and red and white Dardevles are common pike lures.

La Sal Mountain Lakes (Sites 105–111)

The La Sal mountain range east of Moab provides surprisingly good fishing for planted rainbow trout, brook trout, tiger trout, cutthroat trout, and even some grayling. Most lakes are reached via the La Sal Mountain Loop that starts 6 miles south of Moab in the Spanish Valley. Sixty miles later, after going across the west side of the La Sals down to Castle Valley and along the Colorado River and Highway 128, the loop is complete. Considering the hordes of tourists that visit Moab's red rock country, pressure on the La Sals is usually light with the exception of holiday weekends.

105 Hidden Reservoir

Key Species: Rainbow trout.

Best Way to Fish: Bait, lures, and flies.

Best Time of Year to Fish: Summer and fall.

Special Regulations: None.

Description: Take the northern portion of the loop through Castle Valley. Pass the turn for the loop and continue to the east (left) for about 10 miles, then turn on Forest Road 669. Hidden Reservoir is 0.25 mile on the right.

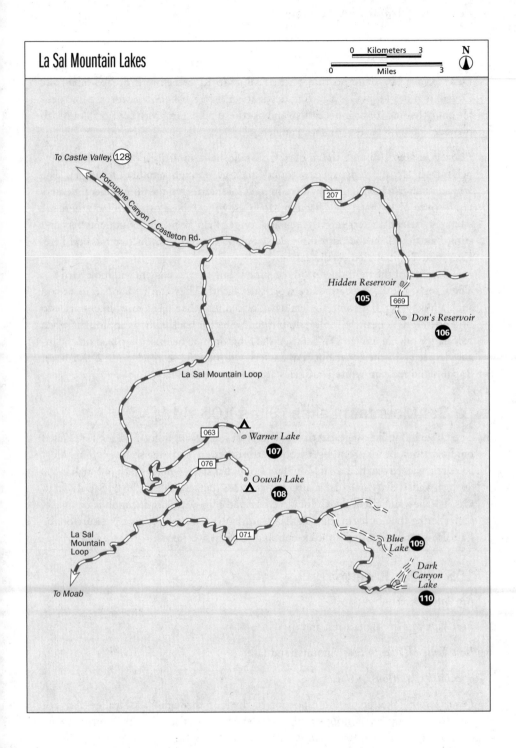

La Sal Mountain Lakes

Fishing Index: A little bigger than Don's Reservoir, Hidden Reservoir also usually receives less pressure. Bait works well here, but lures and wet flies are more effective. Dark leech patterns are the choice of most anglers. Maisie and Jake's spoons are also good choices.

106 Don's Reservoir

Key Species: Rainbow trout and tiger trout.

Best Way to Fish: Bait, lures, and flies.

Best Time of Year to Fish: Summer and fall.

Special Regulations: None.

Description: Don's is reached from the north side of the loop through Castle Valley. Pass the turn for the loop and continue east for about 10 miles to the turn on Forest Road 669. You pass Hidden Reservoir on the right and reach Don's in just over a mile.

Fishing Index: Most fishing at this small lake is from the dam. Power Bait is the most frequently used bait, although gold spinners and spoons can be deadly. Dark leech patterns like the Don's Lake Killer can bring in a fish on every cast.

Don's Reservoir is one of several high mountain lakes in the La Sal Mountains in southeastern Utah.

107 Warner Lake

Key Species: Rainbow trout.

Best Way to Fish: Bait.

Best Time of Year to Fish: Summer and fall.

Special Regulations: None.

Description: Few places are as scenic as this tiny lake. The lake is too small for boats, and there are spots where it is almost possible to cast across it. The fishing is mainly an added bonus to the scenery.

Fishing Index: This is a classic put-and-take fishery. It is stocked with catchable rainbows on a regular basis. In the evenings and early mornings, when an insect hatch is possible, a fly and bubble outfit will work. Those who prefer catch-and-release fishing can also use a variety of spinners—Panther Martin and Mepps are effective here. But the most productive method is to simply use an old-fashioned night crawler or Power Bait fished from the shoreline. After the hatchery trucks have visited, angling can be fast.

108 Oowah Lake

Key Species: Rainbow trout and brook trout.

Best Way to Fish: Bait, small lures, and flies.

Best Time of Year to Fish: Summer and fall.

Special Regulations: None.

Description: This is a popular lake reached by taking Forest Road 076 from the south end of the Loop Road. There are six Forest Service campsites at the lake.

Fishing Index: Dry flies in the evenings are the ticket at Oowah. Rainbows and brookies will both hit slow-moving dries fished behind casting bubbles. Bait works well during the day.

109 Blue Lake

Key Species: Rainbow trout, brook trout, and grayling.

Best Way to Fish: Flies and bait.

Best Time of Year to Fish: Summer and fall.

Special Regulations: None.

Description: Blue Lake is reached via the La Sal Mountain Loop on Forest Road 071 and four-wheel-drive road 242.

Fishing Index: Blue Lake traditionally provides excellent fishing for rainbows with bait, spinners, and flies. Some anglers catch brook trout, and lucky ones will land a grayling. Dry flies like Adams work best in the evenings. Black, olive, and brown leech patterns fished behind a casting bubble can produce fast fishing.

110 Dark Canyon Lake

Key Species: Rainbow trout and brook trout.

Best Way to Fish: Bait, lures, and flies.

Best Time of Year to Fish: Summer and fall.

Special Regulations: None.

Description: Although it can be reached from the Loop road, the quickest way to Dark Canyon is east on Highway 46 south of Moab through La Sal, and then right on Forest Road 208 about 3 miles east of town. After 5 miles on FR 208, take Forest Road 129 to the right. You will reach the lake in another 5 miles.

Fishing Index: Dark Canyon is stocked with rainbows and also has a healthy population of brook trout. Bait fishing is best during the hottest times of the day. Spinners work well in the late morning and early afternoon. Fishing with dry flies is great in the evening hours.

111 Medicine Lake

Key Species: Rainbow trout and brook trout.

Best Way to Fish: Bait, lures, and flies.

Best Time of Year to Fish: Summer and fall.

Special Regulations: None.

Description: This out-of-the-way little lake is planted with rainbows and has a healthy population of brook trout. Medicine is reached on the south end of the La Sals. Take Highway 46 south of Moab through La Sal and then turn right on Forest Road 208 about 3 miles east of town.

Fishing Index: Power Bait and night crawlers will work for the rainbows. The brook trout are fond of red and gold spinners and spoons.

112 Ken's Lake

Key Species: Rainbow trout, brown trout, largemouth bass, and bluegill.

Best Way to Fish: Bait and lures.

Best Time of Year to Fish: Spring, summer, and fall.

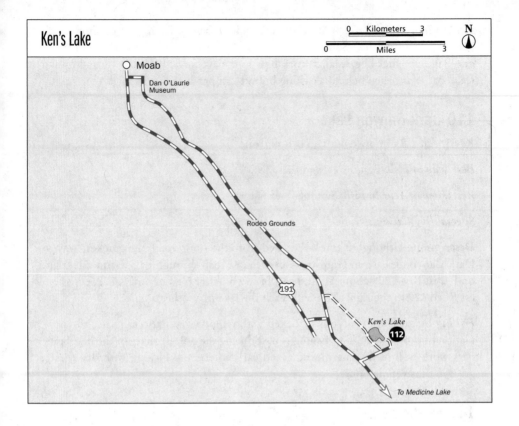

Ken's Lake

Special Regulations: The lake is closed from 11:00 p.m. to 5:00 a.m.

Description: Ken's Lake is 13 miles southeast of Moab. From milepost 118 on U.S. Highway 191 (8 miles south of Moab), turn east on Old Airport Road and follow the sign to Ken's Lake and the La Sal Mountain Loop. After 1 mile, turn right when the road terminates. Go south for 1.5 miles to Flat Pass Road. It is unmarked and unpaved. You should be able to see the dam at this point. Camping is only permitted in designated areas.

Fishing Index: Ken's is planted with rainbows and has some big browns. Fishing is best with night crawlers from shore. Fishing for the bass is best in the early spring when the largemouth are staging for the spawn. Look for them near gravel or flat rock. Spinnerbaits, jig-n-pigs, plastic lizards, spider jigs, and curly-tail grubs are the best bet. After the spawn, fish weed edges and along points. Topwater baits work well in low-light conditions. Medium-size plastic baits can also be productive.

Rainbows are usually caught in the spring and fall by anglers fishing with traditional trout baits from shore. Some large browns can be caught on minnow-imitating lures, especially in the colder months. Fish up to 10 pounds are caught.

Bluegill fishing is best in the spring. Look for these panfish to be schooled on weed flats. Small jigs, spinners, flies, and night crawlers will work from shore. Fly fishing with poppers from a float tube is an option.

113 Blanding Reservoir #4

Key Species: Rainbow trout and largemouth bass.

Best Way to Fish: Bait and lures.

Best Time of Year to Fish: Spring, summer, and fall.

Special Regulations: No internal combustion engines are allowed, but electric trolling motors are.

Description: Blanding #4 is 4 miles north of the town of Blanding. Camping is not allowed at the reservoir.

Fishing Index: Blanding #4 was rebuilt and enlarged in 2004 and offers about 80 surface acres. Rainbow and tiger trout are stocked in #4. Fishing with night crawlers or Power Bait works well for the rainbows. The tigers will hit flashy spinners.

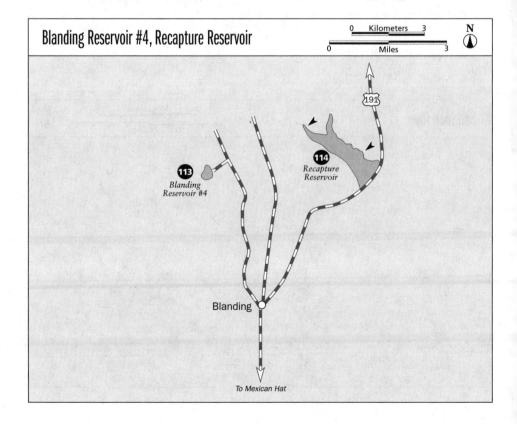

Blanding Reservoir #4, Recapture Reservoir

114 Recapture Reservoir

Key Species: Largemouth bass, bluegill, and northern pike.

Best Way to Fish: Lures and bait.

Best Time of Year to Fish: Spring, summer, and fall.

Special Regulations: None.

Description: Recapture is about 3 miles north of Blanding on U.S. Highway 191, which crosses the dam. Several unimproved roads lead to the reservoir. There are two boat ramps at Recapture: one on the north side and one on the south side. Primitive camping is allowed near the reservoir.

Fishing Index: Perhaps the most interesting thing about Recapture is its population of goldfish. People on shore can see large schools of the bright fish, some up to 12 inches, cruising the reservoir. Largemouth bass hold in areas that provide cover. Spinnerbaits and weedless plastic worms fished near flooded vegetation should produce fish. Bluegill are also found in Recapture. Look for them to hold near weeds and flooded brush where they'll hit jigs. Northern pike were illegally stocked in the reservoir and have successfully reproduced. Rainbow trout stocking has been discontinued because of the presence of the pike.

115 San Juan River

Key Species: Channel catfish.

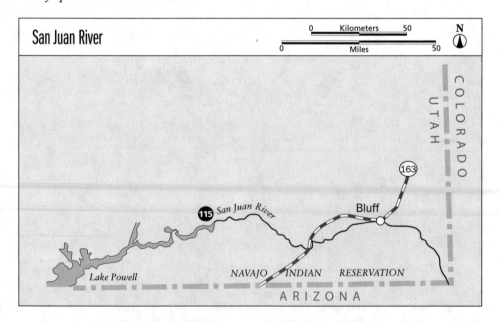

Best Way to Fish: Bait.

Best Time of Year to Fish: Summer, fall, and winter.

Special Regulations: Channel catfish limit 24

Description: The San Juan is a slow-moving river heavy with sediment; it enters Utah in the Four Corners area of the state. It receives little fishing pressure, but some people on float trips fish the river from Bluff to Mexican Hat. The river eventually dumps into Lake Powell. The upper portion of the river is on the Navajo Indian Reservation. Access to the river is difficult.

Fishing Index: Fishing with night crawlers and stink bait in back eddies is the best method.

Southern Utah

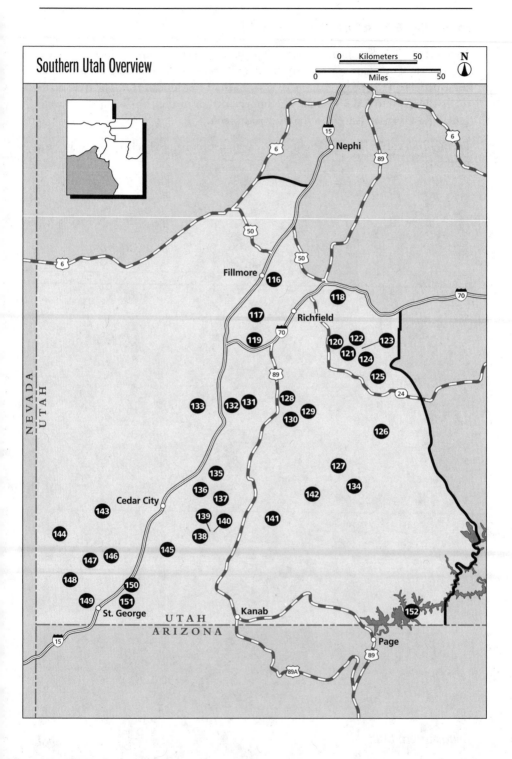

Southern Utah Overview

116 Chalk Creek

Key Species: Rainbow trout, cutthroat trout, and brown trout.

Best Way to Fish: Flies, lures, and bait.

Best Time of Year to Fish: Summer and fall.

Special Regulations: None.

Description: Directly east of Fillmore, Chalk Creek is accessible along Forest Road 100 as it winds up the canyon. The four picnic sites located up the canyon provide good places to park.

Fishing Index: Most people fish the main portion of Chalk Creek in the canyon, but the north fork is a good place to get away from the road and crowds. You can hike along it. Rainbow trout and browns rule the main canyon, but wild cutthroat and rainbows, as well as their hybrids, are plentiful in the upper reaches of the north fork. Dry fly fishing is good when the water drops and clears after spring runoff. Terrestrial patterns are exceptional choices, especially on the north fork. Bait fishing is best, with traditional trout choices, for the rainbows in the canyon area. Small spinners and spoons will bring in some browns.

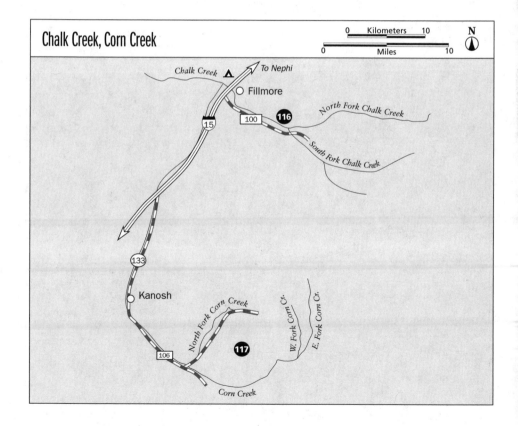

117 Corn Creek

Key Species: Brown trout.

Best Way to Fish: Dry flies, nymphs, and bait.

Best Time of Year to Fish: Fall and summer.

Special Regulations: None.

Description: This small stream east of the tiny Millard County town of Kanosh has been plagued by problems from flooding in the past but recovers each time to provide an excellent fishery.

Fishing Index: Corn Creek is a wild brown trout fishery. Caddis and hopper patterns work well for fly fishers, as do nymphs. Bait is legal, and night crawlers are usually the most effective. Those who hike a ways will be rewarded with more, and possibly larger, fish.

118 Salina Creek

Key Species: Rainbow trout and cutthroat trout.

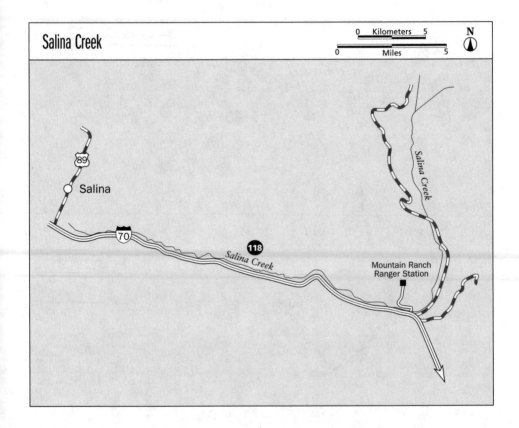

Best Way to Fish: Flies, lures, and bait.

Best Time of Year to Fish: Summer and fall.

Special Regulations: None.

Description: Access to Salina Creek is via Interstate 70, east from the town of Salina. There is some private property along the river.

Fishing Index: Most anglers ignore this creek due to its proximity to the freeway, but it does provide some good fishing. Bead-head nymphs are a good choice early and late in the year. Terrestrials and attractors are good bets from midsummer to late fall. Bait angling is best with night crawlers fished through deeper holes.

119 Clear Creek

Key Species: Rainbow trout and brown trout.

Best Way to Fish: Flies, lures, and bait.

Best Time of Year to Fish: Spring, summer, and fall.

Special Regulations: None.

Description: Clear Creek runs just north of Interstate 70 about 23 miles southwest of Richfield. It is also reached from Interstate 15 and is about 18 miles east from the I–15 and I–70 interchange. Most of the fishing on Clear Creek is done in Fremont

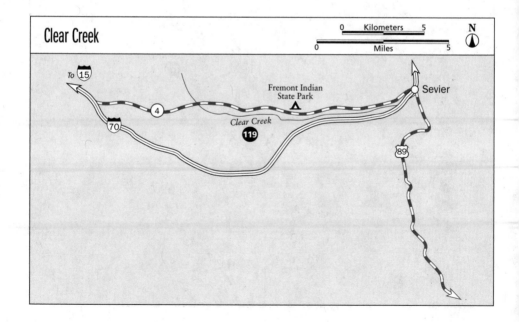

Indian State Park, but it is also accessible on Highway 4 just west of the park in Clear Creek Canyon. There are 31 campsites and some picnic sites at the state park.

Fishing Index: When I–70 was designed to run through central Utah, Clear Creek meandered along part of the proposed roadway. Engineers discussed covering most of the small trout stream with box culverts, straightening other sections, and otherwise making the stream difficult to fish. Instead, Division of Wildlife Resources (DWR) officials obtained mitigation monies from the highway project and got road officials to go around the creek. The result is a classic southern Utah stream with populations of wild browns and rainbows. Look for caddis and mayfly hatches in the early summer and then terrestrials later. Small spoons and spinners will work for the browns. Bait is a good choice for the rainbows.

120 Koosharem Reservoir

Key Species: Rainbow trout and Bear Lake cutthroat trout.

Best Way to Fish: Bait, flies, and lures.

Best Time of Year to Fish: Year-round.

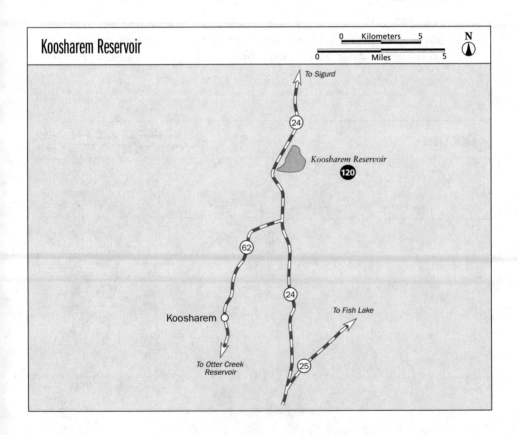

Special Regulations: None.

Description: Located just off of Highway 24 about 5 miles north of the town of Koosharem, this reservoir sees a lot of local pressure. There is a restroom.

Fishing Index: This shallow but fertile reservoir grows fish fast, but it is frequently overrun with nongame fish and has been chemically treated many times throughout the years. To deal with the rough fish, wildlife officials have planted Bear Lake cutthroat, an aggressive predator. Fishing with bait on the bottom is good from the dam and on the west shore. Dark-colored flies like woolly buggers can be effective during the ice-off period and in the fall. Ice fishing is best soon after the reservoir is safe. Use small jigs and ice flies tipped with salmon eggs or Power Bait.

121 Fish Lake

Key Species: Lake trout, splake, rainbow trout, and yellow perch.

Best Way to Fish: Trolling and ice fishing.

Best Time of Year to Fish: Year-round.

Special Regulations: Trout limit four, no more than two may be lake trout and only one can be a lake trout larger than 20 inches. Yellow perch limit 50. The size of a hole when ice fishing may not exceed 18 inches. Possession of a gaff while fishing is unlawful.

Description: Fish Lake is the largest natural mountain lake in Utah. Resting at 8,843 feet on the Fish Lake Plateau, it is also one of the highest. Fish Lake is arguably the state's best ice-fishing destination. On the same day, ice fishers can fill a 5-gallon bucket of tasty yellow perch and then fight a 20-pound lake trout. Fishing for splake is much easier through the ice than in the summer months.

Fish Lake is also one of the most scenic places in the state to fish. In the fall, vast stands of quaking aspen turn the forest ceiling, and eventually the forest floor, gold. Elk, deer, and raptors are a common sight along the shores. Hiking trails, equestrian campgrounds, small marinas, and mountain-biking routes add to Fish Lake's reputation as a quiet, cool place where families gather to enjoy the outdoors.

Forest Service campgrounds include Doctor Creek (29 family sites, 2 group), Bowery (31 family, 12 group), and Mackinaw (53 family, 15 group). Private resorts include Bowery Haven Resort and Fish Lake Lodge/Lakeside Resort. Bowery Haven rents cabins, RV parking spots, motel rooms, and boats from Memorial Day weekend to the end of September. Fish Lake Lodge/Lakeside Resort rents cabins, has an RV park, supports two marinas, and rents boats. A restaurant in the main lodge is open during peak season. Deluxe cabins are available year-round.

Fish Lake is reached by driving east on Highway 24 from U.S. Highway 89 to its junction with Highway 25. At that point, drive north about 7 miles to Fish Lake. The road is plowed in the winter, but conditions can be dangerous. Avoid driving on Highway 25 during storms.

Warm clothes and a good attitude paid off for this wintertime perch double at Fish Lake.

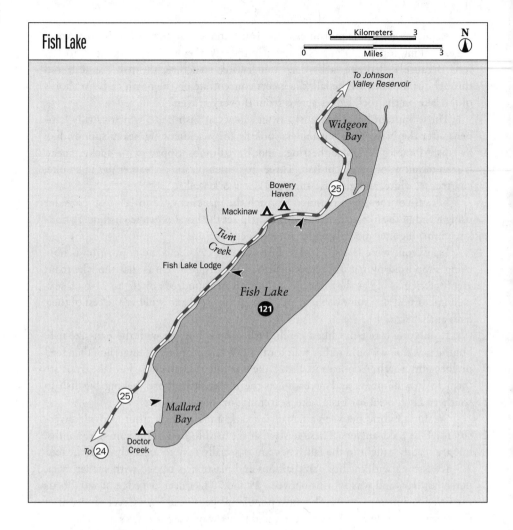

Fishing Index: Who could have known that a plant of a few mackinaw in what was then remote Fish Lake in 1906 would reap benefits for generations of Utah anglers? Fish Lake has become one of Utah's legendary trophy trout waters.

By 1950 fishing for mackinaw, or lake trout, was so popular that the Liars' Table at the Bowery Haven was needed for the anglers to share stories. Traditional summer mackinaw anglers start fishing around 5:00 a.m. and head for the cafe at sunup. Some anglers use a specially shaped piece of board wrapped with copper wire. The wire sinks quickly to the depths of Fish Lake, bouncing a lure along the bottom where the macks roam. The longtime lake record, a 37-pounder caught in 1989, hangs over the Bowery Haven cafe fireplace. A 41-pound fish was caught in 2004.

Most anglers today use steel line and downriggers trailing large and mid-size Rapalas, flatfish, and Kwikfish. The best colors are rainbow, chartreuse, red and white, and perch. In the mornings, lake trout often cruise the shallows along weed edges looking for small rainbows. Later in the day, they can be found at 70 to 100 feet. Because Fish Lake lacks deep underwater structure, the fish are scattered throughout the lake. In the fall, the lakers concentrate on the north and east shores of the lake on the rock ledges across from Bowery Haven.

Those without boats anxiously await safe ice at Fish Lake, which usually happens after the New Year. Ice anglers looking for mackinaw jig heavy spoons, like Swedish Pimples, crippled herring, and BuzzBombs tipped with sucker meat, frozen minnow, or perch cut bait. Three- to 5-inch plastic or feather jigs in smoke, chartreuse, white, and glow-in-the-dark also work well.

Because of the depth required to reach the mackinaw, 70 to 100 feet, consider using a rod in the 5- to 6.5-foot range to help set the hook when ice fishing. A nonstretch fishing line and fish finder are also helpful.

Lake trout were last stocked in Fish Lake in 1991, and the population is now being supported by natural reproduction. The only problem is that the lake trout aren't getting as big as they once did. Officials net hundreds of 16- to 21-inch sexually mature adults; some of them are 10 to 20 years old and will live the rest of their lives at that size.

If only the lake trout liked perch. Fish Lake is busting with the pan-size fish, but the mackinaw would rather wait for the DWR to plant trout fingerling than feed on the spiny perch. At one time, Fish Lake was full of Utah chub, but lake trout ate them to low numbers and perch filled the niche. Still, those seeking big fish in southern Utah head for Fish Lake, searching for monster lakers.

Splake, a hybrid between a female lake and a male brook trout, provide diversity for Fish Lake anglers. These feisty fish are hard to find in the summer months, but are readily caught in the fall. They are especially easy to catch through the ice.

Ice fishing with medium-size spoons and plastic jigs tipped with sucker meat, perch cut bait, and wax worms between 25 and 70 feet near the edge of weed beds can provide nonstop action. The most popular place is near Twin Creeks in front of the marina. Fish up to 26 inches are caught this way. Larger splake are caught by anglers fishing for lake trout.

A state record splake of 15 pounds, 4 ounces was caught at Fish Lake in early 1999. Because splake look similar to lake trout, close inspection is required. Anglers are allowed only two lake trout, only one more than 20 inches.

Rainbow trout, traditionally not a species sought at Fish Lake, have become a staple. The DWR plants 200,000 each year. Some of the planted fingerling escape the lake trout and grow to credible sizes. Because of the thick weed beds, fishing from shore for the rainbows is difficult.

Most anglers seek out the Cheese Hole—the northeastern corner of the lake—where they use, what else? Cheese. Power Bait and night crawlers also work. The southern and northern corners are effective bait areas as well. Trolling along the weed beds in 30 feet of water (or less) is also productive. Flatfish in perch, frog, black, copper, and chartreuse colors are the best bet. Pop gear trailing colored spinners with worm or Triple Teazers can also work.

Fly fishers find double renegades, woolly buggers, damselfly nymphs, and mid-size bead-head nymphs useful when fished along the edge of the weed beds.

Many rainbows are caught while anglers are fishing for perch through the ice. Small jigs and ice flies tipped with wax worm, night crawler, or Power Bait work when ice fishing for rainbows.

Perch are the reason most anglers head for Fish Lake in the winter. Hiding in the vast weed bed on the west side of the reservoir—dubbed the Fish Lake Reef by some anglers—you'll find thousands and thousands of perch. These panfish provide an excellent opportunity to create an all-important successful first memory of fishing for children.

During the winter, a fish per cast is not uncommon; in fact, some people set up two hooks and bring up two perch at a time. In the summer, fishing from shore with a bobber and a jig tipped with night crawler or perch cut bait provides fast action. Fishing over weeds from a boat on the west side is also effective, but be ready for a rainbow or splake as well.

One of the most exciting ways to fish for perch is to bring a tarp and lay it on the ice. Pull something over your head to block out sunlight. Release the bail on the reel and hand-jig the line as deep as you can see it, or until you see perch come out of the weeds to observe, then hit your lure. Occasionally, a rainbow or splake will show up, making it even more exciting to watch. A portable ice shelter blocks more light and makes it even easier to see the fish.

Perch are fond of small jigs and ice flies tipped with mealworm or perch meat. Lightly jig the bait just off the top of the weed bed down to 20 feet. A short, sensitive rod works best. Sometimes perch only nibble on the bait and the hook needs to be set.

122 Johnson Valley Reservoir

Key Species: Yellow perch and tiger muskie.

Best Way to Fish: Bait from shore for perch.

Best Time of Year to Fish: Summer.

Special Regulations: Limit, one tiger muskie; must be over 40 inches long.

Description: This pretty reservoir is surrounded by pine and aspen. It is located 7 miles northeast of Fish Lake, its more famous neighbor. Near the dam, anglers can find a large parking area, cement boat ramp, picnic tables, and restrooms. There are also turnoffs along the road to fish. Forest Service campgrounds can be found in the vicinity.

Fishing Index: Once managed for rainbow trout, problems with stunted yellow perch, chubs, and suckers have made it difficult for the trout to survive. Since the perch are small, there is little angler interest, though this is a good place to bring children to catch good numbers of fish using a worm fished off the bottom.

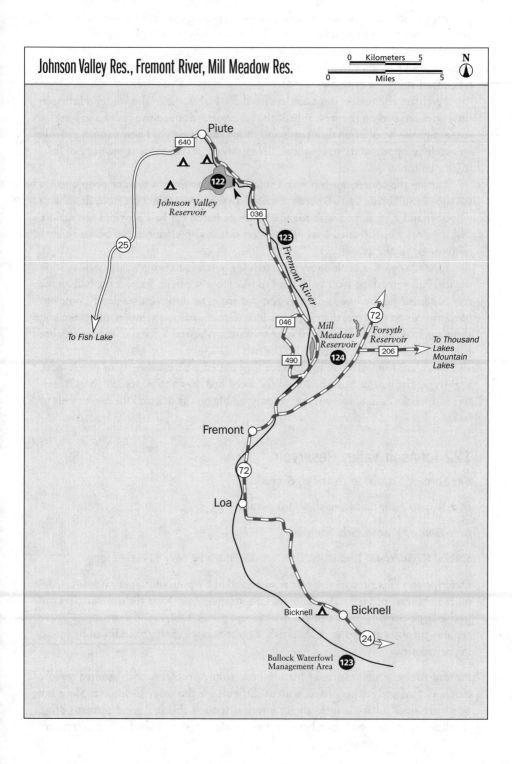

0   Kilometers   5

0   Miles   5

N

Piute

640

Johnson Valley
Reservoir

122

25

To Fish Lake

036

123

Fremont River

046

72

Mill
Meadow
Reservoir

Forsyth
Reservoir

490

124

206

To Thousand
Lakes
Mountain
Lakes

Fremont

72

Loa

Bicknell

Bicknell

24

Bullock Waterfowl
Management Area

123

Whirling disease has also made it difficult for biologists to manage this as a fishery, so in an effort to control the suckers and help solve the perch-stunting problem, biologists have introduced tiger muskie, a predator fish that has been successful in improving panfishing at Pine View in northern Utah. Introduced in 1999, the muskies are growing fast. Anglers can catch a number of small perch and a few holdover trout. The spillway below the dam that turns into the Fremont River can also be productive for small trout and perch. Worms are best, though cheese and Power Bait work as well.

123 Fremont River

Key Species: Brown trout and rainbow trout.

Best Way to Fish: Lures, flies, and bait.

Best Time of Year to Fish: Spring and fall.

Special Regulations: None.

Description: The river starts at Johnson Valley Reservoir Dam in the Fishlake National Forest and flows southeast through Mill Meadow Reservoir before passing the towns of Fremont, Loa, and Bicknell. Access below Johnson is along Forest Road 036 down to Mill Meadow. However, the river is de-watered for irrigation below Johnson. There is a spring about halfway between the reservoirs, which produces a large enough flow to sustain trout. The river is once again shrunk by irrigation demands below Mill Meadow. The best fishing on the Fremont is in the Bicknell Bottoms on the DWR-run Bullock Waterfowl Management Area. Private property is common along the rest of the river. Respect the landowners.

Fishing Index: Before it was poisoned in an effort to rid the river of whirling disease, the Fremont had a good population of large brown trout. As time passes, planted browns should take up that niche again. Fishing for the browns and rainbows is good with Panther Martin and Mepps spinners. Bait anglers do well floating a worm with a sinker through deep holes. Terrestrial patterns work well in the summer, but bead-head nymphs work throughout the year.

124 Mill Meadow Reservoir

Key Species: Rainbow trout, splake, tiger trout, yellow perch, and tiger muskie.

Best Way to Fish: Lures, flies, and bait.

Best Time of Year to Fish: Year-round.

Special Regulations: Tiger muskie limit eight; no size restrictions on tiger muskies.

Description: Mill Meadow is northeast of Loa at the base of the Fish Lake Mountains. From Highway 72 in Fremont via Forest Road 036, the reservoir is 2 miles up the road. Nearby Forsyth Reservoir seems to be in a constant state of low water because of dam problems. Check with officials before fishing at Forsyth.

Fishing Index: Mill Meadow was once fondly dubbed "Monster Meadow" because of all the freaky hybrid trout that DWR officials were planting there in an attempt to fight whirling disease. Biologists planted brownbows, brakes, splake, and tiger trout. Today the splake and tiger trout remain, along with some rainbow trout. Fishing at Mill Meadow is best with spoons and spinners fished from shore. Bait works in the middle of the day. Leech patterns fished deep will also turn up some fish.

125 Thousand Lakes Mountain Lakes

Key Species: Rainbow trout, brook trout, cutthroat trout, and tiger trout.

Best Way to Fish: Lures, flies, and bait.

Best Time of Year to Fish: Summer and fall.

Special Regulations: None.

Description: A surveyor in the early 1900s made the mistake of switching the name of this range with the one south of here. So relatively dry Thousand Lakes Mountain got the name meant for much wetter Boulder Mountain. Fishing is only popular at a few lakes here. Access is from Fremont, north of Loa on Highway 72, about 8.5 miles to Forest Road 206 and then east. The six-site Elkhorn Campground is about 8 miles in, on FR 206.

Fishing Index: Like other mountain lakes stocked with trout, lures and flies are the best bets, but bait fishing has its moments. Maisie and Jake's spoons are good choices. Fishing with leech patterns in dark colors is also effective. Float tubers tend to have better success than shore anglers. Ants are always a good choice in the late summer and into fall. Salmon eggs, Power Bait, and night crawlers fished near the bottom are traditional ways to catch trout while bait fishing from shore. The DWR stocks most of the lakes with rainbows, but there are healthy populations of brook trout. Some lakes have tiger trout and cutthroat. Expect company, especially on the weekends.

Meeks Lake—Water fluctuations hurt fishing for rainbow trout and brook trout here. The lake is reached from FR 206, 4 miles northeast to Forest Road 020, then 3.5 miles on Forest Road 019. The lake is a short hike east from the end of the road.

Morrel Pond—This lake is reached by taking FR 206, 4 miles northeast to FR 020, then less than a mile on FR 019 to a road which leads to the lake. Fishing here is good for rainbow and brook trout.

Floating Island Lake—Tiger trout are abundant, as well as cutthroat trout and splake. From Meeks, hike less than 0.5 mile west and a little south to Floating Island.

Farrell Pond—Has a tendency to develop moss, but there are a lot of rainbows and brook trout here. Take FR 206, 4 miles northeast to FR 020, then head 3.5 miles

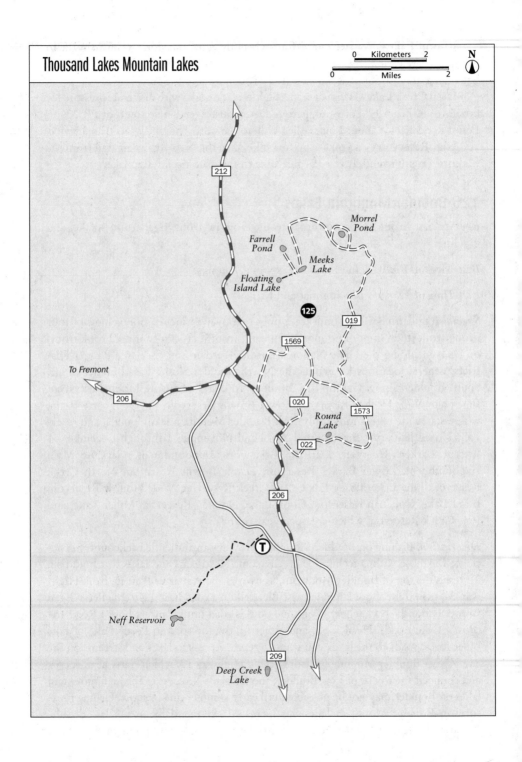

0   Kilometers   2

0   Miles   2

N

212

Morrel
Pond

Farrell
Pond

Meeks
Lake

Floating
Island Lake

125

019

1569

To Fremont

206

020

1573

Round
Lake

022

206

T

Neff Reservoir

209

Deep Creek
Lake

on FR 019 to Forest Road 568. Although it is less than 0.5 mile to the lake, it is rough. You might consider walking.

Round Lake—You will need four-wheel drive if you don't want to walk to Round, where brook trout are the catch. Take FR 206 to Forest Road 022 and head less than a mile to Forest Road 211. It is a rough mile to the lake.

Deep Creek Lake—This is a scenic high-elevation lake with moderate pressure for brook trout. From Elkhorn Campground, head just over 1 mile south of FR 206 to Forest Road 209 for about 2 miles, then walk to the west. The lake is less than 0.5 mile.

Neff Reservoir—If you are up to a hike, take the Neff Reservoir trail from the Elkhorn Campground. It is a 3.5-mile hike to the brookie-infested lake.

126 Boulder Mountain Lakes

Key Species: Brook trout, cutthroat trout, rainbow trout, tiger trout, splake, and grayling.

Best Way to Fish: Bait, flies, spinners, spoons, and jigs.

Best Time of Year to Fish: Summer and fall.

Special Regulations: Trout limit four, only two over 14 inches, bonus limit of four brook trout (total limit of no more than eight trout if at least four are brook trout) on lakes including the Dixie National Forest, Teasdale and Escalante Ranger Districts: general locations known as the North Boulder Slope, East Boulder Slope, South Boulder Slope, Griffin Top, Boulder Top, and Escalante Mountain (except Pine Lake, Wide Hollow Reservoir, Lower Bowns Reservoir, and Dougherty Basin, where statewide regulations apply). All Boulder Mountain lakes, ponds, and reservoirs closed January 1 through mid-April and November 1 through December 31 (except Barker Reservoir, Garkane East Fork Impoundment, Garkane Main Impoundment, Lower Barker Reservoir, Lower Bowns Reservoir, North Creek Reservoir, Pine Lake, Posey Lake, Oak Creek Reservoir, Wide Hollow Reservoir, Blind Lake, Coleman Reservoir, Cook Lake, Donkey Reservoir, Miller Lake, and Pine Creek Reservoir, which are open year-round).

Description: Fishing on Boulder Mountain provides an authentic backcountry experience for those willing to hike. There are some 80 streams and lakes that hold fish. To reach the top of Boulder Mountain, known as the Aquarius Plateau, from Highway 24, turn right about 2.5 miles past Bicknell on a road heading to the Perry Egan Brood Station Fish Hatchery. Continue on this road until it meets Forest Road 154 (Posey Lake Road). Head south and either follow the road to Posey Lake or take other forest roads to the lakes you want to reach. Access to lakes and streams on the east side of Boulder Mountain is from Scenic Highway 12, which starts near Torrey and connects the towns of Loa, Boulder, and Escalante. Access to the high mountain lakes on Boulder may not be possible until early summer due to snow. Fishing pressure on Boulder Mountain lakes has increased exponentially in the last decade. Catch-and-release is vital to ensure a fishing future on the mountain. Unethical

The Boulder Mountain lakes offer an authentic backcountry experience.

anglers taking advantage of susceptible fish in the winter forced the closure of the mountain to fishing from November to mid-April.

Fishing Index: Earlier in the season, cold water will keep insect activity to a minimum. Look for the fish to concentrate in shallower, warmer water at this time. Fishing will be best with lures and flies fished below the surface. Good options are Maisie, Jake's, Dardevle, and Krocodile spoons in gold, copper, black, and orange. Spinners like Panther Martin, Mepps, and Rooster Tails will work in shallow water. Large brook trout are caught frequently with feather and plastic jigs in black, purple, brown, olive, and white. Fly fishing is better from shore at this time. Wet flies and nymphs, like woolly buggers, mohair leeches, prince nymphs, hare's ear nymphs, and scuds, are all good bets. Black, brown, purple, olive, and peacock are good color choices.

As the water warms, insect activity increases, and fish will take advantage of easy meals like damselfly nymphs heading for shore. On the surface, look for mayfly and midge hatches. Blue-winged olive, parachute Adams, Griffith's gnat, renegade, black gnat, and small Royal Wulff patterns are good for rising fish. Later in the season, terrestrial patterns will work. Try ants, hoppers, and beetles.

In late summer, the fish scatter. This is when a float tube or small boat will come in handy. The fish may not always be in the middle of the lake, but being on the water allows you to cover more area than fishing from shore. Fly fishing with a sinking line can help you reach fish holding in deeper water. Some lakes may be difficult to fish as the summer wears on due to heavy weed growth in shallow fisheries.

Fishing in the fall can be good because the brook trout start feeding aggressively as they prepare to spawn. Larger and brighter-colored lures and jigs are more effective at this time. Fly fishing with white, yellow, red, or black streamers near inlets should work well. Bait anglers will do best at lakes with rainbows, but natural baits like night crawlers or grasshoppers will work for all species.

These techniques are somewhat brook trout specific, but should work on all species on the Boulder. However, cutthroat are more aggressive in the spring during their spawn and are likely to be caught around stream inlets early in the season. Grayling have smaller mouths than trout. Use small spinners and flies when fishing for them. Splake are more aggressive than most trout, and larger bright-colored spoons and flies work best for them. They also tend to hold deeper and are most common in the larger lakes on the mountain.

Beaver Dam and Fish Creek Lakes—Forest Road 520 provides the best access to the lakes. Beaver Dam has brook trout and cutthroat trout. Splake and cutthroat trout are found in Fish Creek Lake.

Bess—This small lake has a good population of brook trout and is reached southeast from Elbow Lake on Forest Road 1782, and then a short distance north on Forest Road 1322 to the lake.

Big—About 1 mile north of Pleasant Lake, take your four-wheel-drive vehicle onto FR 1782. Big Lake can also be reached from due west of Meeks. This is a shallow lake with brook trout, but it may suffer from winterkill.

Blind—The biggest lake on the mountain, Blind has rainbows, brookies, cutthroat, and splake. From Highway 12 southeast of Torrey, take Forest Road 179 southwest to Green Lake. A 1-mile-long trail (140) leads to the lake. Blind gets a lot of pressure. A float tube may help you cover water.

Boulder Creek—This stream flows off the east side of Boulder Mountain. The lower reaches are located on Bureau of Land Management (BLM) ground, while the upper portions flow on Dixie National Forest. Some private land prevents fishing the part of Boulder Creek that is around the town of Boulder. Access on the mountain is via Forest Road 166 from Highway 12, 4 miles north of Boulder. FR 166 connects with Forest Road 165 and eventually, Forest Road 508. Kings Pasture Reservoir is a good place to start fishing the stream above the lake. Those more willing to hike a ways can take FR 508 to its end and hike in to fish the stream as it comes off the Aquarius Plateau. A beaver pond on the way makes for a good lunch spot. Don't forget to try for cutthroat trout in the pond. Pressure is light and fishing for them can be fast. Brook trout are the prevalent catch on Boulder Creek, but rainbows, browns, and cutthroat can also be landed.

Bullberry—From Highway 12 south of Teasdale, take Forest Road 521 to Coleman Lake. Then hike 1 mile due south on Trail 124 to Bullberry. The lake is loaded with tiger trout and cutthroat trout.

Calf Creek—This spring-fed stream is situated about halfway between the towns of Escalante and Boulder. It is entirely located on BLM land. A BLM campground is available off Highway 12 at Calf Creek Falls. Other access points can be found off Highway 12 out of Boulder; they require a hike. Look for the Upper Calf Creek

Falls trailhead. The stream flows through red rock and is popular with swimmers. The stream is about 3 miles long and contains brown trout. Beavers are plentiful, and small dams create natural fishing holes. Fall is the best time to fish Calf Creek, as temperatures in the summer are severe.

Coleman—From Highway 12 south of Teasdale, take FR 521 to Coleman. The lake has rainbow and brook trout and receives a lot of pressure.

Cook—Off the Posey Lake Road, take Forest Road 1781 southeast to Forest Road 542 to the lake. Cook is planted with rainbows and also contains brook trout and grayling.

Crescent—This lake is a 2-mile hike east of Spectacle Lake on Trail 114. Cutthroat trout reside in Crescent.

Deer Creek Lake—From Highway 12 on the southeast side of the mountain, take Forest Road 554 to the Great Western Trail and hike 3 miles west to the lake. Fishing is good for cutthroat and brook trout.

Deer Creek—This stream flows off the east side of Boulder Mountain across the Dixie National Forest and onto BLM land where it meanders near the town of Boulder. Deer Creek is most accessible along Highway 12 and along the Burr Trail road starting in Boulder and heading east. Brook, cutthroat, and rainbow trout are common on the upper stretches. The more accessible lower portion of Deer Creek contains browns. Watch for private property on the stream between the USDA Forest Service and BLM property.

Donkey—Just south of Teasdale on Highway 12, take FR 521 to Forest Road 525 and head south past Bob's Hole, Grass Lake, and Round Lake to Donkey Reservoir. Donkey is under heavy pressure for brook trout.

Garkane Power Plant Reservoir—This small reservoir is planted with rainbows. Fishing can be good with traditional trout baits and dry flies in the evening. Flashy spoons and spinners are also effective. Named Powerhouse on some maps, the Garkane Power Plant Reservoir is reached on FR 166 about 0.5 mile off of Highway 12, about 4.5 miles north of the town of Boulder.

Halfmoon—From Horseshoe Lake, take Trail 138 about 1 mile south past East Lake to Halfmoon. A self-sustaining population of brook trout is here.

Horseshoe—From the Bowns Point Trailhead take FR 1782 to FR 1302 and head south 4.5 miles to the lake. A large population of brook trout provides fast fishing here.

Kings Pasture—Once stocked with rainbows, the DWR has discontinued that practice in favor of allowing naturally reproducing brook trout. Dry and wet flies as well as Jake's and Maisie spoons work well here. It is reached via FR 166 off Highway 12 just north of Boulder. About 1.5 miles up FR 166, take FR 165 for approximately 2.5 miles.

Lost—This lonely lake is reached from Coleman via a 2.5-mile hike on Trail 124. Brook trout live here.

Lower Bowns—This 125-acre reservoir on the east side of Boulder Mountain is planted frequently with rainbow trout. Lower Bowns, also called Bowns Reservoir, is easily seen from Highway 12. The reservoir is reached on Forest Road 186; it originates near the Pleasant Creek Campground on Highway 12. Fishing is good

Boulder Mountain Lakes

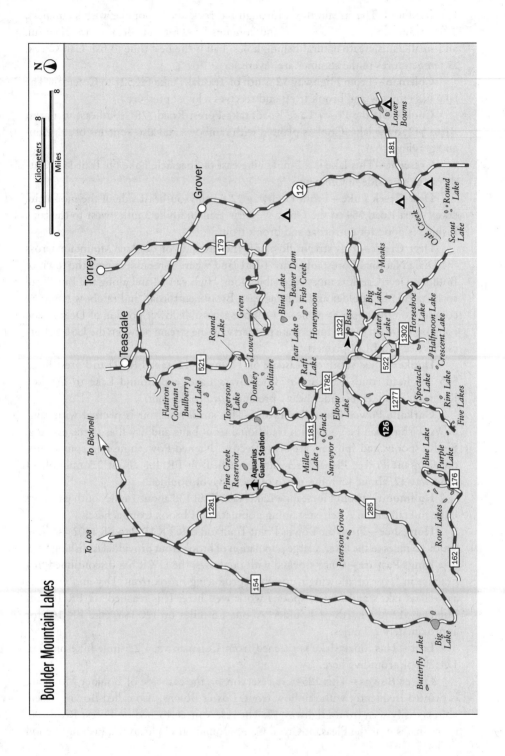

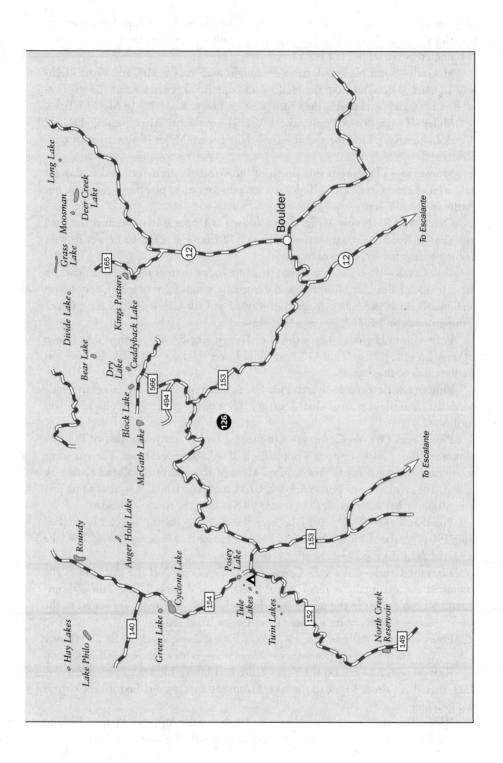

from shore, but many people use small rafts, boats, or float tubes. No launching facilities are located here. Primitive camping is allowed around the reservoir. Four camping areas are set up, but no water.

McGath—Some big brook trout are caught each year at McGath. From Highway 12 west of Boulder, take the Hell's Backbone Road (Forest Road 153) to Forest Road 566 and head north, then turn west on Forest Road 494 to McGath Lake.

Miller—From Bown Point take FR 1781 southeast. After passing FR 542 (Cook Lake Road), look for a spur road heading west. Miller is planted with rainbow trout.

Moosman—This lake is just north of the Great Western Trail and is about 1 mile west of Deer Creek Lake. Biologists have discontinued planting tiger trout, but cutthroat are still here.

Oak Creek Reservoir—This is also known as Upper Bowns because the road to it (Forest Road 567) starts across Highway 12 from the access to Lower Bowns. Fishing here is for large brook trout.

Oak Creek—Brook and cutthroat trout are found in this creek, which flows on the east side of Boulder Mountain and eventually winds its way into Capitol Reef National Park. It is reached from Highway 12 at Oak Creek and Pleasant Creek Campgrounds on FR 567, a four-wheel-drive road.

Pear—From Highway 12 southeast of Torrey, take FR 179 southwest to Green Lake. A 1.5-mile hike on Trail 140, past Blind Lake, will take you there. Brook trout are the catch of the day.

Pine Creek Reservoir—Reach Pine Creek Reservoir by hiking less than 1 mile northeast from the Aquarius Guard Station. The reservoir contains Colorado River cutthroat.

Pine Creek (Wayne County)—Originating on the northwest side of Boulder Mountain, Pine Creek supports a population of wild cutthroat trout. There is some access near the Aquarius Guard Station. Most of the stream is only accessible by hiking. The creek crosses Forest Service, BLM, and state lands, as well as some private property, before meeting the Fremont River near the town of Bicknell.

Pleasant Lake—This small lake near the east edge of the plateau is reached from FR 1782, about 7 miles beyond where it's crossed by Pleasant Creek. The lake is northeast of the road and contains brook trout.

Pleasant Creek—Like Oak Creek, this stream comes off the east side of the mountain and eventually enters Capitol Reef National Park. The stream is dominated by brook trout in the upper stretches, while rainbow trout are found in the lower reaches, which can be accessed from Forest Road 168.

Posey—From Escalante, take FR 153 (Hell's Backbone Road) to FR 154 (Posey Lake Road). There is a campground at the lake. Fishing is for rainbow and brook trout.

Raft—From Bicknell on the Posey Lake Road, take FR 1781 southeast to FR 1324, then drive about 1 mile to the lake. Fishing at Raft is sporadic for brook trout and grayling.

Rim—This aptly named lake rests on the edge of the Aquarius Plateau. Fishing is good for brook trout. Access is best on Forest Road 1277 from FR 1782.

Round—There's heavy pressure for brook trout here. Reach the lake by taking FR 521 just south of Teasdale on Highway 12 to FR 525. Round is about 1 mile past Grass Lake.

Scout—From Highway 12, take FR 554 near the Great Western Trail and head northwest about 3 miles. Expect company when fishing for brook trout.

Solitaire—Start on FR 521 from Highway 12, just south of Teasdale. Then take FR 525 south past Bob's Hole, Grass Lake, and Round Lake. About 0.5 mile past Round Lake, Trail 141 takes you to Solitaire. Cutthroat trout and tiger trout are the catch at Solitaire.

Spectacle—Access is best on FR 1277 from FR 1782. Fishing is good for brookies.

Tule Lakes—Hike half a mile southwest of the Posey Lake Campground. There is good fishing for brook trout.

127 North Creek Lakes (Barker Reservoirs)

This group of lakes at the head of the North Creek Drainage northwest of Escalante is reached from Forest Road 149, which heads northwest from Highway 12 about 5 miles west of town. You will reach the Barker Reservoirs and the campground that

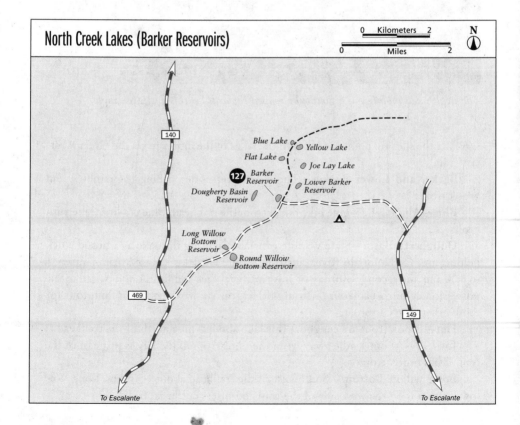

The stealth and mobility of a float tube reaped rewards for this flatwater angler.

serves as the starting point for hikes to the lakes in the drainage via the Great Western Trail.

Barker and Lower Barker—These reservoirs offer fishing for rainbow and brook trout.

Blue—About a 1.25-mile hike north from the trailhead, Blue is a little lake with brookies.

Dougherty Basin—State wildlife officials are using this lake as a brood stock holding area for Colorado River cutthroat trout. The lake is closed from January 1 to 6:00 a.m. the second Saturday of July; artificial flies and lures only; closed to the possession of cutthroat trout or trout with cutthroat markings; trout limit four for those other than cutthroat.

Flat—Brook trout are caught at this lake about 1 mile north of the trailhead.

Joe Lay—About 1 mile away from the campground, Joe Lay is just east of the trail. It has brook trout.

Long Willow Bottom—Southwest of the trailhead about 1.5 miles, Long Willow Bottom is on the west side of the trail and offers cutthroat trout.

Round Willow Bottom—Just opposite the trail from Long Willow Bottom, Round provides fast fishing for cutthroat trout and tiger trout.

Yellow—This lake may suffer winterkill but can provide good fishing for brook trout. It is opposite Blue Lake.

128 Piute Reservoir

Key Species: Rainbow trout, brown trout, and smallmouth bass.

Best Way to Fish: Trolling and from shore.

Best Time of Year to Fish: Spring and fall.

Special Regulations: None.

Description: Located just off U.S. Highway 89 between Marysvale and Junction, this fishery is serviced by Piute State Park on the north end of the reservoir. Conditions are primitive.

Fishing Index: After being drained for dam repairs in 2000, the reservoir was stocked with rainbow trout and smallmouth bass. Trout fishing has traditionally been good from shore with Power Bait, dead minnows, and night crawlers. Flashy

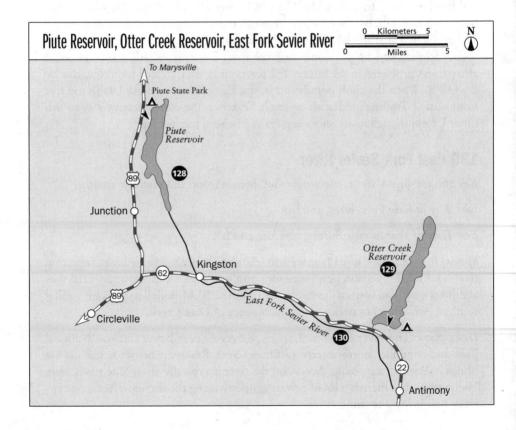

Piute Reservoir, Otter Creek Reservoir, East Fork Sevier River

spinners can also be effective from shore. Trolling is best with needlefish, Jake's, and Z-Rays. Look to catch the smallmouth off points with crankbaits. Topwater lures work well in low-light conditions.

129 Otter Creek Reservoir

Key Species: Rainbow trout, cutthroat trout, brown trout, and smallmouth bass.

Best Way to Fish: Trolling.

Best Time of Year to Fish: Summer.

Special Regulations: None.

Description: State park facilities that include a campground, modern restrooms, and a boat dock coupled with a nearby commercial lodge offering boat rentals make this a popular destination for southern Utah boaters and anglers. The reservoir, located in Piute County, has an open feel to it. Afternoon winds can be a problem, just as they are at Strawberry Reservoir. And, on most summer weekends, reservations are suggested at the state park campground.

Fishing Index: Otter Creek is one of those Utah waters with the ability to grow fat and feisty rainbow trout quickly. The DWR normally plants 200,000 7-inch rainbow trout each fall. By the time the ice is off, most have put on weight and length. The problem is that the lake becomes infested with Utah chubs on a fairly regular basis, and they end up out-competing the trout for food. Whirling disease could also present problems in the future. The reservoir is often treated with rotenone by the DWR. When the chub population is low, this can rank among Utah's top five trout waters. Trolling needlefish or Triple Teazers is the most effective way to fish Otter Creek, though many shore anglers can be seen bait fishing.

130 East Fork Sevier River

Key Species: Brook trout, cutthroat trout, brown trout, and rainbow trout.

Best Way to Fish: Flies, lures, and bait.

Best Time of Year to Fish: Spring, summer, and fall.

Special Regulations: Closed January 1 to 6:00 a.m. the second Saturday of July from the feeder canal diversion near Antimony to Otter Creek Reservoir; artificial flies and lures only and a trout limit of two from the BLM boundary (about 4 miles south of Antimony) upstream to the confluence of Deer Creek.

Description: This river flows into Tropic Reservoir near Bryce Canyon National Park and continues northeasterly to Otter Creek Reservoir before irrigation use brings it down to a dwindle. Access on the river is typically along side roads from Highway 22, but there is a lot of private property along the corridor. Access is typically best below the dams.

Fishing Index: The upper stretches of the river contain primarily brook trout and cutthroat. Small dries fished in pocket water work for both species. Small spoons will also produce fish. The river eventually dumps into Otter Creek Reservoir. Fishing below Otter Creek in Kingston Canyon is good with night crawlers and medium-size spoons and lures. Large terrestrials, especially hoppers, work well in late summer. The section between Antimony and Osiris in Black Canyon typically runs low and clear. Caddis hatches are common. Fishing with flies and small spinners has worked well for brown trout. Fishing below Osiris is spotty at best.

131 Beaver River

Key Species: Brown trout, rainbow trout, cutthroat trout, and brook trout.

Best Way to Fish: Bait, flies, and lures.

Best Time of Year to Fish: Spring, summer, and fall.

Special Regulations: Upstream from Minersville Reservoir to the bridge at Greenville is closed January 1 to 6:00 a.m. the second Saturday of July.

Description: The portion of the stream most anglers fish is in Beaver Canyon east of the town of Beaver. Much of the river is accessible from Highway 153, which runs up

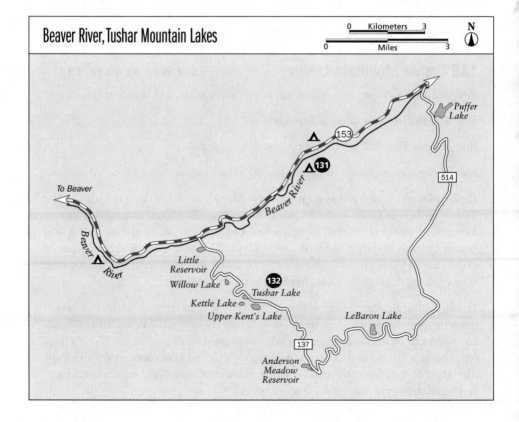

the canyon to Puffer Lake. This is a beautiful canyon with an excellent fishery. The headwaters of the Beaver are near Puffer, but the river is fed by dozens of small tributaries. There are three campgrounds in the canyon. Little Cottonwood, the lowest, has 14 sites and restrooms. Little Reservoir and Mahogany Cove are located about midcanyon. Little Reservoir has five family units and two group sites. Mahogany Cove has seven sites. The Elk Meadows Ski area is also near the head of the canyon, so the road is plowed, and it isn't uncommon to see people fishing in the winter.

After the river flows past Beaver, it is hard to access because of the private property in the valley. In the summer, the Beaver is de-watered in many places between the town of Beaver and Minersville Reservoir for irrigation purposes.

Below Minersville, there are about 3 miles of river to fish. After that, access is hit and miss, and de-watering occurs.

Fishing Index: Cutthroat and brook trout rule the headwaters of the Beaver River. They can also be found high in the tributaries. Browns and wild rainbows are the predominant catch in the main canyon. The DWR plants catchable rainbows near the campgrounds. Browns and rainbows are also found throughout the valley and below Minersville.

There are some good hatches of caddis flies and mayflies here. Small elk hair caddis, Wulff, and terrestrial patterns are local favorites. Small spinners are also a good choice. Fall is the best time to fish for browns. A local favorite is the peacock lady, a fly that can be fished dry or wet. Near the campgrounds, bait fishing with night crawlers, salmon eggs, and Power Bait is popular for planted rainbows.

132 Tushar Mountain Lakes   See map on page 191.

Key Species: Rainbow trout, brook trout, cutthroat trout, and brown trout.

Best Way to Fish: Bait, flies, and spinners.

Best Time of Year to Fish: Late spring, summer, and fall.

Special Regulations: Some of these lakes do not allow boats.

Description: Although not as popular as Boulder Mountain, fishing the lakes of the Tushar up Beaver Canyon can be just as rewarding. The lakes, often called Beaver Mountain Lakes, are reached from the town of Beaver east on Highway 153 into Beaver Canyon, and then south on Forest Road 137. There are several campgrounds in the canyon. As with any high country area, don't overlook fishing in the streams. When fishing slows on the lake, head for a nearby stream.

Fishing Index: Besides fishing with traditional trout baits from shore, float tubing is the most popular way to fish these lakes. Stripping in small flashback bead-heads and size 14 to 16 woolly buggers in olive, brown, and black is effective. Dry fly fishing is good with dun and mosquito patterns. Maisie and Jake's spoons are also popular. Most of the lakes are planted with catchable rainbows. Cutthroat, brown, tiger, and brook trout are also found in some waters.

Anderson Meadow Reservoir—This 9-acre reservoir offers good fishing from shore for stocked rainbows and pan-size brook trout. It is accessible via FR 137 from Highway 153 in Beaver Canyon. Boats with motors are not allowed. The Forest Service maintains a nearby campground with 10 family units, restrooms, and water in the summer months. The lake is set in a high meadow and is one of the prettiest on the mountain. Fishing from a float tube is popular here with dun and mosquito patterns. Leech patterns are also a good choice. Bait fishing is good with night crawlers and Power Bait.

LeBaron Lake—Brook trout are the predominant catch at this 23-acre lake (spelled LaBaron on some maps), but rainbows are also planted here. It's on FR 137. Fishing with bait from shore is slow here; float tubers do well with small woolly buggers.

Little Reservoir—One of the more popular fisheries on the mountain, Little Reservoir is planted with rainbows and browns. Some large browns are caught here. In the mid-1990s, the DWR electroshocked the reservoir and a 15- to 20-pound fish came up. Anglers have seen and hooked the fish since, but no one has landed it. Little Reservoir is the first reservoir along FR 137 from Highway 153. The Forest Service maintains a campground with five family units and two group spots near the reservoir. Restrooms are available. Fishing for planted rainbows is good with bait from shore. Anglers after the big browns throw Rapalas or fish with streamers or leech patterns.

Puffer Lake—It's possible to launch a boat here, but the ramp is private and you may be asked to pay to use it. Brook and rainbow trout are caught here. Fish with bait from shore for the planted rainbows. The brook trout are caught most frequently at ice-off with silver and gold spoons and spinners. Fly fishers strip in leech patterns later in the summer for some quick action. Trolling with pop gear or flatfish should also work.

Kent's Lake (Upper and Middle)—A 32-site campground is located near Upper Kent's Lake. The upper lake has brook, rainbow, and cutthroat trout. Fish up to 4 pounds are possible. Lower Kent's has brookies and cutthroat and is best fished at ice-off—as the summer wears on, the lake tends to develop a moss problem which makes fishing difficult.

Tushar Lake—Shown as Lower Kent's on most maps, Tushar also offers good fishing for planted rainbows, primarily with bait from shore.

133 Minersville Reservoir

Key Species: Rainbow trout, cutthroat trout, and smallmouth bass.

Best Way to Fish: From shore or from a float tube.

Best Time of Year to Fish: Spring and fall.

Special Regulations: Artificial flies and lures only. Trout limit one over 22 inches; all trout under 22 inches must be released. Cement outlet channel between dam and spillway is closed.

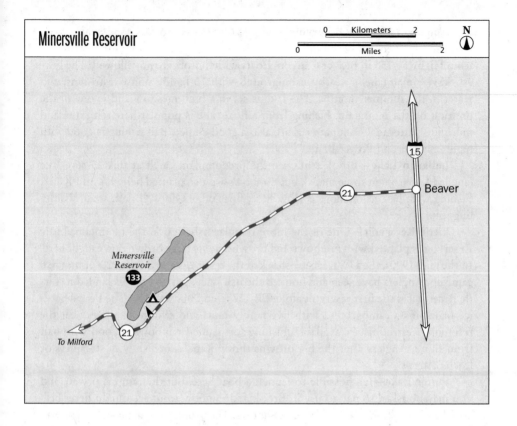

Minersville Reservoir

Minersville Reservoir

To Milford

Beaver

Description: Minersville is 12 miles west of Beaver (Interstate 15 exits 109 or 112) on Highway 21. Access on the north shore of the reservoir is a dirt road from Adamsville. Minersville State Park has a 29-unit campground and also offers showers, a launching ramp, potable water, and electrical hookups for a fee.

Fishing Index: Minersville Reservoir has the dubious distinction of being Utah's most often chemically treated body of water. The 1,130-acre reservoir 12 miles west of Beaver has been treated numerous times to rid it of the prolific Utah chub. In between poisonings, it traditionally provided some of the state's best rainbow fishing thanks to large plants of the trout.

Overzealous anglers cramming their freezers full of trout, coupled with a large population of fish-eating birds and increasing chub numbers, forced the DWR to treat the reservoir repeatedly. It soon became apparent that it was too costly (about $20,000 each treatment) and time consuming (the reservoir was treated about every five years) to give trout anglers just two good years of fishing. Special regulations have now turned Minersville into a trophy fishery.

Float-tubing is the most popular way to fish Minersville, especially when the ice first comes off the reservoir and the trout look for a place to spawn. Using sinking line and stripping in olive, brown, or black woolly buggers works best for the trout. Damselfly nymph and leech patterns in dark colors, especially black and brown, are also productive. Bead-head nymphs and wet flies can work. The only real opportunity for dry fly purists comes in June during large but infrequent midge hatches.

Smallmouth bass congregate on rocky points and near the dam. They hit plastic baits jigged off the bottom. Topwater lures will work in the early morning and late evening hours. Diving crankbaits are also a good bet.

134 Wide Hollow Reservoir

Key Species: Rainbow trout, largemouth bass, and bluegill.

Best Way to Fish: Trolling from a canoe.

Best Time of Year to Fish: Spring.

Special Regulations: None.

Description: This reservoir, just west of Escalante on the edge of the Grand Staircase–Escalante National Monument, is part of Escalante State Park. A boat ramp, restrooms with showers, covered picnic tables, and plenty of grass coupled with an interesting hiking trail make this a popular camping area. Some even enjoy swimming in the cool water here. In the spring, the shallow wetlands on the edge of the reservoir are filled with migrating birds, including ospreys that show up each year around Easter.

Fishing Index: The DWR plants several thousand catchable rainbow trout in this water right after ice-out, and the trout fishing holds up through Memorial Day.

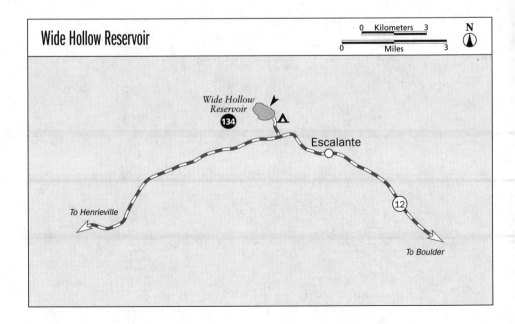

Management strategies have changed because of illegal plants of bluegill and bass. Biologists are now also managing for those species. Bass and bluegill fishing is good during the summer and fall months when the water warms. That is a rarity in this trout-oriented part of the world. Most shore anglers fish with bait from the long, earthen dam. Jigs and traditional bass lures work for the warm-water species; boat fishing is more effective.

135 Paragonah Reservoir

Key Species: Rainbow trout.

Best Way to Fish: Bait, lures, and flies.

Best Time of Year to Fish: Spring and fall.

Special Regulations: Tributaries are closed January 1 to the second Saturday of July.

Description: Known as Red Creek Reservoir by locals, Paragonah Reservoir is a 70-acre fishery found east of Paragonah. It is accessed through Paragonah Main Canyon on Forest Road 078. Small boats can be launched from shore.

Fishing Index: Once a put-and-take fishery, the reservoir now sustains a naturally reproducing population of rainbow trout. Fly fishers typically have the best success. In the spring, try bead-head nymphs, dark-colored wet flies, and damselfly nymphs. As the water warms, midge and mayfly hatches will occur. Try an Adams, Griffith's gnat, and ants. Small spoons and spinners fished from shore should also work.

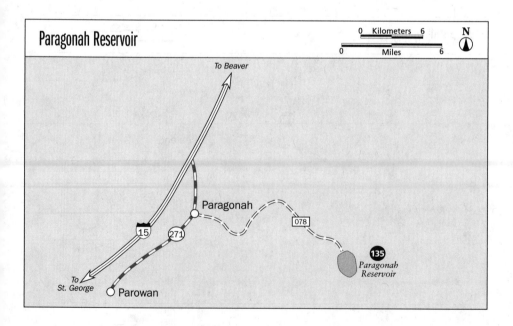

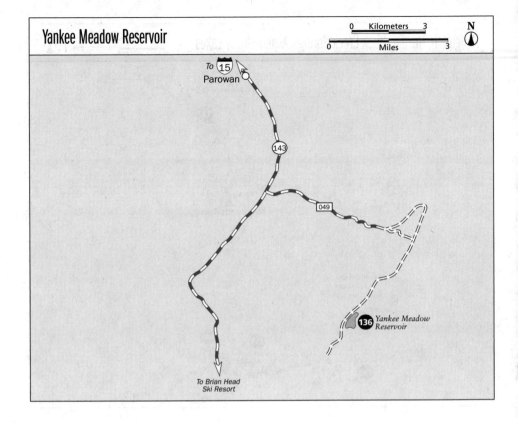

Kilometers

Miles

N

To 15
Parowan

143

049

Yankee Meadow
Reservoir

To Brian Head
Ski Resort

136 Yankee Meadow Reservoir

Key Species: Rainbow trout, cutthroat trout, and brook trout.

Best Way to Fish: Bait, lures, and flies.

Best Time of Year to Fish: Spring and fall.

Special Regulations: None.

Description: Yankee Meadow is southeast of Parowan off Highway 143 via Forest Road 049. Small boats can be launched from shore.

Fishing Index: Popular with locals, Yankee Meadow produces some nice rainbows. Power Bait and worms work well from shore. Float tubers do well stripping in woolly buggers and scuds. Maisie, Jake's, and small Krocodile spoons can all be effective, casting or trolling.

137 Panguitch Lake

Key Species: Rainbow trout, cutthroat trout, and tiger trout.

Best Way to Fish: Trolling and from shore.

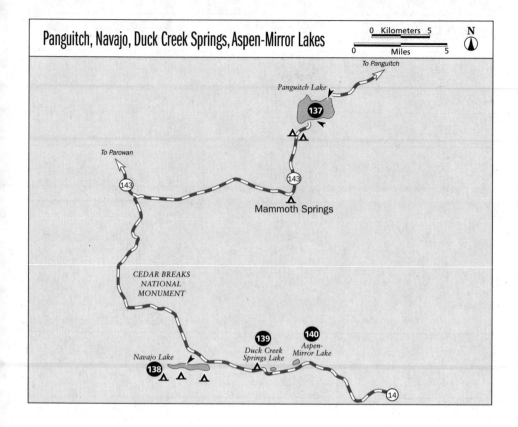

Panguitch, Navajo, Duck Creek Springs, Aspen-Mirror Lakes

Best Time of Year to Fish: Year-round.

Special Regulations: None.

Description: Panguitch Lake was chemically treated in the spring of 2006 to remove a high concentration of Utah chubs in the productive reservoir. Rainbow trout were planted within a month of the treatment, and fishing at Panguitch is expected to be good for trout in the coming decades. Fisheries officials have also decided to stock the aggressive Bear Lake cutthroat in Panguitch Lake to help battle the chub problem. Tiger trout were also introduced to provide some diversity for anglers. Regulations are sure to change as the fishery recovers; be sure to check the proclamation.

Panguitch is one of the most popular lakes in southern Utah. In addition to local pressure, Panguitch also sees plenty of anglers from the Wasatch Front and even more from the Las Vegas area and as far away as southern California (a 2001 survey showed that 68 percent of the anglers at Panguitch were not residents of Utah).

About 18 miles west of Panguitch on Highway 143, this 1,250-acre fishery is a reliable fish producer. In fact, translated from Paiute, the local Native American tribe, the word *Panguitch* means "big fish." A number of small commercial stores surround Panguitch Lake, making it easy to rent a cabin or a boat. The Forest Service operates three large campgrounds in the area: White Bridge, North Panguitch Lake, and South Panguitch Lake.

Fishing Index: Panguitch Lake was the first fishery in the state to allow ice fishing. Anglers just couldn't wait for the ice to thaw to experience the good fishing here. Businesses along the lakeshore supported the idea. Things went so well in the winter at Panguitch, officials eventually decided to open the rest of Utah's fisheries to ice fishing.

However, Panguitch gets most of its pressure in the late spring, throughout the summer, and into fall. While trolling is productive, most anglers here fish with bait from shore or still-fish from anchored boats. Vegetation can be a problem in late summer, especially for those trying to fish from shore. Night crawlers and Power Bait are the baits of choice among Panguitch Lake anglers. Trolling is good with pop gear and a worm, Z-Rays, or flatfish.

Due to the pressure, most fish are in the 14- to 20-inch range, but every once in a while, a trophy fish is landed. The DWR plants 20,000 fingerling cutthroat and 200,000 fingerling rainbow each year.

Casting spoons and spinners from shore or from a boat works well in the spring and fall. Float tubers strip leech patterns in black, olive, and brown for some big fish. A sinking line helps immensely.

138 Navajo Lake

Key Species: Rainbow trout, brook trout, and splake.

Best Way to Fish: Trolling.

Best Time of Year to Fish: Summer and fall.

Special Regulations: None.

Description: The scenery and cool high alpine setting is the big draw at Navajo Lake, a popular place for southern Utah and Las Vegas residents to escape the heat. The turquoise blue water is beautiful. Facilities are plentiful with a boat ramp, two commercial lodges, and three Forest Service campgrounds located on the shoreline.

Fishing Index: Planted rainbow trout in the 10- to 14-inch range are the staple here, though an occasional brook or larger splake can be caught. The lake is big enough for trolling with lures such as needlefish, Triple Teazers, flatfish, and Z-Rays being quite effective. Many anglers fish from the easily accessible shoreline with traditional baits such as Power Bait or worms. Biologists say some fly fishing is also possible on the west end of the lake, especially on still evenings. Again, with the scenery this pretty, catching fish is a bonus. Angling here is spotty, but patience is rewarded.

139 Duck Creek Springs Lake

Key Species: Rainbow trout and brook trout.

Best Way to Fish: Bait, lures, and flies.

Best Time of Year to Fish: Summer and fall.

Special Regulations: Boats and float tubes are not allowed.

Description: East of Navajo Lake and just north of Highway 14 on Cedar Mountain, Duck Creek Springs gets a lot of local pressure as well as anglers from nearby states. The lake is stocked regularly with catchable rainbows and fingerling brook trout. Duck Creek Springs Lake is shown as Duck Creek Reservoir on some maps.

Fishing Index: For better success at this shallow and weedy fishery, try lightweight spinners and spoons. Help the fish find your bait by using a bobber to suspend it just above the weeds. Power Bait, night crawlers, and salmon eggs are the most popular baits. The trout at Duck Creek readily take flies, and small dry flies work exceptionally well when the fish are rising. Parachute Adams, Griffith's gnat, ants, and renegades are solid choices. Bead-head and damselfly nymphs work when there's no surface action.

140 Aspen-Mirror Lake

Key Species: Rainbow trout, brook trout, and brown trout.

Best Way to Fish: Bait, spinners, and flies.

Best Time of Year to Fish: Summer and fall.

Special Regulations: Closed January 1 through mid-April. Boats and float tubes are not allowed.

Description: Aspen-Mirror Lake is a 0.25-mile hike from Highway 14 near Navajo Lake and Duck Creek Springs Lake. It sees an incredible amount of pressure because people from Las Vegas and southern California have marked it as the place to fish in southern Utah. The lake is set in timber at a high elevation. Even if you aren't fishing, you should make the short hike.

Fishing Index: Aspen-Mirror is heavily stocked throughout the summer with catchable rainbow trout. Fishing is best with traditional trout baits. Spinners work well in the late morning and early afternoon. Dry flies fished in the evenings behind a casting bubble can provide some fast action.

141 Tropic Reservoir

Key Species: Rainbow trout, cutthroat trout, and brook trout.

Best Way to Fish: Flies, lures, and bait.

Best Time of Year to Fish: Summer and fall.

Special Regulations: None.

Description: Just outside of Bryce Canyon National Park, Tropic shares the beauty the national park is known for. It is located off Highway 12 and is accessed by For-

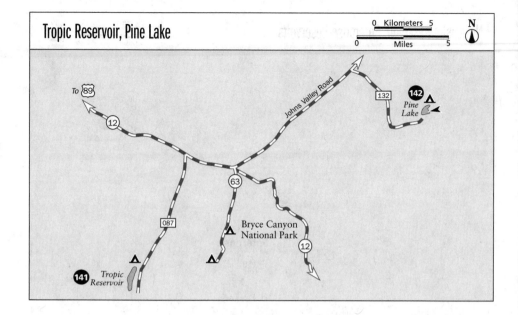

est Road 087, which takes you 8 miles to the reservoir. The King Creek Campground has 34 sites with toilets and picnic areas.

Fishing Index: Fishing is best with traditional trout baits fished on the bottom. Small gold-colored spoons can also work well. Flies fished behind casting bubbles are also productive.

142 Pine Lake

See map above.

Key Species: Rainbow trout, brook trout, and cutthroat trout.

Best Way to Fish: Bait, lures, and flies.

Best Time of Year to Fish: Spring, summer, and fall.

Special Regulations: None.

Description: Pine Lake is reached from Forest Road 132, which intersects the road from Bryce Canyon to Antimony, 11 miles north of Highway 12. The lake is 6 miles east of Highway 12. There is a 33-site campground, a boat ramp, and toilets.

Fishing Index: Pine Lake is a good place to fish for trout. Bait is the best bet, but some anglers have success with Kastmasters, woolly buggers, and marabou jigs. Mealworms seem to work better than night crawlers when it comes to bait.

143 Newcastle Reservoir

Key Species: Rainbow trout, smallmouth bass, and wiper bass.

Best Way to Fish: From a boat and from shore.

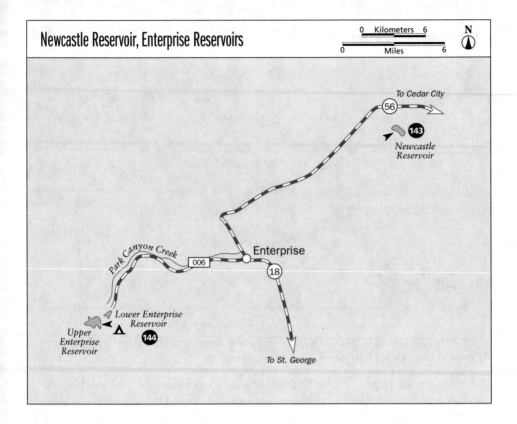

Newcastle Reservoir, Enterprise Reservoirs

0 Kilometers 6
0 Miles 6

N

To Cedar City

56

143
Newcastle
Reservoir

Park Canyon Creek

006

Enterprise

18

Lower Enterprise
Reservoir

Upper
Enterprise
Reservoir

144

To St. George

Best Time of Year to Fish: Spring and fall.

Special Regulations: Wiper limit two.

Description: Thirty miles west of Cedar City on Highway 56, Newcastle has a boat ramp and restrooms. Although the shoreline is owned by the Newcastle Irrigation Company, public access is unrestricted.

Fishing Index: Early spring is the best time to fish for rainbows. Salmon eggs and Power Bait are the best baits. Fishing is best near stream inlets, gravel shoreline, and points. As the summer progresses, trolling pop gear and flatfish is a good method. Large gold spinners and lures can be effective from shore.

Smallmouth bass fishing is good spring to fall when the water is warm. In the spring, fish gravel flats or rock ledges with plastic tubes or grubs in smoke, pumpkin, watermelon, chartreuse, or black. Crankbaits are a good option as the water warms. Topwater lures work in low-light conditions summer and fall.

Wipers were planted in Newcastle in 2005, and it did not take long for the hybrid between a white bass and a striped bass to grow to catchable lengths. Trolling in the main lake in 10 to 15 feet of water with crankbaits, jigs, and spoons is an effective method for wipers. Look for wiper boils to begin in July, occurring most frequently at first and last light.

144 Enterprise Reservoirs

Key Species: Rainbow trout, smallmouth bass, and green sunfish.

Best Way to Fish: From a boat.

Best Time of Year to Fish: Summer and fall.

Special Regulations: Tributaries to the upper and lower reservoirs are closed January 1 to 6:00 a.m. on the second Saturday of July. Limit in Little Pine Creek outflow is 8 trout, 12 smallmouth bass with no size restriction.

Description: These reservoirs are located about 12 miles west of the town of Enterprise and are reached by taking Highway 18 north out of St. George. Drive west through Enterprise to Hebron and turn south on the Veyo Shoal Creek Road. The reservoirs are about 5 miles down the road. The Honeycomb Rocks Campground has 21 sites. There is a boat launch. The upper reservoir is maintained as a conservation pool for fishing. The lower reservoir fluctuates with irrigation needs.

Fishing Index: Fishing for smallmouth picks up in late June. Tube jigs and lizards are popular bass methods. Fishing for the planted rainbows is primarily with Power Bait and night crawlers. Some trout are caught by trollers using pop gear and a worm. Fishing for the green sunfish is a good way to entertain children; fish in or near cover with a worm suspended below a bobber. Green sunfish populations have been greatly reduced in recent years.

145 Kolob Reservoir

Key Species: Rainbow trout and cutthroat trout.

Best Way to Fish: Flies and lures.

Best Time of Year to Fish: Spring, summer, and fall.

Special Regulations: Artificial flies and lures only; only one trout over 18 inches.

Description: Kolob Reservoir feeds the river that flows through the Zion Narrows of Zion National Park. Access is from Highway 9 in Virgin, where you head north on the Kolob Reservoir Road for about 20 miles. Primitive camping is allowed in the area. There is a small unimproved ramp at the reservoir.

Fishing Index: Once a highly used put-and-take fishery, special regulations were put into use to take advantage of the reservoir's natural productivity to grow large fish. Managing the reservoir with a population of larger fish will reduce stocking costs, help control numbers of nongame fish in the reservoir, and provide an opportunity to catch a larger fish. Anglers are happy with the results. Kolob is known as a trophy trout fishery. Fishing is usually done from a float tube, though some troll from small boats.

Stripping in woolly buggers in olive and brown imitates the crayfish in the

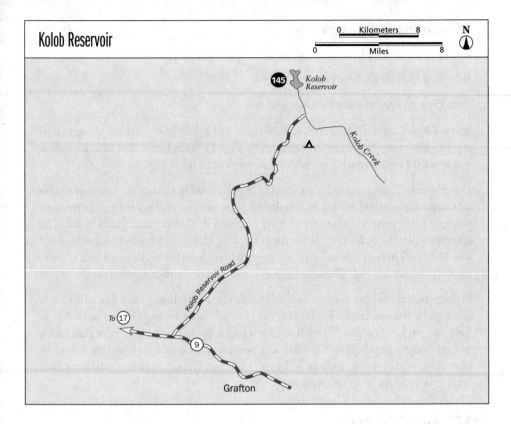

Kolob Reservoir

145 Kolob Reservoir

Kolob Creek

Kolob Reservoir Road

To 17

9

Grafton

reservoir. Egg-sucking leech patterns are also effective. There is some dry fly action with mayfly and caddis hatches. Black jigs and dark spinners are good hardware choices.

146 Pine Valley Reservoir

Key Species: Rainbow trout.

Best Way to Fish: Bait from shore.

Best Time of Year to Fish: Summer.

Special Regulations: Trout limit four. Fishing from a boat or float tube is unlawful.

Description: The draw here is the excellent camping. Pine Valley Reservoir is surrounded by about a half-dozen beautiful Dixie National Forest campgrounds. Located on the edge of Utah's second-largest Forest Service wilderness area, this little pond gets heavy use from Las Vegas and southern Utah campers trying to escape the desert heat. It's surrounded by pine trees in a definite alpine setting. A commercial lodge is located nearby. Pine Valley Reservoir is accessed from Highway 18 about halfway between Enterprise and Veyo. A well-marked turn to the east on Forest Road 035 will lead you to the reservoir.

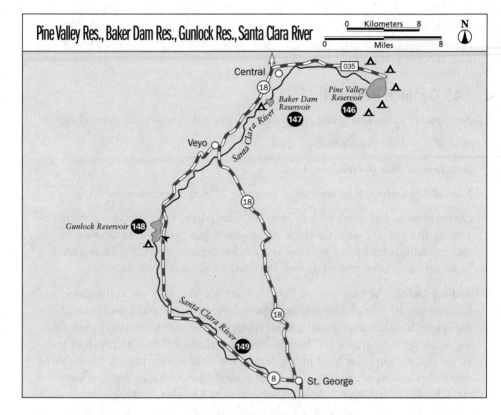

Pine Valley Res., Baker Dam Res., Gunlock Res., Santa Clara River

Central

Pine Valley Reservoir

Baker Dam Reservoir

Veyo

Santa Clara River

Gunlock Reservoir

Santa Clara River

St. George

Fishing Index: This is a put-and-take fishery where the angling will only be fast if the hatchery truck has paid a recent visit. Due to the popularity of this spot, the truck visits every two weeks between Memorial Day and Labor Day. Most anglers simply use bait from shore to catch the small catchable rainbows, though there is no reason a fly and bubble would not work just as well.

147 Baker Dam Reservoir

Key Species: Rainbow trout and brown trout.

Best Way to Fish: Bait.

Best Time of Year to Fish: Year-round.

Special Regulations: None.

Description: Surrounded by a pinyon-juniper forest, Baker Dam Reservoir is located just off Highway 18 between St. George and Enterprise. There is a small BLM campground on the property, but no boat ramp.

Fishing Index: Fishing here tends to be better when the weather is not too hot. Therefore, it's a good fishery from September through May, though fish can be caught during the hot summer months. While this is mainly a place to catch rainbows with bait, some large brown trout are to be had as well. Browns tend to bite more frequently in the winter season. Most fishing is done from shore at this relatively small 62-acre reservoir on the Santa Clara River, but there is no reason a raft, float tube, or canoe would not work.

148 Gunlock Reservoir

Key Species: Largemouth bass, green sunfish, bluegill, crappie, and channel catfish.

Best Way to Fish: From a boat or shore.

Best Time of Year to Fish: Year-round.

Special Regulations: Bass limit six, four under 10 inches and two over 20.

Description: In scenic red-rock country, 15 miles northwest of St. George on Highway 8, lies the 240-acre Gunlock Reservoir, where year-round boating, water sports, and quality fishing for bass and catfish attract visitors. Facilities include a boat-launching ramp and pit privies. Primitive camping is available.

Fishing Index: The best time to fish Gunlock for bass is in the early spring and fall. During the heat of summer, the bass are usually deep and hard to reach. Fishing is best from a boat, throwing spinnerbaits, rubber worms, jig-and-pigs, floating worms, plastic tubes, and lizards. Look for shallow flats with brush or trees. In the fall, try topwater lures in low-light conditions and diving crankbaits along weed lines and windy points. Fish smaller plastic baits on a jig-head or Carolina rig. Channel catfishing is best from late March to October. Some fish as big as 25 pounds have been reported. Try night crawlers, frozen minnows, and cut baits in the warmer months. Rattling and bright-colored lures work in the rocky areas during the spawn, usually in May. In the colder months, try stink bait.

Fishing for crappie is best in late spring when the fish are spawning. Look for flooded brush edges, then use small plastic or feather jigs in 1- to 3-inch sizes. Chartreuse, yellow, white, black, red, and combinations of those colors work best. Suspend the jigs 3 to 6 feet below a colored bobber. If fishing is slow, drop a night crawler in the middle of brush clumps. After the spawn, look for schools of crappie to be suspended on drop-offs adjacent to spawning areas.

Bluegill are easiest to catch in the spring when they are spawning. Float through weed flats looking for spawning beds. Use small plastic or feather jigs, spinners, and night crawlers. Fly fishing can be great at this time while using small poppers, grasshoppers, and other dry flies.

Sunfish are most commonly caught during the summer months. Look for broken rock structure and fish with small spinners, jigs, or night crawlers.

149 Santa Clara River

Key Species: Brown trout, rainbow trout, and channel catfish.

Best Way to Fish: Flies, lures, and bait.

Best Time of Year to Fish: Spring and fall.

Special Regulations: None.

Description: The Santa Clara originates in Pine Valley on the west side of Pine Mountain. There is some access below Pine Valley Reservoir, but in a short distance, the Santa Clara leaves Forest Service land and runs through private land. Soon after leaving Pine Valley, the river again enters national forest. It then flows about 8 miles to the town of Central. Access is primarily by hiking. After that, the river flows into Baker Dam Reservoir, then Gunlock Reservoir, before dumping into the Virgin River south of St. George.

Fishing Index: Most anglers avoid fishing the Santa Clara in the summer due to excessive heat and the presence of rattlesnakes. Common techniques used for other southern Utah streams will work for trout here. Some big catfish are caught in the lower stretches in deep holes with night crawlers.

150 Quail Creek Reservoir

Key Species: Largemouth bass, rainbow trout, bluegill, crappie, and bullhead catfish.

Best Way to Fish: From a boat and from shore.

Best Time of Year to Fish: Spring, fall, and winter.

Special Regulations: Bass limit four under 10 inches and two over 20 inches.

05/07/2006 12:43 pm

Sunny Hawk of Salt Lake City kisses a largemouth from Quail Creek Reservoir for helping him win a youth bass tournament.

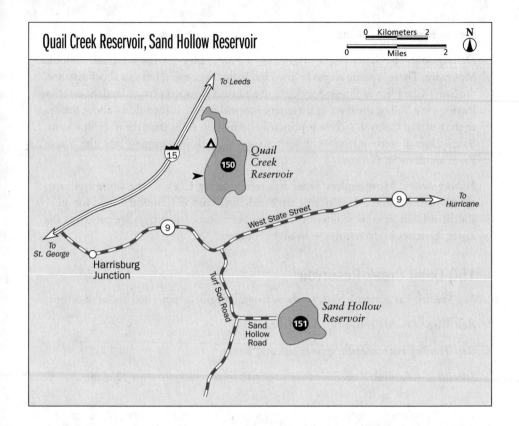

Quail Creek Reservoir, Sand Hollow Reservoir

0 Kilometers 2

0 Miles 2

N

To Leeds

15

150

Quail
Creek
Reservoir

9

To
Hurricane

West State Street

9

To
St. George

Harrisburg
Junction

Turf Sod Road

Sand Hollow
Road

Sand Hollow
Reservoir

151

Description: Quail Creek Reservoir sits just off Highway 9, 3 miles east of Interstate 15 (exit 16). Quail Creek State Park is on the south side of the reservoir and is accessible from the highway. Facilities include 23 campsites, restrooms, and two covered group-use pavilions. Recreational pressure is heavy due to the reservoir's proximity to St. George. Even-odd boat registration number launching restrictions are in effect on weekends and holidays.

Fishing Index: Quail Creek remains ice-free throughout the year, and anglers can be seen here every day. Most Quail Creek anglers are after the big largemouth bass the reservoir is known for. Officials say bass up to 15 pounds have been reported being pulled from the waters at Quail Creek Reservoir. In the early spring, look for flats and flooded brush areas close to deep water. Spinnerbaits, jig-n-pigs, large plastic tubes, lizards, and grubs work well. As it warms, the fish move onto spawning beds, typically in mid- to late April. As summer arrives, the largemouth head into deeper water. Fish diving crankbaits, spinnerbaits, and 4-inch rubber worms or plastic tubes and spider jigs on drop-offs next to the spawning beds. The Harrisburg Arm is a good area to start in. Fall is a good time to try topwater lures fished in the morning and evening hours. Crankbaits work well on windy days. Small plastic baits and rubber worms fished on the bottom can turn up fish. A few large fish are caught in the winter to anglers using jig-n-pigs, jigging spoons, and heavy spinnerbaits.

Rainbow trout fishing is best in the fall, winter, and spring, when recreational pressure isn't as great and the water is cooler. Fishing with traditional trout baits from shore works in cold months. When the water warms, try trolling with pop gear and a worm or flatfish near the dam.

151 Sand Hollow Reservoir

Key Species: Largemouth bass and bluegill.

Best Way to Fish: From a boat.

Best Time of Year to Fish: Spring, summer, and fall.

Special Regulations: Bass limit six, four under 10 inches and two over 20 inches; all bass between 10 and 20 inches must be released.

Description: Water began to fill Sand Hollow Reservoir in 2002. Approximately 100 largemouth bass hit the water in 2003 when DWR officials caught fish from other Utah waters and moved them to this new reservoir 15 miles east of St. George. Sand Hollow State Park provides a concrete launching ramp, two 50-site campgrounds, and four day-use areas.

Fishing Index: The largemouth and bluegill will be centered on trees, sagebrush, and whatever other vegetation was in the area before it was flooded, so look for this structure first. For the largemouth use Senko baits, hula and brush grubs, and the Kreature. Spinnerbaits are another good option. Topwater lures will work in low-light conditions above structure. Bluegill can be caught on small spinners, plastic or feather jigs, and night crawlers. Catching them on light spinning tackle is a hoot.

152 Lake Powell

Key Species: Smallmouth bass, striped bass, largemouth bass, bluegill, green sunfish, black crappie, walleye, channel catfish, bullhead catfish, and northern pike.

Best Way to Fish: From a boat.

Best Time of Year to Fish: Year-round.

Special Regulations: Smallmouth bass limit 20; largemouth bass limit 5; crappie limit 10; channel catfish limit 25; striped bass, no limit; walleye limit 10. An interstate permit for Arizona is needed on the southern portion of the reservoir in that state. Chumming is only allowed for taking striped bass, and only commercially prepared anchovies and sardines may be used. Archery and spear fishing is prohibited within 0.25 mile of developed areas, structures, Rainbow Bridge National Monument, and Dangling Rope Marina and 100 yards of boats.

Description: The Colorado River impounded behind Glen Canyon Dam near Page, Arizona, forms Lake Powell, which is more than 570 feet deep when filled to capacity. The lake follows the flooded river gorge for 180 miles with an ever-changing

Lake Powell

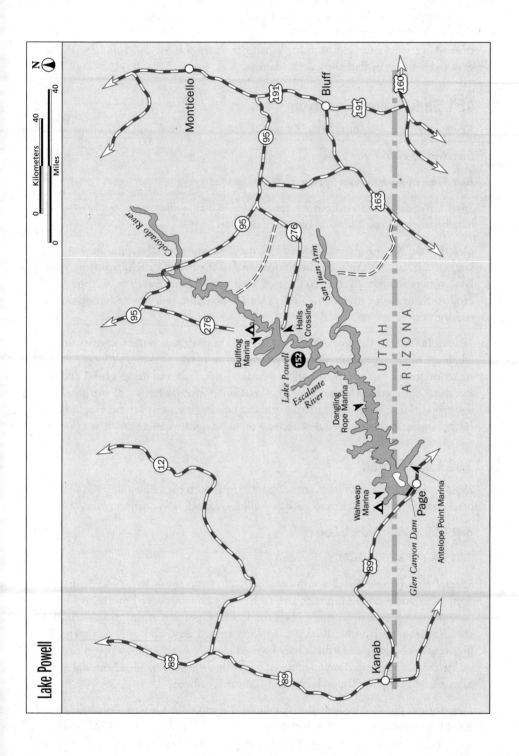

shoreline of nearly 2,000 miles. The lake covers more than 160,000 surface-acres when full. Two inundated rivers, the San Juan and Escalante, branch off the Colorado River and compose major portions of the reservoir.

There are full-service marinas and launch ramps at the following sites: Wahweap Marina and the Glen Canyon Dam, located near Page, Arizona, on U.S. Highway 89. This south end of Powell is less fertile than the upper stretches. Striped bass are the most common catch.

Bullfrog Marina is used by most Utahns. From Salt Lake, head south on Interstate 15 and southeast on U.S. Highway 6 to Interstate 70, then west to Highway 24 (exit 147) to Hanksville. Head south on Highway 95 from Hanksville and then Highway 276 to Bullfrog.

Hite Marina was once the northernmost facility on the lake for getting boats on the water, but the ramp has been closed due to low lake levels.

Halls Crossing is located across the main channel from Bullfrog and is reached by a vehicle ferry that operates year-round.

A midlake marina, Dangling Rope, provides gas and services for boaters traveling the lake. There is no shore-based access to Dangling Rope Marina.

Antelope Point Marina joined the list of marinas on the huge reservoir in the early 2000s and is found near Page, Arizona.

Lodging is located at Wahweap and Bullfrog. Accommodations are available in Page. Trailer rentals are available at Halls Crossing and Hite. There is a National Park Service campground at Lees Ferry. Concessionaire-operated campgrounds are available in Wahweap, Bullfrog, and Halls Crossing on a first-come, first-served basis. RV campgrounds are available at Wahweap, Bullfrog, and Halls Crossing. Primitive camping is available at the following vehicle-accessible shoreline areas: Lone Rock, Stanton Creek, Bullfrog North and South (Bullfrog area), Hite, and Farley Canyon. These sites have no facilities except for pit toilets. Shoreline camping outside developed areas is possible lakewide (campers must have self-contained or portable toilets).

Fees for day-use, boat launching, and camping are collected at Powell March through November. The cost to enter the Glen Canyon National Recreation Area is $30.00 for an annual vehicle pass, one- to seven-day vehicle $15.00; $30.00 for an annual boat pass, $16.00 for a boat one to seven days, and $8.00 for a second boat (including personal watercraft); and individual walk-in $7.00.

Groceries and supplies are available at all marinas, though selection is limited and prices are high. It is best to arrive at the reservoir with everything you will need. The park concessionaire offers numerous services, including lodging, boat tours, boat rental, equipment rental, etc.

Anyone camping within 0.25 mile of Lake Powell is required to carry and use a portable toilet unless their boat or camper is self-contained or toilets are available on the beach. Several commercial portable toilets are available from a variety of sources. Because plastic bags clog and incapacitate portable toilet dump stations, homemade devices such as plastic bag-lined buckets or cans are not acceptable. Also, plastic bags or other containers contaminated with human wastes cannot

Lake Powell is a great place to take kids fishing. The diverse fishery ensures something is always feeding. Photo by Mickey Anderson

legally be placed in dumpsters. Human waste must be disposed of only at designated boat pump-outs and dumps.

Fishing Index by Species

Striped Bass: One of the most common fish at Lake Powell is the striper. They're easy to catch from anchored houseboats or from shore. In some cases all it takes is an anchovy over the side.

Serious anglers have a variety of choices when it comes to catching stripers. In the spring, stripers tend to group in water 30 to 80 feet deep near river inlets—try the Colorado, Dirty Devil, San Juan, and Escalante arms. They also group near the dam and around the water pump for the Navajo Power Plant Generating Station. Fishing at these times is best with heavy spoons, bucktail jigs, and cut anchovy or sardine bait. To help anglers harvest an overpopulation of stripers, of which there is no limit, officials allow chumming with anchovies. Chumming attracts and holds striper schools, making it easier to catch a large number of them.

As the water warms in the spring, stripers leave the deep and stage in spawning areas around rock piles, main lake points, and reefs in water less than 40 feet deep. Fish anchovy cut bait along the bottom or troll Rapala Shadraps or lures with rattles. Casting plastic grubs and tubes in 3- to 5-inch lengths in shad and crayfish colors is also productive. Stripers stay in spawning areas through early summer until warming water forces most of them to go deep.

When fish go deep, they often hold in depths of 60 to 90 feet. Trolling the main channel at faster speeds, up to 5 mph, will trigger strikes with shad-colored crankbaits and spoons. To reach these depths, downriggers or leaded line are needed. Jigging or bait fishing will work, although the stripers will rarely hold in one spot for very long.

In the summer and early fall, look for the stripers to be on the move as they search for schools of shad. Keep your eyes open on the lake surface, as stripers will often force a school of shad to the surface, where a boil occurs. Move to the boil quickly and kill the engine to avoid disturbing the school. The bass are feeding aggressively and will usually take any lure presented. The most exciting way to fish a boil is with topwater lures. Stripers will attack these lures with visually violent explosions. Lures with a side-to-side action resemble shad and attract attention from striped bass, even when no surface activity is present.

Boils can happen at any time and any place. If you plan on fishing for stripers for more than one day, record what time and where a boil happened; they often occur at the same places at the same times. If a boil stops, don't leave. The stripers will linger in the area looking for stunned or wounded shad. Cast spoons and rattling crankbaits and cover the area to pick up any remaining stripers. Boils usually start near the end of June and go through late fall.

Fishing for stripers in late fall and early winter can be fast. They're usually grouped at 60 to 100 feet and are readily caught by anglers jigging heavy spoons or bucktail jigs. Once the water temperature goes below 50 degrees, they become less active.

A Lake Powell angler pauses from fishing to "take it all in."

Largemouth Bass: Largemouth can be caught year-round at Powell, but when the water temperature drops below 50 degrees, the fish become less active and harder to catch. One of the best times to go after big largemouth is as the water starts to warm in the late winter (February and March). You'll find them on short flats and broken rock near deep water with jig-n-pigs, spinnerbaits, plastic lizards, and spider jigs in black, purple, smoke, white, chartreuse, and crayfish colors. Live water dogs (salamanders) are also effective.

As the water continues to warm, more fish concentrate in the shallows preparing for the spawn (April through May). This is the best time to find and catch a lot of fish. Look for flats with brush or trees, flat broken rock, and small, main channel pockets to find spawning fish. They are usually in less than 15 feet of water. Spinnerbaits, jig-n-pigs, spider jigs, and weedless plastic tubes or grubs work well at this time.

After the spawn, the fish pull from the shallows and scatter. They can be hard to find during midsummer, but can still be caught. Fish in the morning and evening with topwater lures and jerkbaits. During the day, look for broken shaded rock, walls, and main lake points. Use 3- to 5-inch plastic grubs, worms, spider jigs, and tube baits. The most productive colors are smoke, watermelon, bluegill, crayfish, and white. Fishing with a split-shot or Carolina rig can produce fish on tough days.

In the fall when the water begins to cool, the largemouth move to main lake shallows and eventually to the back of canyons as they follow shad. The fish sometimes school in areas where there are strong concentrations of shad. Topwater lures, crankbaits, jerkbaits, and small plastic grubs or tubes can be effective. Fish topwater in low-light conditions. Crankbaits are especially effective on windy points and shorelines. If the fish are hard to find, head for deeper water (down to 40 feet) with plastic grubs, spider jigs, and tube baits. The best colors in the fall are white, silver, smoke, chartreuse, pumpkin, bluegill, and shad colors.

Smallmouth Bass: Smallmouth bass are more numerous than largemouth, but they tend to be found in greater numbers on the upper half of Lake Powell. They are even more inactive than the largemouth when the water drops below 50 degrees.

As the water warms, smallmouth group on gravel or smooth rock points, flats, and shallow reefs to spawn. They're more concentrated, so you don't need to cover as much water for them as you do for largemouth. Spinnerbaits, jerkbaits, jig-n-pigs, spider jigs, and plastic tubes, worms, and grubs will produce fish. Smoke, chartreuse, watermelon, pumpkin, white, and black are solid color choices.

The smallmouth spawn lasts longer than the largemouths'. It usually wraps up at the end of May. After the spawn, smallies group on main lake points and rock piles and are caught on topwater lures in low-light periods or with 3- to 4-inch plastic grubs and tubes. Diving crankbaits are also effective.

Like the largemouth, smallmouth will move shallow in the fall as the water cools. Fish shorelines, points, and rock piles with small shad or crayfish-colored plastic baits, topwater lures, and diving crankbaits. The fish tend to school in areas where shad are concentrated and will sometimes cause boils.

Channel and Bullhead Catfish: The best times to fish for catfish are in the summer and early fall. They are perhaps the easiest fish to catch at Lake Powell. Most are caught at night with anchovies and table scraps fished on the bottom. Although they can be caught just about anywhere, catfish prefer shallow sandy flats. Often overlooked, catfish is a tasty dish. Channel catfish up to 20 pounds are not unheard of, but most are less than 3 pounds. Bullhead catfish are not as common, but are often caught on the upper half of the reservoir.

Crappie: These panfish are most readily caught in the spring when they're spawning. Look for them in flooded brush in the back of canyons. Small spinners, crankbaits, plastic or feather jigs, and night crawlers are effective. Cast around the brush to locate schools, and once located, fish for them with small jigs or night crawler suspended below a bobber.

After the spawn, the schools leave the shallows in favor of deeper brush edges and will often suspend on ledges and over flooded trees most of the summer. Crappie are often found near shad in late summer and fall. There are some large ones here and occasionally they're caught by bass anglers using big lures.

Green Sunfish: Sunfish are not targeted by many anglers, but families with small children should consider fishing for them. These aggressive panfish will hit just about anything, including bare hooks. They tend to concentrate in the shade of boats and are commonly found around broken rock in shallow water. Use small plastic or feather jigs and night crawlers. Fly fishing for them with most dry flies provides nonstop action. Rubber-legged patterns are the best.

Bluegill: Spring and summer are the best times to fish for bluegill at Powell. Use small jigs, spinners, flies, and night crawlers. During the spawn, look for shallow flats with vegetation. In the summer, they head for large broken rock. Flies work best when the fish are concentrated in the shallows.

Walleye: Most walleye at Lake Powell are caught by anglers fishing for other species. Early spring through midsummer is the best time to target them. In early spring, usually February or March, walleye concentrate for the spawn. River inlets, rock flats, and shallow points are good spawning areas. Trolling with crankbaits or

Wayne Gustaveson with a daily double at Lake Powell. He caught a smallmouth bass (left) and a largemouth bass (right) on the same cast with one topwater lure. Photo by Charlene Gustaveson

bottom bouncers trailing spinners with a worm can help anglers locate schools of fish. Once located, casting crankbaits or plastic grubs tipped with night crawlers is a better option. Chartreuse, white, yellow, orange, and crayfish colors work best. After the spawn, they move to points and rock piles on the main lake. Trolling with diving crankbaits in chartreuse or shad colors will produce through the early summer. Some walleye are caught while trolling along shaded rock walls during the hot summer months.

Northern Pike: This toothy predator entered Lake Powell from the Colorado River. Pike are rarely caught, or seen, south of Bullfrog Marina. They're most often caught by anglers trolling crankbaits along main channel points and rock piles or in open water by striper anglers in the summer.

Lakes of the Uinta Mountains

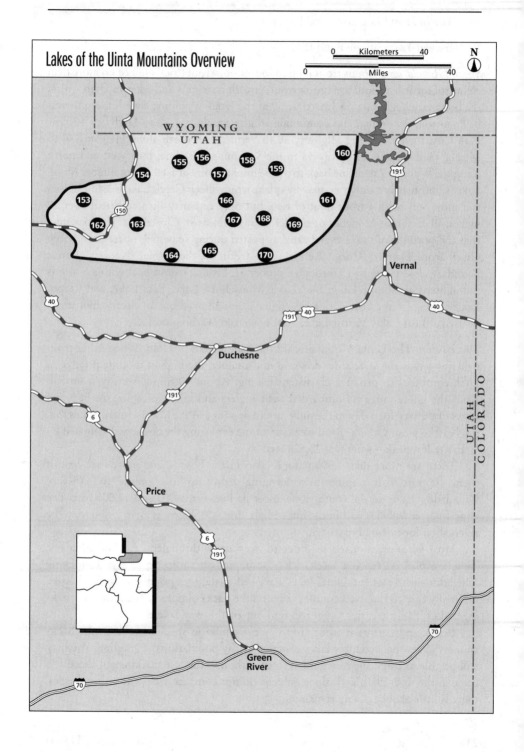

Lakes of the Uinta Mountains Overview

Key Species: Brook trout, cutthroat trout, rainbow trout, grayling, golden trout, and brown trout.

Best Way to Fish: Flies, lures, and bait.

Best Time of Year: Summer and fall.

Special Regulations: Bonus trout limit of four brook trout (total limit of no more than eight trout if at least four are brook trout) covering streams and lakes in Utah within the boundary beginning on Interstate 80 at the Utah-Wyoming state line southwest of Evanston, Wyoming, and continuing southwest along I-80 to Highway 40 near Park City, then east along Highway 40 to Vernal, then north along Highway 44 to Manila, then west on Highway 43 to the Wyoming state line, then west and north along the Wyoming state line back to the beginning point at I-80. Trout limit at Moon Lake is four fish, but only two may be splake trout; Sheep Creek Lake is artificial flies and lures only with a trout limit of two, but only one may be a cutthroat over 22 inches; all cutthroat 22 inches or smaller must be released. Closed near the spawning trap and portions of the lake and canal as posted during spawning operations; Sheep Creek from Flaming Gorge Reservoir upstream to the Ashley National Forest boundary closed August 15 through October 31. Fishing from a boat with a motor is not allowed at Bonnie Lake, Bud Lake, Moosehorn Lake, Pass Lake, and Teapot Lake; fishing from a boat with a gas engine is not allowed but an electric motor can be used at Lost Lake, Mirror Lake, Trial Lake, and Washington Lake.

Description: The Uinta Mountains are the fishing gem of Utah. When other trout fisheries across the state slow down in midsummer, the highest mountain range in Utah continues to produce consistent fishing. About 90 minutes away from Salt Lake, the Uinta range is bombarded with anglers and hikers escaping the heat and stress of the city for a day in the only mountain range in the lower United States that runs east to west. Others spend weeks at a time exploring the country dominated by Utah's tallest peak—King's, at 13,528 feet.

There are more than 1,000 natural lakes in the Uintas, and more than half of them support fish populations. Ranging from pothole ponds to 175-acre Grandaddy Lake on the south slope, most lie between 9,000 and 12,000 feet. The largest percentage lies within the huge High Uintas Wilderness Area and have to be reached on foot or by horseback.

Most lakes are stocked in order to keep up with anglers. Around holidays, some are planted twice a week, while some are on three- to five-year stocking schedules—many of the Uinta lakes have self-sustaining populations. Trout were originally carried into backcountry lakes on the backs of horses. Today, aerial stocking makes it a little easier to get fish into out-of-the-way lakes.

Brook and cutthroat trout are the most common species found in the backcountry. A few backcountry lakes contain healthy populations of grayling. You may still be able to catch the rare golden trout, although the last stockings of those fish came in the mid-1980s and, since goldens do not compete well with other species, there is little chance of any remaining.

Uinta Mountain lakes offer breathtaking vistas and great summertime fishing.

Rainbow trout, a large proportion of them albinos, are planted heavily along the Mirror Lake Highway and other areas easily reached by road.

Because they are primarily self-sustaining, fishing for brook and cutthroat trout often requires a different technique than is used for planted rainbows. Bait works well on hatchery-raised rainbows, but brook and cutthroat are more often caught on flies and lures. In an effort to get Colorado cutthroat off the endangered species list, officials have been trying to find a way to replace the Yellowstone cutthroat planted in the Uintas with the Colorado subspecies. The Colorado River cutthroat is the only trout indigenous to the upper Colorado River watershed in Utah, Colorado, Wyoming, and New Mexico. Because few knew there was a subspecies, the Yellowstone cutthroat trout and other nonindigenous trout were often stocked over existing Colorado River cutthroat populations. Eventually, many of the Colorado River cutthroat died out because of loss of habitat or became hybridized with other cutthroat.

Officials are only able to secure grayling about every other year for planting, so their numbers remain limited. However, some lakes are thriving with this unique fish, and at times, anglers can bring one in on every cast.

The majority of anglers heading to the Uintas drive along the Mirror Lake Highway east out of Kamas, but there are countless points of entry along the fringe of the mountain range. There are numerous USDA Forest Service campgrounds, and open camping is also permitted.

Whether going to the Uintas on a 20-mile hike into a remote lake at 12,000 feet or heading to one of the lakes along the highway for a day of fishing, planning will help you get the most out of your trip. Detailed maps are a must for those leaving the highway area. They are available at any Forest Service office.

Always take a rain jacket, warm clothes, and a change of clothes. Afternoon thundershowers can be a daily occurrence in the Uintas, and it snows year-round. Be prepared for the worst weather conditions and hope for the best.

Mosquito repellent is a must in the warmer months, until it gets too cold for the little pests. Sunscreen is also a must. High-elevation sunlight is intense, especially when it is reflected from the water.

Always leave details with someone explaining where you are going and how long you will be gone. That way, if you don't return on time, he or she can contact officials to begin looking for you.

There are numerous springs in the Uinta backcountry. Drinking from them is safe in most cases, but it is always better to use a water filter or boil water to prevent the chance of picking up the giardia parasite.

Nothing ruins a trip like viewing somebody else's litter in the wilderness. Pack out what you take in, and pick up after others if you can. Use existing fire rings in the backcountry when possible, and use designated fire pits in developed campgrounds. In the backcountry, bury human waste at least 200 feet away from water in 8 to 10 inches of soil.

Those on horseback should practice ethical decisions about pasturing and remember to respect hikers on the trail. There is a Forest Service user fee when using facilities along the Mirror Lake Highway and in the Flaming Gorge National Recreation Area.

Fishing Index: Hatchery trucks are usually the first vehicles into the Uinta Mountain lakes late each spring. Eager anglers follow them closely.

A fair number of these lakes suffer from winterkill. Those expecting good fishing as the Uintas open should head to the larger bodies of water that are able to sustain fish through even the harshest winter, like those easily reached by the Mirror Lake Highway.

Most rainbows in the Uintas are caught with Power Bait, salmon eggs, night crawlers, and grasshoppers. Because water remains cool at these elevations, fishing from shore is productive throughout the summer. Small spinners and spoons work near stream inlets and along deep shorelines for the rainbows. Silver, brass, copper, frog, chartreuse, and red and white colors are the best.

Flies can also be effective. Look for rising fish in the evenings. Try mosquito, Adams, renegade, Griffith's gnat, and ant patterns. During the heat of the day, wet flies or nymphs will work in deeper water. Good choices include woolly buggers, mohair leeches, zug bugs, hare's ear, and damselfly nymphs.

Cutthroat are more predacious than rainbows and will take lures more often than bait. Early in the season, cutthroat are preparing to spawn. They can be found near stream inlets and along gravel shorelines. To prevent snags in these shallow areas, use lightweight spinners, jigs, and spoons. Bright colors like orange, chartreuse, white, and pink are good for spawning fish. Gold, copper, black, and yellow are good colors throughout the summer. Bait anglers have better success with night crawlers than artificial bait.

At times, fly fishing for cutthroat in the Uintas can be exceptional. Most cutthroat are caught with flies fished below the surface. Woolly buggers, Crystal Killers, and mohair leeches in red, brown, black, and olive are top producers. Small nymph patterns like hare's ear, scud, and prince work when fishing is slow. Bright-colored streamers are good during the spawn and in the fall. At times, cutthroat cruise the surface chasing aquatic insects like mayflies, caddises, and damselflies. After strong wind or a rainstorm, cutts move into the shallows looking for ants, beetles, and other insects that have been knocked into the water.

Due to low insect activity early in the season, brook trout fishing will be best with lures and flies fished below the surface. Good options are Maisie, Jake's, and Krocodile spoons in gold, copper, black, and orange. Spinners like Panther Martin, Mepps, and Rooster Tails work in shallow water.

Fly fishing can be better from shore at this time. Wet flies and nymphs like woolly buggers, mohair leeches, prince nymph, hare's ear nymph, and scuds are all good bets. Black, brown, olive, and peacock are good color choices for brook trout.

As insect activity increases, the fish will take advantage of easy meals like damselfly nymphs heading for shore. On the surface, look for midge, mayfly, and caddis hatches. Mosquito, Adams, Griffith's gnat, renegade, black gnat, and gray hackle yellow patterns are good for rising fish. Like the cutthroat, brook trout cruise the shoreline after storms looking for terrestrials. Fishing in the fall can be good because the brook trout start feeding aggressively as they prepare to spawn. Bright-colored lures and jigs are more effective at this time. Fly fish with white, yellow, red, and black streamers on gravel points or near stream inlets.

Grayling are most commonly caught with flies, and they'll go out of their way to take a fly off of the surface. Use Adams, renegade, black gnat, gray hackle yellow, and ant patterns. Grayling have small mouths. Use small spinners and flies to increase your chances of hooking these unique fish.

Anglers often overlook streams and creeks in the Uintas. The time frame for fishing streams is not as long as it is for lakes, due to high water in the spring and low water in the fall, but running water provides a good fishing opportunity when lake fishing is slow.

Inlets are good places to fish in the spring and fall as fish concentrate in them to spawn. Fish in streams and creeks feed aggressively on attractor dry flies. The size of the streams and the fish typically get larger the lower you fish in a drainage.

153 Weber River Drainage

On the western extremity of the Uintas, the Weber is a large drainage with some 59 lakes and 80 to 100 ponds. Access to the drainage is by Highway 213 east of Oakley and Highway 150 east of Kamas. Starting points along Highway 213 include the Erickson Basin Trailhead near the Ledgefork Campground. Take Forest Road 133 from Highway 213 to reach the Ledgefork Trailhead and campground. Holiday

Park is farther up Highway 213 near the Forest Service boundary. Trails originating at Holiday Park extend south into the major forks of the Weber River.

The major access points to the Weber Drainage are scattered along Highway 150 and include the Upper Setting Trailhead, the Crystal Lake Trailhead, the Bald Mountain Trailhead, and the Weber River Trailhead near Pass Lake. There are 42 lakes in the drainage containing game fish. Stream fishing is also good.

Abes—Access is along the Middle Fork Trail south from Holiday Park for 2.5 miles to the junction with the Abes Lake Trail and then a steep 1 mile to the southeast. Fishing for cutthroat is unpredictable.

Adax—This scenic lake is 2.5 miles south of Holiday Park on the Middle Fork Trail and then 1 steep mile west on a faint trail. Another route is 1.5 miles east of Olsen Lake over the pass, with no trail. The lake is hard to find either way. Adax contains natural populations of brook and cutthroat trout.

Anchor—Fishing is fast for small brook trout and pressure is light at this lake, which sits 3 miles southeast from the end of the Gardners Fork Jeep Road on the obscure Anchor Lake Trail over the pass into the Middle Fork.

Arrowhead—Access is 1 mile northeast of Upper Yellowpine on a well-traveled section of the Yellowpine Trail, or 1 mile west of Castle Reservoir over rough terrain. Day-use pressure is moderate on the small brook trout population.

Bench—This lake is subject to winterkill, but is planted with brook trout and sustains moderate pressure. It is 2.75 miles northwest of the Bald Mountain Trailhead, or 2.75 miles around the ridge from Ibantik on the Notch Mountain Loop Trail.

Carol—This small lake is stocked with brook trout and is 0.5 mile northeast of Round Lake. There are no trails, but access on foot is not difficult.

Castle—Brook trout are the catch at this lake, which lies at the base of Castle Peak in the Beaver Creek Drainage. Access is 6 miles north of Highway 150 on the Upper Setting Road to an unmarked turnoff, and then north for 1 mile to the end of the logging road. Follow the Castle Lake Trail northwest for 0.25 mile to the lake.

Cuberant #1—Located 2.5 miles northwest of Highway 150 on the Lofty Lake and Cuberant Basin Trails, this lake usually provides some fast fishing for brook and cutthroat trout.

Cuberant #2—Fishing pressure at this, the second lake in the basin, is not as fast as #1.

Cuberant #3—Pan-size brook trout make up this lake's fishing potential.

Cuberant #4—About 0.125 mile north of Cuberant #1, this lake is planted by aircraft with cutthroat trout.

Dean—Although subject to winterkill, some brook and cutthroat trout are caught here. The lake is 2 miles southwest of the Bald Mountain Trailhead on the Notch Mountain Trail.

Elkhorn—Access is 4.75 miles south of Highway 213 on the South Fork Road and jeep trail past the rock slide area. Then head south for 2.5 miles on a faint trail to the headwaters region where Elkhorn Lake sits. The lake is stocked with brook trout and receives light pressure.

Erickson, North—About 0.25 mile north of Erickson South, this lake suffers winterkill but is frequently stocked with brook trout.

Erickson, South—The water here has a milky green color. Erickson South is stocked with brook trout. Access is 2.5 miles northeast of the Upper Setting Trailhead on the Upper Setting and Erickson Basin Trails. Access is also possible by the Smith-Morehouse and Erickson Basin Trails from the Erickson Basin Trailhead at the Ledgefork Campground.

Fish—Access is 4.5 miles southeast of Holiday Park on the Dry Fork Trail past Round and Sand Lakes. Fish Lake contains a large population of grayling and some brook trout.

Fran—Stocked with brook trout, Fran is 0.75 mile south from the end of Gardners Fork Jeep Road on a good section of the Anchor Lake Trail.

Ibantik—The lake is 3 miles north of the Crystal Lake Trailhead on the Notch Mountain Trail over the notch. The route is well marked, and the lake is stocked with brook trout.

Jean—This lake has been stocked in the past, but there are no guarantees cutthroat will still be in it. Access is 3.5 miles south from the end of the Gardners Fork Jeep Road on an obscure trail over the steep pass into Hell's Kitchen. It's a difficult lake to locate.

Jerry—There are no trails and the lake often winterkills, but Jerry is stocked frequently with brook trout. Access is 1.75 miles south of Anchor Lake.

Kamas—This lake contains a good population of cutthroat trout and sustains a moderate level of pressure. It is reached 1.5 miles northwest of Highway 150 at Pass Lake on the Weber River and Lofty Lake Trails.

Little Hidden—Direct access trails to Little Hidden do not exist. The lake is 0.5 mile over the pass from Divide #2 into the Middle Fork Drainage. Total distance from the Crystal Lake Trailhead in the Provo Drainage is 2.5 miles. Little Hidden has a good population of brook trout.

Lofty—This lake gets significant pressure from Boy Scout troops. It is 2.25 miles west and north of Highway 150 from the Pass Lake area, or 1 mile northwest of Camp Steiner on the Lofty Lake Loop Trail. The lake is stocked with cutthroat.

Lovenia—The first lake over the top of Notch Pass, Lovenia has brook trout and sees heavy pressure. It is 2.75 miles north of the Crystal Lake Trailhead on the Notch Mountain Trail.

Meadow—A large cutthroat population inhabits Meadow. It is 4 miles north of the Crystal Lake Trailhead, or 4.5 miles northwest of the Bald Mountain Trailhead on the Notch Mountain Loop Trail to the Meadow Lake junction, and then 0.5 mile northwest.

Neil—A small, slow-growing population of brook trout live in Neil. It is 0.5 mile directly south of Abes up the ridge, or 1.5 miles northwest of the Notch Mountain Trail near Lovenia Lake over rough terrain.

Notch—At the base of Notch Mountain, 2.25 miles northwest of the Bald Mountain Trailhead, Notch is a popular reservoir for campers and anglers. It suffers from some winterkill, but carries some brook trout.

Weber River Drainage

KEY TO NAMED LAKES

W-20	Divide No. 2 Lake
W-21	Little Hidden Lake
W-22	Peter Lake
W-23	Lovenia Lake
W-24	Ibantik Reservoir
W-25	South Erickson Lake
W-26	North Erickson Lake
W-27	Meadow Lake
W-28	Jerry Lake
W-29	Anchor Lake
W-30	Abes Lake
W-31	Neil Lake
W-32	Olsen Lake
W-33	Rhoads Lake
W-34	Adax Lake
W-35	Dean Lake
W-36	Notch Reservoir
W-37	Bench Lake
W-38	Reids Lake
W-39	Jean Lake
W-40	Kamas Lake
W-41	Lofty Lake
W-42	Cuberant #1 Lake
W-43	Cuberant #2 Lake
W-44	Cuberant #3 Lake
W-45	Cuberant #4 Lake
W-46	Cuberant #5 Lake
W-47	Fish Lake
W-48	Round Lake
W-49	Sand Reservoir
W-51	Carol Lake
W-64	Elkhorn Lake
W-65	Upper Yellowpine Lake
W-66	Lower Yellowpine Lake
W-67	Castle Lake
W-68	Arrowhead Lake

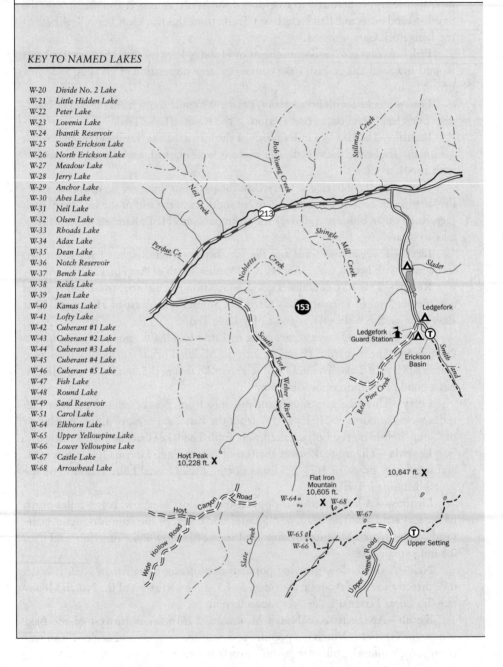

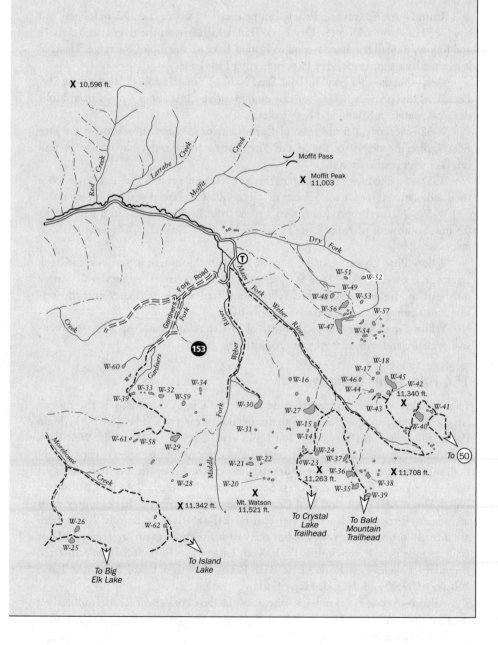

Kilometers

Miles

N

X 10,596 ft.

Red Creek

Larrabe Creek

Moffit Creek

Moffit Pass

X Moffit Peak
11,003

Dry Fork

T

Gardners Fork Road

Main Fork

Weber River

W-51
W-52
W-49
W-48   W-53
W-56
W-47   W-57
W-54

Gardners Fork

Creek

153

W-60

Gardners Fork

Weber River

Middle Fork

W-33 W-32   W-34
W-39   W-59
W-61 W-58
W-29
W-28

W-30

W-31

W-21   W-22
W-20

X 11,342 ft.

W-18
W-17
W-46   W-45
W-44   W-42
W-16   11,340 ft.
W-43   X   W-41
W-40
W-27
W-15
W-14   W-24
W-37
W-23   W-36
11,263 ft. W-35
X 11,708 ft.
W-38
W-39

To 50

Morehouse Creek

W-26

W-25

W-62

X Mt. Watson
11,521 ft.

To Big
Elk Lake

To Island
Lake

To Crystal
Lake
Trailhead

To Bald
Mountain
Trailhead

Olsen—This lake is 0.5 mile due east of Fran Lake in the Gardners Fork Drainage. The lake may suffer from winterkill but is periodically stocked with brook trout.

Rhoads—There are no trails to the lake, but it is situated 0.25 mile due east of Fran Lake in the Gardners Fork Drainage. Rhoads has a good population of brook trout.

Round—Arctic grayling fishing can be excellent at this lake, 3.5 miles east and south of Holiday Park on the Dry Fork Trail, which crosses the river after 1.5 miles and follows a small tributary stream to Round Lake on the top of the ridge. The trail is marked by a sign at Holiday Park indicating Fish Lake.

Sand—Yet another grayling lake, Sand is the second in a row of lakes on the Dry Fork Trail that provide fishing for this unique species. It is about 4 miles from Holiday Park, between Round and Fish Lakes.

W-52—Access is 0.5 mile east of Carol Lake or 0.75 mile northeast of the Dry Fork Trail in the vicinity of Sand Lake. There are no trails, and it may be hard to find this lake with cutthroat in it.

W-57—Stocked with brook trout, this lake is 0.5 mile east of Fish Lake over ledge rock and scattered meadows. Subject to winterkill, it is planted with brook trout.

W-59—Natural reproduction by brook trout keeps this lake as a fishery; it's 0.5 mile southwest of Adax Lake in the Middle Fork Drainage. Obvious trails do not exist.

Yellow Pine Lower—At the base of Flat Iron Mountain in the Beaver Creek Drainage, Lower Yellow Pine is stocked with brook trout. Access is 0.75 mile northeast of Highway 150 on the Yellow Pine Trail which originates near the Yellow Pine Campground. The trail is heavily used.

Yellow Pine Upper—Directly north of Lower Yellow Pine, this lake sees intensive pressure and annual stocks of brook trout.

154 Bear River Drainage

This drainage on the northwest extreme of the Uinta Mountains is the range's largest. Its six major tributary systems include West Fork, Hayden Fork, Main Fork, Stillwater Fork, East Fork, and Mill Creek. Large portions of the West Fork and Mill Creek areas are privately owned and offer no public access. Thirty-eight bodies of water in the Bear River drainage have fish. Access to this drainage is via the Mirror Lake Highway on Forest Service routes Whitney, Gold Hill, Stillwater, North Slope, East Fork, and Mill Creek. Major access points to backcountry areas include the Christmas Meadows and East Fork–Bear River Trailheads. A few lakes are directly accessible to vehicles, but the vast majority of them are remote. Major trails include Bear River–Smiths Fork, Ruth Lake, Main Fork Stillwater, Stillwater, Boundary Creek, East Fork Little Bear River, Kermsuh Lake, Amethyst Lake, Whiskey Creek, and the Left Hand Fork.

Allsop—Access is 8.5 miles southeast of the East Fork–Bear River Trailhead on the East Fork and Left Hand Fork Pack Trails. It is sustained with a naturally reproducing population of cutthroat.

Moose are some of the "other anglers" you may encounter while fishing in the Uintas.

Amethyst—This aptly named lake is 6.25 miles southeast of the Christmas Meadows Trailhead on the Stillwater and Amethyst Lake Pack Trails. There is fast fishing for brook trout and cutthroat here.

Baker—Wary brook trout call Baker home. It is 4.25 miles southeast of the Bear River Boy Scout Camp on the Boundary Creek Trail. The last 0.75 mile of the trail is hard to follow.

Beaver—Because it is easily accessed from the Moffit Pass Road 1.75 miles southwest of the Whitney Reservoir Dam, Beaver gets a lot of pressure. It is stocked with catchable rainbows and may have brook and cutthroat as well.

Bourbon (Gold Hill)—Located 1 mile west of Highway 150 up the steep Whiskey Creek Trail that starts across the highway from the Sulphur Campground. Access is also possible from the Whiskey Creek Road starting across from and slightly north of the Kletting Peak information turnoff. Follow the road north and west for 2.5 miles to the end and then travel 0.25 mile northwest on foot. Feisty brook trout make Bourbon a popular destination.

BR-2—This meadow pond is about 100 yards downstream from Bourbon Lake and has a sizable population of brook trout.

BR-16—Brook and cutthroat trout inhabit this pond, which is accessible immediately below Ryder in the Stillwater Fork Drainage.

BR-17—This spring-fed lake is south of Ryder Lake. It has pan-size brook trout.

BR-18—This glacial lake is 200 yards southeast of Ryder Lake or immediately downstream from BR-17. It has a good population of brook trout, and pressure is usually light.

BR-24—Within sight of Amethyst Lake, BR-24 is 5.125 miles southeast of the Christmas Meadows Trailhead. It has spotty fishing for cutthroat.

Cutthroat—Access is 1 mile west of Ruth Lake through thick timber in the Hayden Fork Drainage. There is no trail. Cutthroat and brook trout are abundant here.

Hayden—No trail goes to Hayden, but it is 0.25 mile due west of Ruth Lake in the Hayden Fork. A small population of cutthroat live here.

Hell Hole—So named because of large numbers of mosquitoes, Hell Hole is 5 miles southeast of Highway 150 on the Main Fork Stillwater Trail, which begins as an unmarked jeep road across the highway from the Gold Hill turnoff. The trail is not always easy to follow. Fishing is good for cutthroat trout.

Jewel—Located 0.5 mile northwest of Ruth Lake over rough terrain, Jewel is stocked with cutthroat trout.

Kermsuh—Access is 4.5 miles south of Christmas Meadows on the Stillwater Pack Trail to the Kermsuh Lake Trail junction, and then 2.25 miles southwest up a steep grade. The lake hosts naturally reproducing cutthroat.

Lily—This large beaver pond east of Highway 150 is 1 mile north of the Bear River Ranger Station on Highway 150 to a well-marked turnoff. After heading southeast for 2 miles on the Lily Lake–Boundary Creek Road, you will reach the rainbow-infested fishery.

Bear River Drainage

0 Kilometers 2

0 Miles 2

N

Elizabeth Mtn.

150

154

Mill

Creek

BR-8

Elizabeth Pass Road

Elizabeth Pass

Deer Creek

West Fork Bear

River

East Fork

Bear River

Whitney Road

BR-5

BR-4

BR-6

Stillwater

BR-11

East

Fork

BR-7

East Fork (B.S.A.)

Bear

Deadman Pass

BR-41

Whitney Reservoir

BR-10

Moffit Pass Rd.

BR-51

Hayden Fork

Beaver View

BR-12

River

BR-45

BR-46

BR-44

BR-53

BR-52

Main Fork

Stillwater Fork

BR-43

BR-26

Right Hand Fork

Left Hand Fork

BR-42

BR-50

BR-1

BR-2

BR-3

Sulphur

BR-30

BR-29

BR-31

BR-25

Lamotte Peak

BR-48

BR-47

Hayden Fork

Kletting Peak

BR-27

BR-24

BR-28

BR-49

BR-35

BR-33

BR-34

BR-32

BR-39

BR-38

BR-22

BR-20

BR-23

Ostler Peak

X

BR-21

BR-14

BR-37

BR-36

BR-40

150

BR-16

BR-15

BR-19

Spread Eagle Peak

X

Hayden Pass

BR-17

BR-18

KEY TO NAMED LAKES

BR-1	Bourbon Lake	BR-14	McPheters Lake	BR-28	Amethyst Lake	BR-40	Ruth Lake
BR-3	Whiskey Island Lake	BR-15	Ryder Lake	BR-31	Seidner Lake	BR-42	Allsop Lake
BR-7	Lym Lake	BR-19	Meadow Lake	BR-32	Teal Lake	BR-45	Baker Lake
BR-8	Mt. Elizabeth Lake	BR-20	Kermsuh Lake	BR-36	Hayden Lake	BR-46	Lorena Lake
BR-10	Beaver Lake	BR-25	Toomset Lake	BR-37	Cutthroat Lake	BR-47	Norice Lake
BR-11	Lily Lake	BR-26	Salamander Lake	BR-38	Jewel Lake	BR-48	Priord Lake
BR-12	Scow Lake	BR-27	Ostler Lake	BR-39	Naomi Lake		

Lorena—Head 2 miles southeast of the East Fork–Bear River Trailhead on the East Fork Trail to some old cabin sites. Then proceed south for 1.5 miles up the steep and rocky ridge to the head of the basin. Lorena is stocked with brook trout and gets little pressure.

Lym—Access is 4 miles south of the Mill Creek Guard Station on the Mill Creek Road, and then 2 miles northeast on the Lym Lake four-wheel-drive road. Brook trout are caught here.

McPheters—A half mile northwest of Ryder Lake, the total distance to McPheters is 9 miles from the Christmas Meadows Trailhead. The lake is stocked with cutthroat.

Meadow—The best route is to head 0.25 mile southeast of the Stillwater Pack Trail from the large meadows due east of Ryder Lake. There's a large population of brookies here.

Mt. Elizabeth—Access is 11.5 miles east of Highway 150 on the North Slope Road to Elizabeth Pass and then 4.25 miles north and west on the Elizabeth Mountain Road to the point overlooking the lake. The lake sees moderate pressure for cutthroat.

Norice—Near the head of the Right Hand Fork, Norice is about 8.25 miles southeast of the East Fork Trailhead on the East Fork–Bear River Pack Trail. Good fly fishing for cutthroat is found here.

Ostler—Boy Scouts enjoy this lake with brook and cutthroat, 5.25 miles southeast of the Christmas Meadows Trailhead on the Stillwater and Amethyst Lake Trails. When you reach the lower meadows, head 0.25 mile up the hillside to the lake.

Priord—There are cutthroat in this small lake, which sits 9 miles east and south of the East Fork–Bear River Trailhead on the East Fork Trail.

Ruth—Frequently stocked with brook trout, Ruth is 0.75 mile west of Highway 150 on the Ruth Lake Trail. Day use is heavy.

Ryder—Access is 8.5 miles south of the Christmas Meadows Trailhead on the Stillwater Pack Trail. The trail is hard to follow at some points, so it is marked with cairns. Fishing is fast for brook trout.

Salamander—Stocked with brook trout, Salamander is 3.5 miles south and east of the Christmas Meadows Trailhead on the Stillwater and Amethyst Lake Trails. From the first meadow in the Amethyst Basin, head southwest up the ridge.

Scow—Due to winterkill, Scow is planted with brook trout. Reach it by hiking for 2.5 miles south of the East Fork of the Bear River Boy Scout Camp on the Boundary Creek Trail past the burn to a small meadow. Continue south 0.75 mile through thick timber to the lake.

Seidner—A large population of wild brook trout is found in Seidner. Head 2.25 miles south of the Christmas Meadows Trailhead on the Stillwater Pack Trail to a minor side drainage and then up 2 steep miles to the head of the basin. Direct trails are not available.

Teal—Regularly stocked with cutthroat, Teal is 1.25 miles northwest of Ruth Lake over rough terrain in the Hayden Fork Drainage.

Toomset—Often overlooked, Toomset is a good place to fish for brook trout. It lies 0.25 mile north of Ostler Lake in the Amethyst Basin.

Whiskey Island—Access is 1.25 miles southwest on the Whiskey Creek timber road, approximately 1.5 miles northwest of Highway 150. There is no direct trail to the lake, which is surrounded by heavy timber. Grayling are the catch.

Whitney—Planted rainbow, cutthroat, and brook trout make this a popular destination. Access is from Highway 150 on the Whitney Road (Forest Road 032).

155 Blacks Fork Drainage

This isolated drainage on the north slope of the Uintas is located between the Bear River and Smiths Fork drainages. The four major tributaries are the West Fork, Middle Fork, East Fork, and Little East Fork. Generally, lakes in Blacks Fork Basin are small and widely scattered. The drainage is about 15 miles south of Highway 150 on the North Slope Road over Elizabeth Ridge, or 18 miles southwest of Robertson, Wyoming, on the Blacks Fork Road.

Trailheads in the drainage include Cache, East Fork Blacks Fork, and West Fork Blacks Fork. Major trails include Bear River–Smith Fork, West Fork Blacks Fork, East Fork Blacks Fork, Little East Fork Blacks Fork, and Middle Fork Blacks Fork. Only 3 of the 22 fisheries in the basin can be reached by road. As a result, lakes in this region see light pressure.

Bobs—At the base of Tokewanna Peak, Bobs is reached 10.25 miles southwest of the East Fork Blacks Fork Road on the sketchy Middle Fork Trail, which begins as a jeep road just south of the Blacks Fork Bridge. Once you have reached the large headwater meadows, follow the tributary toward the west. Bobs rests well above the timberline. The lake is stocked with cutthroat.

Dead Horse—Access is 7.5 miles south of the West Fork Blacks Fork Trailhead on the West Fork Trail to the head of the basin. Dead Horse is stocked with cutthroat.

Ejod—This glacial lake is reached by traveling 0.25 mile northwest of Dead Horse Lake to the top of a small ridge. Open shorelines make Ejod a natural fly-fishing lake for cutthroat.

G-65—Access is 6 miles south of the East Fork Blacks Fork Trailhead on the East Fork and Little East Fork Trails to the large meadow. From the lower end of the meadow, follow a minor tributary stream west for 0.75 mile to a small basin. A healthy population of brook trout inhabits G-65.

G-66—Access is 5 miles south of the East Fork Blacks Fork Trailhead on the East Fork and Little East Fork Trails to a large, dry park. At the lower end of the park is a small stream coming from the west. Follow the stream west and south for 0.75 mile to the lake. Brook trout are waiting for you.

G-67—This lake is occasionally stocked with brook trout and is 1 mile northwest of G-68 around a rocky point.

G-69—Wild cutthroat are found in G-69, which is 7.5 miles south of the East Fork Blacks Fork Trailhead on the East Fork and Little East Fork Trails to the head of a large meadow, and then 1 mile west up a steep slope to the lake.

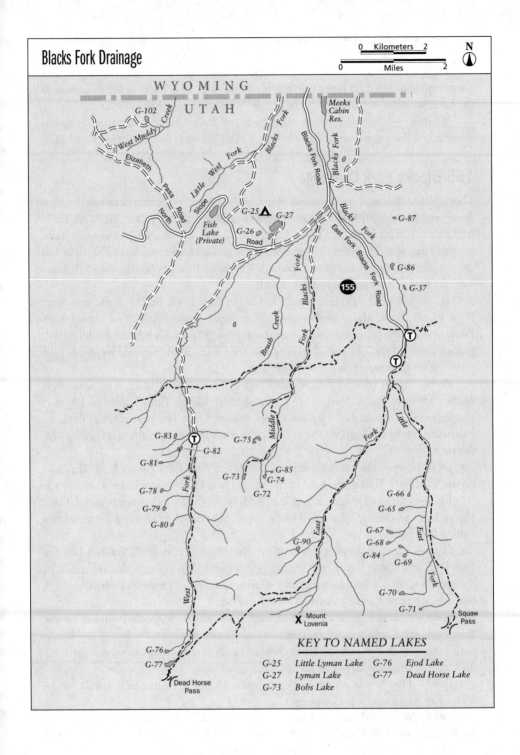

Blacks Fork Drainage

0 Kilometers 2

0 Miles 2

N

WYOMING

UTAH

G-102

West Muddy Creek

Elizabeth

Pass

North

Road

Slope

Fish Lake (Private)

Little West Fork

Blacks Fork

Blacks Fork

Blacks Fork

Meeks Cabin Res.

G-25 ▲ G-27

G-26

Road

Blacks Fork Road

East Fork Blacks Fork Road

G-87

G-86

G-37

155

Fork

Blacks

Fork

Brush Creek

T

T

G-83

T

G-82

G-75

Middle

G-81

G-73

G-85

G-74

Fork

Little

G-78

G-72

G-79

G-66

G-80

G-65

East

East

Fork

G-67

G-68

G-84

G-69

G-90

G-70

West

G-71

Squaw Pass

Mount Lovenia

KEY TO NAMED LAKES

G-76

G-77

Dead Horse Pass

G-25	Little Lyman Lake	G-76	Ejod Lake
G-27	Lyman Lake	G-77	Dead Horse Lake
G-73	Bobs Lake		

G-71—Access is 9 miles south of the East Fork Blacks Fork Trailhead on the East Fork and Little East Fork Trails to the foot of Squaw Pass. Leave the trail and proceed west for 1.25 miles over rough terrain to this lake stocked with bookies.

G-74—Some brook trout make it through the winter here, but not all. Access is 9.5 miles southwest of the East Fork Road on the Middle Fork Blacks Fork jeep road and trail to the head of the Middle Fork Basin. The trail disappears in the head-water region about 1 mile short of the lake, but it can be found by following the easternmost drainage system in the upper basin.

G-80—Brook trout are stocked at G-80, which is reached 2.5 miles south of the West Fork Blacks Fork Trailhead on the West Fork Trail to the upper end of Buck Pasture, and then 0.75 mile west up the steep slope to a small basin.

G-81—Stocked with cutthroat trout, G-81 is 0.75 mile from G-82 at the southern end of the large basin against a talus slope.

G-82—This lake sits in a boggy meadow and has a small population of brook trout. Access is 0.5 mile southwest of the old cabin at the West Fork Blacks Fork Trailhead up a steep timbered ridge. Follow the drainage system to the lake.

Little Lyman—Access to this heavily fished lake is 16 miles east of Highway 150 on the North Slope Road or 24 miles southwest of Robertson, Wyoming, on the Blacks Fork Road. Take Lyman Lake Road 0.5 mile north at the well-marked turnoff. Little Lyman is stocked with rainbow trout and brook trout. There's a small full-service campground here.

Lyman—This large scenic lake is immediately north and east of Little Lyman. The lake often winterkills, but officials plant it with rainbow and albino trout.

156 Smiths Fork Drainage

This small drainage is centered on the north slope of the Uinta Mountains, and it is perhaps the most naturally beautiful drainage in the system. There are two major tributary systems: the West Fork and East Fork. Twenty-eight of the 60 waters in the Smiths Fork sustain fish life. The basin is about 20 miles south of Mountain View, Wyoming, on Highway 410 and the China Meadows Road (Forest Road 072). Access is also possible from the North Slope Road east from the Bear River Drainage on Highway 150.

Major trails in the Smiths Fork Basin are East Fork Smiths Fork Trail, which originates at the China Meadows Trailhead, and the West Fork Smiths Fork Trail, which begins at the end of the Mansfield Meadows Road south of the Hewinta Guard Station. Access is also possible from the Cache Trailhead in the Blacks Fork Drainage to the west or the Yellowstone Drainage to the south on the Bald Mountain–Smiths Fork Pass Trail. The interbasin Highline Trail, the Big Meadows Trail, and the Sargent Lake Trail provide access to the lower basin.

Bald—This lake lies at the base of Bald Mountain in the West Fork Smiths Fork. It is 2.5 miles south of the Hewinta Guard Station on the Mansfield Meadows Road to the wilderness boundary and 2.5 miles south of the West Fork Smiths Fork

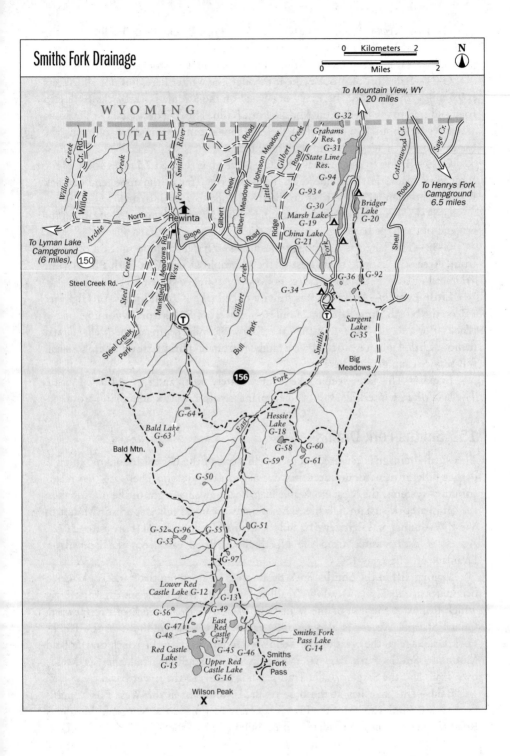

Smiths Fork Drainage

Trail to the junction with the Highline Trail. Leave the trails and continue southwest 1.5 miles overland, following the outlet to Bald Lake. There is moderate pressure for a large population of brook trout.

Bridger—This is a popular lake, which receives substantial fishing pressure. Bridger is 25 miles south of Mountain View, Wyoming, on Highway 410 and improved FR 072. There is a 32-unit campground at the lake and a summer guard station. Shore fishing can be difficult due to extensive beds of pond lilies. A small boat, canoe, or raft is the best way to fish here. The lake is stocked with rainbows, catchable throughout the summer, and is also planted with brook trout.

China—Access to China Lake is 0.125 mile north of the North Slope Road on foot, following an old road closed to vehicles. The route begins at a small turnoff and parking area 0.5 mile west of China Meadows. The lake has cutthroat and brook trout and has been planted with grayling. The China Meadows Campground has 9 campsites, and another at the trailhead has 12.

G-13—Because it sometimes suffers from winterkill, G-13 is stocked frequently with brook trout. The lake is reached by trail, 1 mile southeast of the footbridge immediately below Lower Red Castle Lake on the Bald Mountain–Smiths Fork Trail. G-13 lies to the south and within sight of the trail.

G-34—Near the junction of the China Meadows and North Slope Roads, this lake sits at the lower end of China Meadows. Its brookies and rainbows see heavy pressure due to easy access.

G-45—This small glacial lake is 0.125 mile northwest of Smiths Fork Pass Lake. Fishing can be unpredictable for stocked brook trout because of occasional winterkill.

G-49—Despite having rainbow, brook, and cutthroat trout, G-49 is often overlooked by anglers. It is 100 yards east of the East Fork Smiths Fork Trail from the stream crossing 0.5 mile south of Lower Red Castle Lake. G-49 is located on the major drainage system between Red Castle and Lower Red Castle Lakes.

G-50—A naturally reproducing population of brook trout make up G-50's angling opportunity. Access is 6.25 miles southwest of the China Meadows Trailhead on the East Fork Smiths Fork Trail to Broadbent Meadow, and then 0.5 mile west up a steep ridge to the lake.

G-51—This scenic lake sits at the western flank of Flat Top Mountain in the Smiths Fork Basin. It is 7.25 miles southwest of the China Meadows Trailhead on the East Fork Smiths Fork Trail to the second footbridge. Without crossing the footbridge, follow an obscure trail south and east around the timbered ridge and across an open meadow for about 1 mile to the lake. G-51 has a good population of brook trout.

G-52—Potential winterkill doesn't stop anglers from pursuing stocked cutthroat here. The lake is 0.125 mile northwest of G-53.

G-53—Cutthroat and brook trout are caught on this lake, which is 8.5 miles southwest of the China Meadows Trailhead on the East Fork Smiths Fork Trail to the junction with the Bald Mountain–Smiths Fork Trail. Head 1 mile northwest on this trail to the point where it crosses a timbered ridge, then leave the trail heading southwest for another 0.5 mile to the lake.

G-56—At 11,460 feet, this lake sits well above the timberline. It is seldom visited despite its solid brookie populations. It is 1.5 miles southwest of Lower Red Castle Lake in the Smiths Fork Drainage.

G-58—This shallow lake maintains its fishery through nearby Hessie Lake. The lake is 25 yards east and below Hessie.

G-59—Stocked with brook trout, G-59 sometimes winterkills. It is 0.5 mile south of Hessie Lake along the base of a talus ridge.

G-60—This lake with brook trout is 250 yards south of the steam crossing in Hessie Lake Basin, some 5.25 miles south of the China Meadows Trailhead on the East Fork Smiths Fork and Highline Trails.

G-61—It is located 0.125 mile south of G-60. Follow G-60's inlet stream up a steep timbered ridge. The lake is stocked with brook trout.

G-64—Good fishing for cutthroat is possible here during years when the lake doesn't winterkill. It is 0.25 mile south of the junction of the West Fork Smiths Fork and Highline Trails in the West Fork Drainage. Total distance from the Hewinta Guard Station is 5.75 miles. From the Cache Trailhead in the East Fork Blacks Fork Drainage, it is 4.5 miles.

Hessie—Aerially planted with cutthroat trout, Hessie is a popular destination in the East Fork Smiths Fork Drainage. Access is 3.5 miles southwest of the China Meadows Trailhead on the East Fork Smiths Fork Trail to the junction with the Highline Trail heading east. Follow the Highline Trail south and east for 1.5 miles to the Hessie Lake cutoff and proceed west 0.25 mile to the lake.

Marsh—This lake gets heavy fishing and camping pressure because it's easily reached by driving 26 miles south of Mountain View, Wyoming, on FR 072. There are two Forest Service campgrounds at the lake with 38 units between them. Pressure for the stocked rainbow, albino, and brook trout is intense, especially on weekends.

Red Castle—At 168 acres and a depth of 103 feet, Red Castle is one of the largest and deepest natural lakes in the Uinta Mountains. With an elevation of 11,295 feet at the base of Wilson Peak, it is also one of the windiest. Many people pack blow-up rafts or float tubes to the lake, but extreme caution must be used, as strong winds can pick up at any time. The lake is stocked with cutthroat trout. It is reached with an 11-mile hike southwest of the China Meadows Trailhead on the East Fork Smiths Fork Trail, about 2 miles beyond Lower Red Castle Lake.

Red Castle, East—Fishing for cutthroat at Red Castle East is a little more difficult than at other lakes. It is slightly more than 0.25 mile northwest of Smiths Fork Pass Lake against a steep talus ridge.

Red Castle, Lower—Nine miles south and west of China Meadows on the East Fork Smiths Fork Trail, Lower Red Castle is found just beyond the switchbacks. This is a popular lake and fishing is good for rainbow, cutthroat, and brook trout.

Red Castle, Upper—On the top of a rocky ridge 0.125 mile south of Red Castle Lake, this lake can be difficult to access due to steep slopes and vertical cliffs. It's stocked with cutthroat and has a reputation for being slow, but it also yields some big fish.

Smiths Fork Pass — This lake is well suited to fly fishing its good population of cutthroat trout. From the footbridge below Lower Red Castle Lake, proceed southeast for 2.5 miles on the Bald Mountain–Smiths Fork Pass Trail to the large cirque basin in which the lake sits.

State Line — This is the largest body of water in the Smiths Fork Drainage. State Line looks like it should produce big fish given its size, but the reservoir can't support a large population of fish because of its sterile environment. It receives less pressure than the surrounding fisheries, which are more productive.

157 Henrys Fork Drainage

This is a small drainage on the north slope about 25 miles south of Mountain View, Wyoming. The Henrys Fork Drainage is composed of 50 natural lakes and numerous ponds, of which 19 hold fish. Access to the drainage is provided from Mountain View, Wyoming, from Utah Highway 410 to Forest Road 072, then to Forest Road 017. From Lonetree, Wyoming, take County Road 208 to Forest Road 077. Henrys Fork Trailhead is the major access point into the drainage. The Henrys Fork Trail follows the drainage system south over Gunsight Pass into the Uinta River Drainage. Henrys Fork can also be reached via Smiths Fork to the west or Beaver Creek to the east on the interbasin Highline Trail. Dollar Lake is popular stopover for groups hiking in to climb King's Peak. There are seven campsites at the trailhead. A picnic area is located north of the trailhead on FR 077.

Alligator — Due to easy access, Alligator is fished intensively. Thick timber makes fly fishing difficult. The lake is slightly more than 0.25 mile west of the Henrys Fork Trail on an unmarked side trail that begins about 2.25 miles southwest of the Henrys Fork Trailhead.

Bear — This is a popular lake that receives moderate to heavy pressure on its stocked brook and cutthroat population. Bear is 6.5 miles from the Henrys Fork Trailhead or 8.25 miles from the China Meadows Trailhead in the Smiths Fork Drainage. From the Henrys Fork Trailhead follow the Henrys Fork Trail southwest to Elkhorn Crossing and then proceed west on the Highline and Basin Trails to the lake.

Blanchard — Good fly fishing for pan-size cutthroat can be had at this lake, 1 mile southwest of Henrys Fork Lake. Blanchard can be located by following the stream connecting the two lakes.

Castle — Access is 0.75 mile northwest of Blanchard Lake over rocky terrain, or 1 steep mile southwest of Island Lake. The lake is planted with brook trout from aircraft.

Cliff — Fishing for cutthroat is more difficult here than in most Uinta lakes. Cliff is above timberline at the head of the Henrys Fork Drainage. Access is 1 mile south of Blanchard Lake up a gently sloping ridge to the large cirque basin the lake sits in.

Dollar — A popular place to camp on a hike to or from King's Peak, Utah's tallest mountain, means moderate to heavy fishing pressure on Dollar's brook and cutthroat trout populations. Dollar is 7 miles southwest of the Henrys Fork Trailhead on the

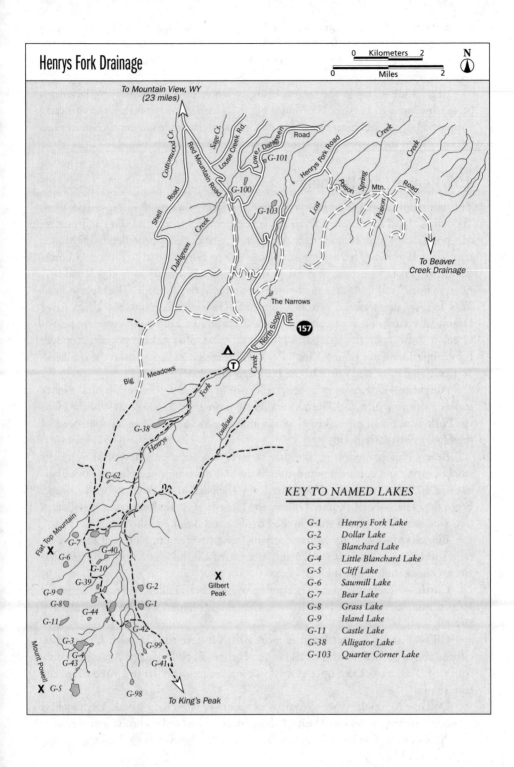

Henrys Fork Drainage

KEY TO NAMED LAKES

G-1	Henrys Fork Lake
G-2	Dollar Lake
G-3	Blanchard Lake
G-4	Little Blanchard Lake
G-5	Cliff Lake
G-6	Sawmill Lake
G-7	Bear Lake
G-8	Grass Lake
G-9	Island Lake
G-11	Castle Lake
G-38	Alligator Lake
G-103	Quarter Corner Lake

Henrys Fork Trail to the last patch of tall timber on the trail before breaking into open alpine meadows at the head of the basin. Dollar is about 250 yards east of the trail from this point.

G-10—There is potential here for winterkill, but the lake is planted with brook trout. Access is 1.25 miles south of Bear Lake on the Basin Trail. G-10 is visible from the trail and lies about 350 yards northeast at the lower end of a large alpine meadow.

G-39—Fishing can be spotty here for brook trout. G-39 is adjacent to the Basin Trail, 2 miles south of Bear Lake or 0.5 mile northwest of Henrys Fork Lake.

G-42—This shallow lake in open terrain, 0.5 mile south and east of Henrys Fork Lake on the Basin Trail, does not support fish life year-round, but brookies and cutthroat come in from the adjacent stream in the summer.

G-44—One-half mile southwest of Henrys Fork Lake, G-44 has been stocked with cutthroat trout.

G-62—Stocked brook trout make up the catch at this small lake. It is 4.25 miles southwest of the Henrys Fork Trailhead on the Henrys Fork Trail to a point where two small streams cross the trail in close proximity. Leave the trail and follow the northernmost of the streams west for 0.75 mile to the lake.

Grass—This lake can provide some excellent evening fly fishing for pan-size brook and cutthroat trout. It is in a broad alpine meadow within sight of the Basin Trail 0.5 mile northwest of Henrys Fork Lake.

Henrys Fork—This beautiful high-elevation lake is popular, but it continues to provide good to excellent fishing for cutthroat trout. Trail access is 8 miles southwest of the trailhead on the Henrys Fork Trail to the junction with the Basin Trail, and then west for 1 mile to the lake.

Island—Shallow water means sneaky fishing at this small lake slightly more than 0.25 mile west of Henrys Fork Lake. There are no direct trails to Island, but it is easy to find from Henrys.

Little Blanchard—Immediately upstream 50 yards east of Blanchard Lake, Little Blanchard has a large population of cutthroat trout. Open shorelines make this a good place to fly fish.

Sawmill—Brook trout have out-competed the cutthroat for dominance here. An old sawmill site nearby gave this lake its name. It is 0.75 mile south and west of Elkhorn Crossing on the obscure trail that follows the minor drainage to Sawmill. Sawmill is popular; expect company.

158 Beaver Creek Drainage

This remote medium-size drainage on the north slope is about 10 miles south of Lonetree, Wyoming. The three major drainage systems in the basin are the West Fork, the Middle Fork, and the East Fork. Because of the isolated nature of this basin, fishing pressure is limited, and it's a good place to go for solitude.

There are 40 natural lakes in the basin, and about half of them support fish. Major roads to the drainage include Hole in the Rock Road (Forest Road 078) from County Road 264, and the North Slope Road from either Henrys Fork Drainage to

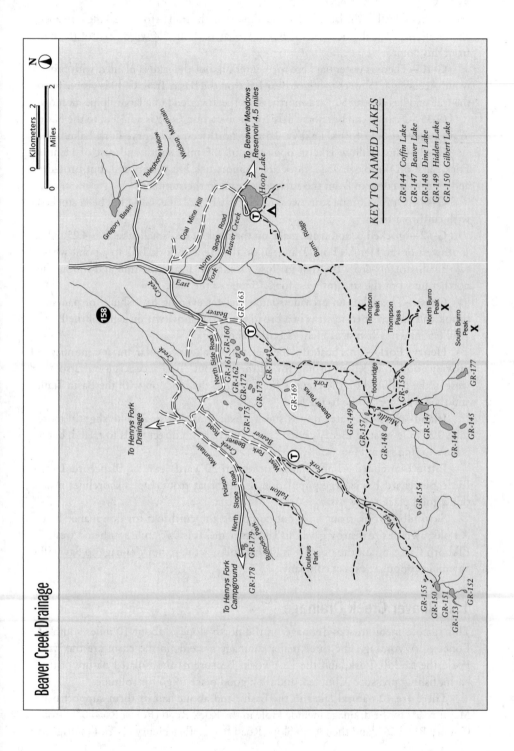

Beaver Creek Drainage

KEY TO NAMED LAKES

GR-144 Coffin Lake
GR-147 Beaver Lake
GR-148 Dine Lake
GR-149 Hidden Lake
GR-150 Gilbert Lake

N

0   Kilometers   2
0   Miles   2

To Beaver Meadows
Reservoir 4.5 miles

Hoop Lake

Gregory Basin

Telephone Hollow

Widdup Mountain

Coal Mine Hill

North Slope Road

Beaver Creek

East

Fork

Creek

158

Beaver

GR-163

GR-160

GR-161

North Side Road

GR-162

GR-172

GR-175

GR-173

GR-164

GR-169

Beaver Parks

Fork

To Henrys Fork
Drainage

Creek

Poison

Mountain

North Slope Road

West Fork Beaver Creek Road

Fork

Fallon

To Henrys Fork
Campground

GR-178

GR-179

Bullocks Park

Joullous Park

West

Fork

GR-154

Burn Ridge

Thompson
Peak

Thompson
Pass

North Burro
Peak

South Burro
Peak

footbridge

GR-156

GR-177

Middle

GR-149

GR-157

GR-148

GR-147

GR-144

GR-145

GR-155

GR-150

GR-151

GR-153

GR-152

the west or Burnt Fork Drainage to the east. Foot access to the wilderness area is on the West Fork Beaver Trail from the West Fork Road, the Middle Fork Beaver Trail from Georges Park Trailhead, and the Burnt Ridge and Thompson Peak Trails from the Hoop Lake Trailhead. The Hoop Lake Trailhead also provides access to the Burnt Fork Drainage via the Kabell Meadow Trail. A full-service 44-site campground with water is located at Hoop Lake. The Middle Fork Beaver Trail is poorly routed and difficult to follow in some areas. The North Slope Road near Fallon Creek is rough, as is the West Fork Road.

Beaver — Access is 5 miles southwest of the Georges Park Trailhead in the Middle Fork Trail to the footbridge at the lower end of Long Meadow, then 1.75 miles south on the Beaver Lake Trail to the lake. Beaver is a popular lake, full of brook trout and cutthroat.

Coffin — This scenic alpine lake sits in rugged rocky terrain at the head of the Middle Fork Drainage. There is no trail to the lake, and the going is tough. From Beaver Lake follow the drainage south and west for 0.75 mile to the lake. Angling pressure is light for stocked cutthroat.

Dine — This shallow lake has been known to winterkill, but it is planted with brook trout. It is 0.5 mile west of Long Meadow up the steep timbered ridge, or 1 mile south and west of Hidden Lake following the drainage.

Gilbert — Despite shallow water, Gilbert maintains excellent populations of self-sustaining brook and cutthroat trout. Access is 2.75 miles southwest of the North Slope Road on the West Fork Beaver Road, and then 6.5 miles south and west on the West Fork Beaver Trail to the headwaters area. The trail departs from the road before the road ends and is marked by a sign. Open shoreline allows for fly casting at Gilbert.

GR-145 — It has been stocked in the past with brook trout. Take your chances. GR-145 is 0.125 mile south of Coffin Lake up a talus ridge.

GR-151 — A little more than 0.25 mile south of Gilbert Lake in the West Fork Basin, GR-151 has a healthy population of naturally reproducing brook trout and receives light angling pressure. This is also a good place to fish the inlet and outlet streams.

GR-152 — This lake usually doesn't become ice-free until mid-July, but it is stocked with brook trout and rarely sees any pressure. It is slightly more than a 0.25 mile south of GR-151 following the stream to the top of the ridge. Total distance from the North Slope Road is 10 miles.

GR-153 — Few make the trip here, but fly fishing is good for pan-size brook trout and some cutthroat. The lake is 150 yards west of GR-151.

GR-155 — About 0.25 mile northeast of Gilbert Lake and out of sight of the West Fork Beaver Trail, GR-155 is stocked with brook trout.

GR-160 — This is one of many pothole lakes situated in a broad and heavily timbered basin, which makes it difficult to locate. It is 0.25 mile east and just a bit north of GR-162 in the lower Middle Fork Basin. It has been planted with brook trout.

GR-161 — About 250 yards east of GR-162, this lake is rounded and should not be confused with nearby GR-164, which is elongated and contains no fish. GR-161 has been planted with brook trout.

GR-162—Access is 0.5 mile southeast of the North Slope Road near Willow Park, over the timbered ridge. The lake has a small population of wary brook trout. Pressure is light, angling is difficult, and the lake may suffer from winterkill.

GR-163—About 0.25 mile south and slightly west of GR-162, this lake has been stocked with brook trout.

GR-172—Yet another of the pothole lakes in the lower Beaver Drainage, GR-172 is 0.75 mile south of Willow Park. It was once planted with brook trout, but it may periodically winterkill.

GR-173—One hundred yards southwest of GR-172, this lake is difficult to fish due to heavy cover and deadfall.

GR-177—Near the head of the Middle Fork Basin, GR-177 is 1.5 miles southeast of Beaver Lake over rough terrain. Light fishing pressure is for cutthroat trout.

Hidden—There is no direct trail to Hidden, but access is not difficult. It is 0.5 mile north of Long Meadow in the Middle Fork Drainage. A brook trout population is bolstered by aerial planting.

159 Burnt Fork Drainage

Immediately east of the Beaver Creek Drainage and south of Hoop Lake on the north slope of the Uintas, Burnt Fork is a relatively small drainage with only 15 major lakes. The 11 lakes that sustain fish are all at elevations higher than 10,500 feet.

The best road entry to the area is just east from Lonetree, Wyoming, on Forest Road 078 going south for about 7 miles to Forest Road 058. Hoop Lake, which serves as the primary access point into the Burnt Fork Drainage, is about 4 miles down the road. The eastern portion of the drainage can also be reached from Spirit Lake.

Lower Bennion—At the base of North Burro Peak in the southwestern corner of the drainage, Lower Bennion is stocked with brook trout, but it also has some cutthroat. The lake is just under 1 mile west of Island Lake across a large meadow and up a timbered slope. There is no trail to Lower Bennion.

Upper Bennion—The lake is not stocked, but fish migrate from Lower Bennion only a few hundred yards upstream.

Boxer—A faint trail to Boxer begins at the western end of Fish Lake and eventually cuts south across a ridge to Burnt Fork Lake. Boxer is against a talus slope less than 0.5 mile to the southeast. Fishing pressure is moderate for cutthroat trout.

Burnt Fork—One mile from the western end of Fish Lake on a faint trail gets you to Burnt Fork. The lake has a naturally reproducing population of cutthroat trout. It is 6 miles from Spirit Lake and more than 10 miles from Hoop Lake.

Crystal—Just over 0.5 mile southwest of Burnt Fork, Crystal lies at the bottom of a steep talus slope. Another way to reach the lake is to follow the outlet from Burnt Fork Lake down to a meadow. The outlet from Crystal flows into Burnt Fork Creek on the west side of the wet meadow. Cutthroat inhabit Crystal.

Fish—This relatively large lake sits atop the divide between the Burnt Fork and Sheep Creek drainages. The Burnt Fork Trail ends at the lake's western tip. It is just over 5 miles from Spirit Lake and more than 9 miles from Hoop Lake.

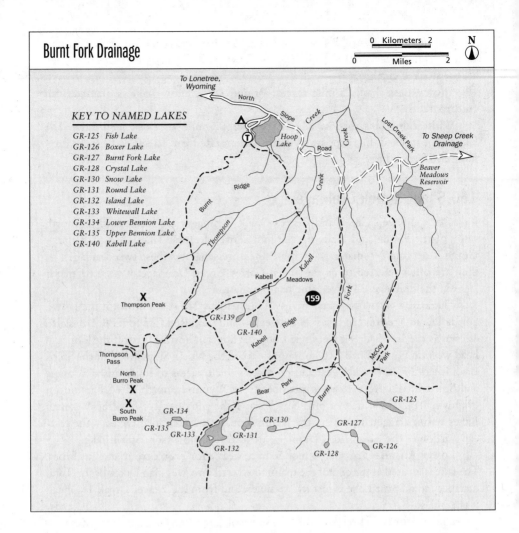

KEY TO NAMED LAKES

GR-125	Fish Lake
GR-126	Boxer Lake
GR-127	Burnt Fork Lake
GR-128	Crystal Lake
GR-130	Snow Lake
GR-131	Round Lake
GR-132	Island Lake
GR-133	Whitewall Lake
GR-134	Lower Bennion Lake
GR-135	Upper Bennion Lake
GR-140	Kabell Lake

Hoop Lake—There is a 44-unit campground at Hoop Lake. This is another popular Uinta fishery. A small boat ramp makes it easy to find the rainbows and cutthroat that have been planted here.

Island—This lake in the southwest corner of the Burnt Fork Drainage is used for water storage, and it fluctuates accordingly. Despite the level changes, Island provides good fishing for self-sustaining cutthroat and a fair number of brook trout. Pressure is heavy. The lake is about 9 miles from Hoop Lake via the trail across Kabell Ridge.

Kabell—This is another popular lake, especially with large groups. Stocked cutthroat make up the fishing opportunity here. From Hoop Lake, a maintained trail leads south to Kabell Meadows; at the upper end of the meadows, a trail splits off to the southeast and begins to climb the eastern tip of Kabell Ridge. A short distance down this trail, a spur cuts to the right and terminates at Kabell Lake.

Round—Less than 0.5 mile southeast of the Island Lake outlet sits Round Lake. It is just over 9 miles from Hoop Lake via Kabell Ridge. Pressure is moderate for stocked cutthroat.

Snow—Less than 0.5 mile east of Round Lake, Snow Lake is planted with cutthroat.

Whitewall—This shallow lake is less than 0.5 mile west of Island Lake. The lake is not stocked, but brook and cutthroat migrate from Island and Lower Bennion. Pressure is light.

160 Sheep Creek Drainage

Lakes of the Sheep Creek and Carter Creek Drainages are located on the north slope of the Uintas and make up the first series of alpine lakes west of Flaming Gorge Reservoir. No major geographical feature separates these two drainages, so they are often referred to as the Sheep-Carter Creek Drainage. Of the 62 major lakes in the drainage, 34 have game fish populations

There are two major access points. Forest Road 218 starts north of the Dowd Spring Picnic Area on Highway 44 between Manila and Red Canyon. FR 218 is also known as the Sheep Creek Geologic Loop. At Summit Springs, get off the loop and head west on Forest Road 221, commonly called the North Slope Road or the Spirit Lake Road. FR 221 heads west and provides vehicle access to trailheads at Browne and Spirit Lakes. Access is also possible from Wyoming north of McKinnon on Highway 414. Trails that originate at Spirit Lake provide access to the Weyman Lakes Basin, Daggett Lake, and the Jesson-Tamarack Lakes area. Lakes in the eastern portion of the Burnt Fork Drainage are also accessible from Spirit Lake.

Lower Anson—Pressure is moderate to heavy for brook trout and cutthroat. The lake is located at the end of the maintained trail into Weyman Lakes Basin. Total distance from Spirit Lake is just over 6 miles, and from the Beaver Creek Trailhead it is 8 miles.

Upper Anson—This lake is 0.2 mile south of Lower Anson Lake in the Weyman Lakes Basin. Naturally reproducing brook trout are caught from Upper Anson.

Browne—About 10 miles west of Highway 44 via the Sheep Creek Loop and FR 221 (the North Slope Road), follow the signs to the lake. A 14-unit campground is located at the lake. There is no ramp, but it is possible to launch small boats. Brook trout and rainbows are planted here. The stream below Browne provides good fly fishing.

Bummer—Periodically planted with brook trout, Bummer is a shallow lake on the east side of the Lamb Lakes Basin about 6.5 miles from Browne Lake. There is no maintained trail for the last 1.5 miles. The most direct access is from the junction of Potter-Lamb Lakes and Browne-Spirit Lake Trails southwest up the bottom of the basin. The going is rough through rocky timber and boulder fields.

Clear—Located in Weyman Lakes Basin and aptly named, Clear Lake is less than 0.5 mile west of Lower Anson Lake through timber. Fishing pressure is light for stocked cutthroat trout.

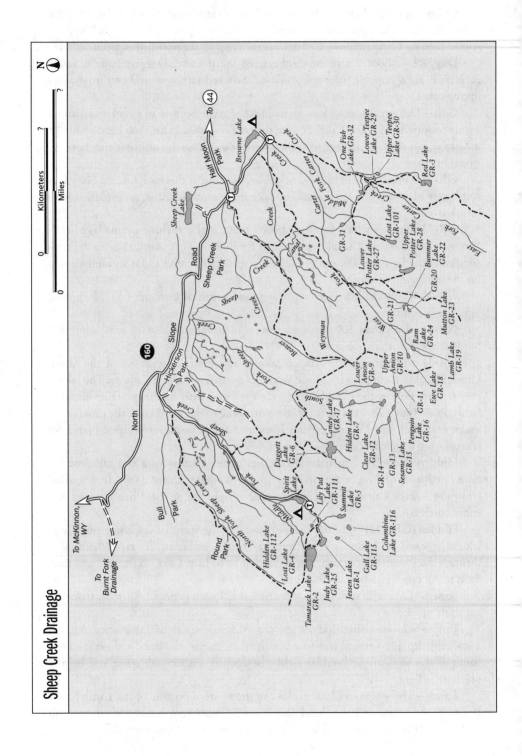

Sheep Creek Drainage

Columbine—Follow the Middle Fork of Sheep Creek upstream from Spirit Lake until the stream goes underground. The lake is across the boulder fields to the south. Despite being shallow, Columbine manages to support brook trout.

Daggett—About 2.5 miles southeast of Spirit Lake, Daggett Lake is easily accessible and a popular fishing destination. Stocked rainbows and cutthroat make up the catch.

Gall—This small and seldom-visited lake is at the bottom of a rock slide, about 1 mile southwest of Spirit Lake. Follow the trail to Jessen Lake, then head south 0.2 mile to across downed timber to Gall, where you can catch cutthroat and an occasional brookie.

GR-11—Pressure is light for stocked brook trout at this lake, located 200 yards southwest of Upper Anson Lake. The lake may winterkill, but it is stocked with brook trout.

GR-13—Strong winds await the brook trout angler at this moraine lake in the Weyman Lakes Basin. The lake is less than 1 mile west of Anson Lakes up the rock slide and boulder field. The outlet of the lake is underground and is a visible siphon on the northeastern shore.

GR-20—This shallow lake is just west and south of Bummer Lake. Fishing is light for brook trout.

GR-21—Less than 200 yards northwest of Bummer, this lake may winterkill but is stocked with brook trout.

GR-31—The irregularly shaped lake is an on-stream portion of the Sheep Creek Canal that supplies irrigation water to northern Daggett County. The lake is easy to find. Follow the canal for just over 1 mile northwest of its junction with the Leidy Peak Trail. GR-31 is the first lake you come to directly below the canal's first major waterfall. Total distance from Browne Lake is just over 4 miles. Naturally reproducing brook trout are caught here.

Hidden (GR-7)—This natural lake lies at the bottom of a wet meadow 0.7 mile northwest of Lower Anson Lake in the Weyman Lakes Basin. It is 9 miles from the Beaver Creek Trailhead. Pressure is light for stocked brook trout and some cutthroat.

Hidden (GR-112)—Just 0.8 mile northwest of the Spirit Lake Campground, this lake is stocked with brook trout and has some cutthroat. To avoid hoofing it through thick timber from the campground, hike to Lost Lake via the trail and then head north cross-country about 0.2 mile.

Jessen—One mile southwest of Spirit Lake, Jessen is popular. Brook trout are regularly stocked.

Judy—Seldom-visited Judy is less than 0.5 mile south of Tamarack Lake. It's a scramble up 400 vertical feet to a bench from Tamarack. Judy, a short distance south at the base of the boulder fields, is stocked with brook trout and fishing pressure is light.

Lamb—There is no trail to this lake in the western portion of the Lamb Lakes Basin. From Bummer Lake, head about 1 mile west across downed timber and rocks. The lake is stocked with cutthroat, but may suffer from winterkill.

Lost (GR-101)—Follow the south bank of the Sheep Creek Canal downstream from the Leidy Peak Trail, about 0.2 mile upstream from GR-31. The trail cuts up the slope to the south. Lost Lake, also called Mystery Lake, is just over 1 mile up the trail. It is 5 miles from Browne Lake. Cutthroat and brook trout are caught here.

Mutton—There is no trail but it is easy to reach by following the inlet to Bummer Lake just over 0.5 mile. Mutton rarely sees anglers for its stocked brook trout.

One Fish—Dense timber lines One Fish Lake, which is just a few yards to the north of the Sheep Creek Canal about 0.3 mile downstream from where the canal crosses the Leidy Peak Trail. Brook trout are stocked.

Penguin—Just to the west of Upper Anson Lake in the Weyman Lakes Basin, Penguin has a good population of brook trout.

Lower Potter—A few yards northeast of Upper Potter, this lake sees moderate fishing pressure for its brook trout.

Upper Potter—Follow the trail from Browne Lake to the bottom of the Lamb Lakes Basin. About 1 mile beyond where the trail crosses the West Fork of Carter, a faint trail cuts off to the south. Upper Potter Lake lies at the end of the trail. It is about 6.5 miles from Browne Lake. There is a naturally reproducing population of brook trout in Upper Potter.

Ram—Just over 0.5 mile west-southwest of Bummer Lake, Ram is stocked with cutthroat trout by aircraft.

Red—Stocked brook trout are the catch of the day at Red. The lake is just over 1 mile south of the Teepee Lakes. The trail to Red Lake diverges from the Leidy Peak Trail just south of its junction with the Sheep Creek Canal.

Sesame—The lake may suffer from winterkill, but it is stocked with brook trout. It is 0.4 mile west of Upper Anson Lake, but the most direct access is due west from Penguin Lake up a rock slide and a boulder field.

Sheep Creek—The DWR uses Sheep Creek Lake as a wild hatchery for native Colorado River cutthroat trout and runs a spawning capture station at the fishery. The fish here are big and beautiful, but special regulations allow artificial flies and lures anglers keep two fish, with only one cutthroat longer than 22 inches. All cutthroat 22 inches and under must be released. The reservoir is closed near the spawning trap and on portions of the lake as posted.

Spirit—Spirit Lake is one of the most popular fishing destinations in the Uintas. Spirit Lake Lodge provides rooms and a convenience store, as well as horseback rides. The Spirit Lake Campground has 24 camping sites. Spirit is stocked with catchable rainbow trout, and pressure is heavy. The lake is about 11 miles west of Highway 44 via the Sheep Creek Loop and the North Slope Road (sometimes called Spirit Lake Road).

Summit—Winterkill has been a problem here. Grayling may be introduced. The best access is to travel due south from Spirit Lake until you reach a line of steep cliffs.

Tamarack—This is by far the largest lake in the Sheep Creek–Carter Creek Drainage. It is 1.5 miles west of Spirit Lake via a rock trail. It is popular with day hikers and Scout groups. Pressure is heavy for naturally reproducing brook trout.

Lower Teepee—At the head of the Sheep Creek Canal, Lower Teepee is 3 miles from Browne Lake. Follow the canal upstream 0.2 mile from its junction with the Leidy Peak Trail. Pressure is moderate to heavy for stocked brook trout.

Upper Teepee—About 250 yards southeast of Lower Teepee, this lake sometimes winterkills but is stocked with cutthroat trout.

161 Ashley Creek Drainage

This drainage is not as steep as its sister drainages on the south slope. It is divided into three basin areas: Dry Fork Creek and the South and North Forks of Ashley Creek. At last count, 27 of the 70 lakes and ponds in the drainage supported fish populations. Access is via three trailheads. The Dry Fork access begins at the Paradise Park Reservoir Campground. Another point of access is Blanchett Park, reached by a 3-mile four-wheel-drive road from the campground. Ashley Twins Reservoir serves as a major takeoff point for lakes in the South Fork. The reservoir is reached by driving 5.5 miles on Forest Road 027 from the Red Cloud Loop out of Vernal. Hacking Lake, 7.75 miles on Forest Road 043 from the Trout Creek Guard Station, is another point of entry.

Ashley Twins Reservoir—These three lakes have brook and cutthroat and are reached 5.5 miles from the Red Cloud Loop on FR 027.

Bert—Follow the Marsh Peak Trail 1 mile to the ridge. Turn southeast and go down the east side of Chimney Rock Basin. You will see Chimney Rock Lake, which does not support fish. Bert is 1 mile south of Chimney Rock Lake, has brook trout, and receives little pressure.

Blue—Hike 5 miles from Blanchett Park to Deadman Lake, then head southeast for 1.75 miles. Brook trout are abundant.

Deadman—From Blanchett Park, Deadman is 5 miles. You will find brookies and cutthroat here.

DF-4—Follow Dry Creek for 2.75 miles above Blanchett Park to Reynolds Creek. Follow Reynolds to its spring source, then head west over boulder terrain to the lake. DF-4 gets very little pressure and contains cutthroat trout.

Fish—From North Twin Lake, follow a small trail along the east inlet stream toward Marsh Peak for 2.25 miles. Pressure is heavy for naturally reproducing cutthroat trout.

Goose Lakes—Half a mile north of Ashley Twins, two of the three lakes may or may not have fish, depending on winterkill.

GR-52—From North Twin Lake, follow the north stream inlet 1.25 miles into a meadow and turn east; follow the tributary for 125 yards to the lake, which has a few brookies.

Hacking—Drive west on FR 043 from the Trout Creek Guard Station on the Red Cloud Loop Road for 7.75 miles. Brook and rainbow trout provide good fishing, but the lake gets heavy pressure on weekends.

Hooper—Access is 1.25 miles northwest of Ashley Twins Reservoir on a well-marked trail. Hooper provides excellent fly fishing for cutthroat.

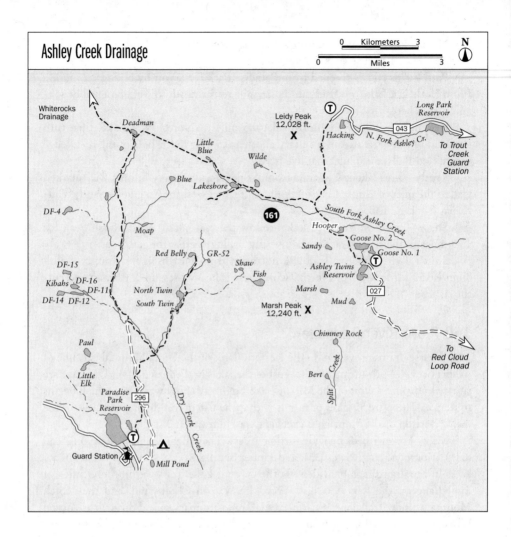

Kibah Basin—Four of the five lakes in this basin have fish. They are reached from Blanchett Park by heading cross-country (no trail) northwest for 1 mile. East Kibah (DF-11) is the first lake you'll come to; it has brook trout and a few rainbows. Ninety yards to the southwest is Finger Kibah (DF-12). It has brook trout. West Kibah (DF-14) is located 0.5 mile in a southwest direction from East Kibah. It is stocked with brook trout. Island Kibah (DF-16) is reached by following the west inlet of DF-11 about 300 yards. It too has brook trout and gets only marginal pressure.

Lakeshore—This lake with brook and cutthroat trout is 4.5 miles from Ashley Twins Reservoir, or 5 miles southwest on the Hacking Lake Trail.

Marsh—Go 1 mile west from Ashley Twins Reservoir into the basin on the northwest side of Marsh Peak for brook trout.

Mud—Access is 0.5 mile south through timber from Ashley Twins Reservoir. Cutthroat trout have been stocked here.

North Twin—Abundant brook and cutthroat await. Go 6 miles northeast on Trail 296 from Paradise Park Campground. Fishing pressure is high.

Paul—This lake is reached from Paradise Park Reservoir by hiking 2.25 miles. From Little Elk Lake (no fish), head 0.25 mile to the north to Paul. Stocked brookies do well here.

Red Belly—Follow the north inlet 0.5 mile to North Twin Lake, then turn north and follow the stream tributary another 0.5 mile to the base of the rock ledge where Red Belly sits. Cutthroat live here.

Sandy—This lake is 0.66 mile from Ashley Twins Reservoir on a well-marked trail to the inlet of Goose Lake #2. Follow the inlet west for 0.5 mile to Sandy. Cutthroat live here, too.

Shaw—From North Twin Lake, follow the east inlet toward Marsh Peak for 1.75 miles to the second large meadow. Fly fishing is great for cutthroat.

South Twin—Follow Trail 296 northeast from Paradise Park 6 miles. South Twin is 150 yards south of North Twin. There is heavy pressure for brook and cutthroat trout.

162 Provo River Drainage

This diverse drainage system on the western flank of the Uinta Mountains is one of the major water-producing zones. Most of the lakes in the Provo River Drainage are situated north and west of the Mirror Lake Highway (Highway 150), which begins in Kamas. There are 55 lakes or ponds with game fish in this drainage. Access to the major portion of the drainage is excellent via Highway 150.

Major Forest Roads provide further access. They include Spring Canyon Road (041), Norway Flats Road (035), and Upper Setting Road. Access to backcountry lakes in the drainage is provided via the Crystal Lake Trailhead in the vicinity of Trial Lake on the Lake Country Trail, the Watson-Clyde Trail, and the Notch Mountain Loop Trail. The Watson-Clyde Trail is unmarked and difficult to locate; it begins at the northwestern end of Upper Lily Lake near the Crystal Lake Trailhead. Other established take-off points in the drainage include the Bald Mountain and Upper Setting Trailheads, which provide access primarily into the Weber Basin Lakes. Other trails in the drainage include Norway Flats, Shingle Creek, North Fork, Weir Lake, and Upper Setting.

Alexander—Access is 3 miles north on the Spring Canyon Road from the Mirror Lake Highway and then 0.25 mile southeast on a well-marked trail. The lake is situated in heavy timber and is stocked by aircraft with brook trout.

Azure (Lock)—Stocked with cutthroat trout, this lake sits on a glacial basin. It is slightly more than 0.25 mile west of Haystack Lake and about 200 yards north and slightly west of Rock Lake.

Beaver—This remote lake is a little more than 0.25 mile southwest of Duck #6 Reservoir. It is subject to winterkill, but can produce good fishing for brook trout.

Beth—Access is 6.5 miles north on the Spring Canyon Road from Highway 150 and then west for 0.25 mile on a marked spur road. Pressure is heavy for a sizable population of brook trout.

Big Elk—From Highway 150, proceed north on the Norway Flats Road and then the Lake Country Trail. The last mile of the road is four-wheel drive only. Access is also possible from the Crystal Lake Trailhead on 7 miles of the Lake Country Trail. That trail is difficult to follow between Island and Big Elk. Cutthroat and brook trout can be caught at Big Elk.

Blue—Access to Blue is 1.25 miles beyond Buckeye Lake on a well-marked jeep road (Forest Road 531). Blue has brook trout and has been planted with grayling.

Booker—This is one of three lakes situated on the Provo-Weber Drainage Divide at the foot of Mt. Watson. Booker is about 200 yards northwest of Clyde Lake. The lake has a small population of brook trout.

Brook—Winterkill is a problem here, but fishing can be good for brook trout. Access is 4 miles south and west of the Crystal Lake Trailhead on the Lake Country and Weir Lake Trails.

Buckeye—This lake receives intense pressure for planted brook trout. Access is 4.75 miles north from Highway 150 on the Spring Canyon Road to the Buckeye Lake turnoff, then 0.25 mile north on a rough road. Catch-and-release is a good ethic to practice here due to heavy pressure.

Clegg—The major portion of this lake is shallow, so winterkill is always possible. However, the lake is planted with brook trout and reached 1.5 miles northwest of the Bald Mountain Trailhead on the Notch Mountain Trail.

Cliff—Pan-size cutthroat trout are the norm at this lake 0.5 mile north of the Crystal Lake Trailhead on the Watson-Clyde Trail. The trail is not marked, but it is easy to find on the northwestern extremity of Upper Lily Lake.

Clyde—Fishing pressure is moderate for cutthroat at Clyde. It is reached 1.5 miles north of the Crystal Lake Trailhead on the unmarked and indistinct Watson-Clyde Trail that begins near Upper Lily Lake.

Crystal—This lake is 200 yards west of the Crystal Lake Trailhead on the North Fork Trail. The lake sees intense pressure and is stocked heavily with brook trout.

Cutthroat—Contrary to its name, brook trout are the fish you will catch here. Cutthroat is 1 mile west of the Long Lake Dam within sight of the Lake Country Trail. It is 3 miles from the Crystal Lake Trailhead.

Diamond—A productive lake with brook trout, Diamond lies in a large meadow at the head of the easternmost tributary to Trial Lake.

Divide #1—This is one of three lakes on the drainage divide between the Weber and Provo Basins. It is slightly more than 0.25 mile northwest of Clyde Lake on an indistinct trail. The lake has brook trout, and pressure is light.

Duck—With brook trout and cutthroat, Duck gets moderate to heavy pressure. It is 1.25 miles beyond Long Lake on the Lake Country Trail. Duck is 3.25 miles from the Crystal Lake Trailhead.

Fire—Access to Fire is 150 yards south of Junior Lake in the North Fork Drainage. Pressure is moderate to light for cutthroat trout.

Provo River Drainage

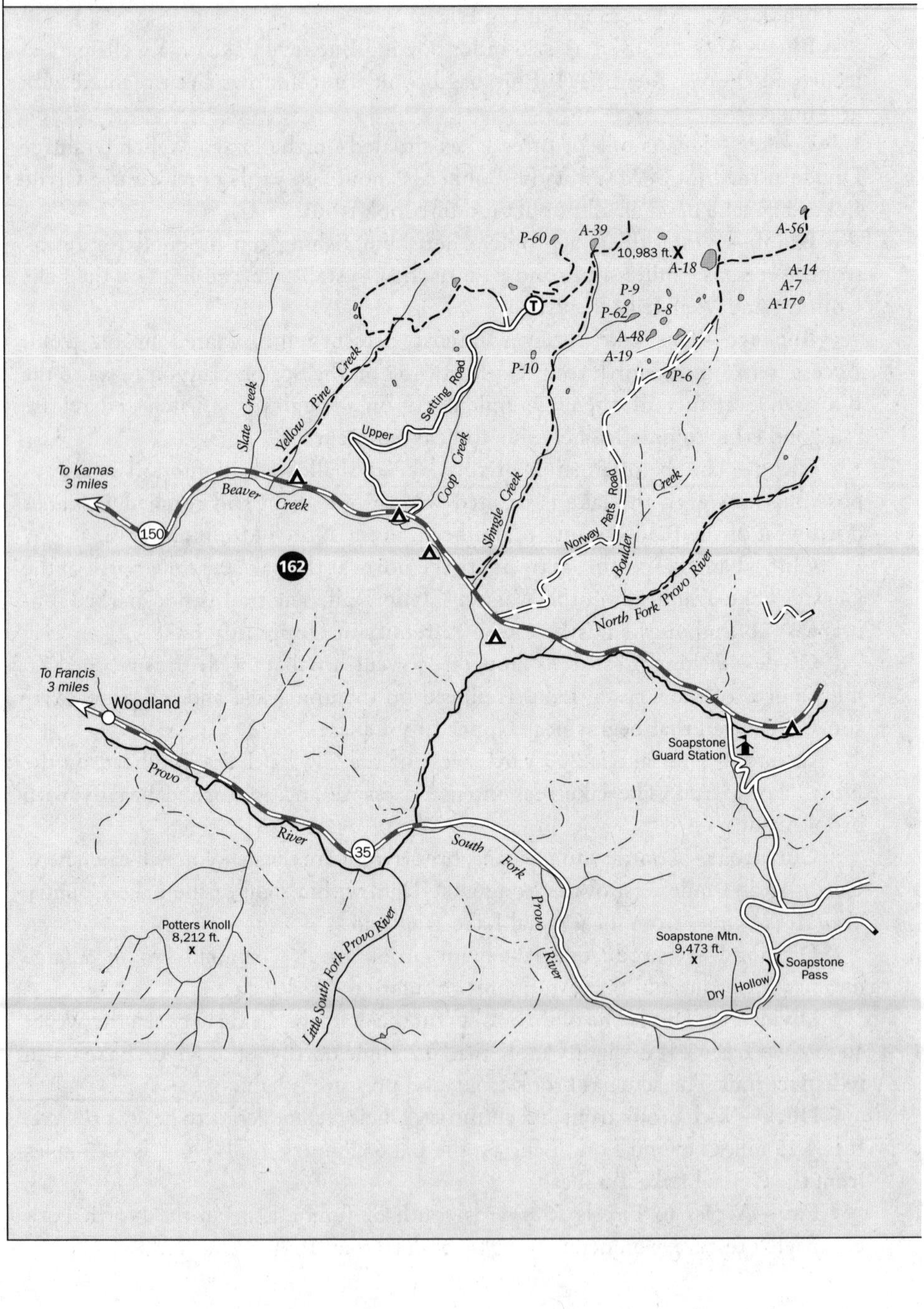

To Kamas
3 miles

150

162

To Francis
3 miles
Woodland

P-60   A-39   A-56
        10,983 ft. X   A-14
             A-18   A-7
         P-9   A-17
    P-62   P-8
       A-48
      A-19   P-6
P-10

Slate Creek
Yellow Pine Creek
Beaver   Creek
Upper   Setting Road
Coop Creek
Shingle Creek
Norway Flats Road
Boulder   Creek
North Fork Provo River

Soapstone
Guard Station

Provo

River

35

South   Fork

Provo   River

Little South Fork Provo River

Potters Knoll
8,212 ft.
X

Soapstone Mtn.
9,473 ft.
X

Dry Hollow

Soapstone
Pass

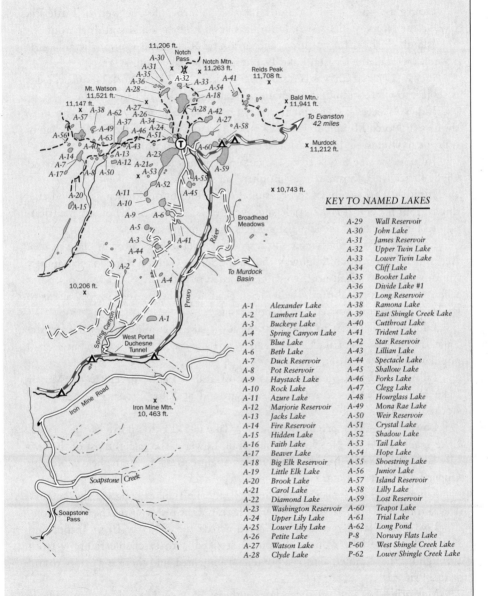

Haystack—Expect company when fishing Haystack. It is 0.5 mile west of the Spring Canyon Road on a side road limited to four-wheel-drive vehicles. The lake has brook and cutthroat trout.

Hidden—Stocked brook trout are the catch at Hidden. Access is 2.25 miles south of Weir Lake on a poor portion of the Weir Lake Trail. It is 5 miles from the Crystal Lake Trailhead.

Hourglass—Set at the base of a talus slope 0.25 mile due west of Little Elk Lake in the Norway Flats Area, Hourglass has both brook and cutthroat trout.

Island—Fishing for cutthroat and brook trout at Island is unpredictable. It is 3.5 miles west of the Crystal Lake Trailhead on the Lake County Trail.

Jacks—Located 200 yards east of Weir Lake in the North Fork Drainage, Jacks is subject to winterkill but it maintains a small population of brook trout.

James—Access is 0.25 mile north of Divide #1 Lake along the inlet stream to the foot of Notch Mountain. It is 2.25 miles from the Crystal Lake Trailhead. James is prone to winterkill, but it is stocked frequently with brook trout.

John—Pan-size brook trout are common at this lake 0.125 mile northeast of Clyde Lake. The lake appears as "Booker" on some maps.

Junior—This is subject to occasional winterkill, but is known as a good cutthroat trout fishery. It is 0.25 mile southwest of Island Lake. The outlet is a tributary to Fire Lake, so if the lake fishing gets slow, hit the stream.

Lambert—Pond lilies make this a scenic but sometimes difficult place to fish. Access is 2 miles north of Highway 150 on the Spring Canyon Road to the Lambert Meadows turnoff. Head northwest on this road past the large meadow to a point where the road turns abruptly west. Then head northeast on foot for 300 yards to the lake. Lambert is stocked with brook trout.

Lillian—Trail access to this pretty meadow lake is 2 miles west of the Crystal Lake Trailhead on the Lake County and Weir Lake cutoff trails. Lillian has a small population of brook trout.

Lilly—This lake is just 300 yards east of Teapot Lake adjacent to the Mirror Lake Highway. There is a 14-unit campground at Lilly. Pressure is heavy for stocked catchable rainbow and brook trout.

Lower Lily—This productive meadow lake is 200 yards north of the Crystal Lake Trailhead on the Notch Mountain Trail. Lower is the easternmost of the two Lily lakes. Lower Lily has brook trout, and angling pressure can be heavy. Nearby Upper Lily is not stocked.

Long—Access is 2 miles west of the Crystal Lake Trailhead on the Lake Country Trail. Brook and cutthroat trout are caught here, but the reservoir sees heavy pressure.

Lost—This large reservoir is located across the highway from Teapot and Lilly Lakes. The lake winterkills, but is stocked with catchable rainbow trout throughout the summer. This is a popular fishing area, and there is a campground with 34 sites.

Marjorie—Located on the ridge southeast of Weir Lake, Marjorie contains grayling that survive despite low water in the winter. Access is 2.5 miles west of the

Crystal Lake Trailhead on the Lake Country and Weir Lake Trails. At Weir, head 0.125 mile to the southeast. Pressure is moderate.

Petite (Junior #5)—Access is 0.75 mile north of the Crystal Lake Trailhead on the unmarked Watson-Clyde Trail. The lake has a small and wary population of brook trout.

Pot—Stocked with brook trout, Pot is 0.25 mile southwest of Weir on the Weir Lake Cutoff Trail. It is 2.75 miles from the Crystal Lake Trailhead.

Ramona—Light pressure and stocked brook trout should make for good fishing here. Ramona is on a ridge 0.25 mile northeast of Island Lake in the North Fork Drainage. It is 3.75 miles from the Crystal Lake Trailhead.

Rock—Stocked frequently with brook trout, Rock provides good fishing despite suffering winterkill. It is slightly more than 0.25 mile west of Haystack Lake. There is no clearly defined trail to the lake.

Shadow—A half mile south of Washington Reservoir, Shadow has a good population of brook trout. Fishing pressure can be heavy.

Shingle Creek, East—Access is 6.5 miles north of Highway 150 on the Upper Setting Road to the trailhead, then 1.5 miles northeast on the Upper Setting Pack Trail. Access is also possible on the Shingle Creek Pack Trail from Highway 150. Brook trout compete with rough fish in this lake.

Shingle Creek, Lower—Trails do not go to Lower Shingle Creek. Head east from the Upper Setting Trailhead for 1.5 miles over steep terrain to the lake. Pressure is light for brook trout.

Shingle Creek, West—Access is 1.75 miles north of the Upper Setting Trailhead along a logging road blocked to vehicles. The lake is stocked with brook trout.

Spectacle—Large expanses of yellow pond lilies cover the lake. Brook trout live under them. Access is 4.5 miles north of Highway 150 on the Spring Canyon Road to a small roadside pond, and then west for 0.25 mile to Spectacle.

Star—Located 1 mile northeast of Trial Lake, Star has cutthroat and brook trout. At Trial, find the major inlet stream and follow it north to a small pond on the tributary. The reservoir is located at the top of this tributary stream.

Tail—Pressure is heavy at this lake 0.5 mile southwest of the dam at Washington Reservoir. Tail has a good population of brook and rainbow trout.

Teapot—This natural lake is 1 mile east of the Trial Lake turnoff on Highway 150, about 27 miles east of Kamas. The lake gets heavy pressure due to its proximity to the highway. Teapot is stocked with rainbow and albino trout, as well as brook trout.

Trial—This popular lake is 0.5 mile off of the Mirror Lake Highway. At the Trial Lake turnoff, follow FR 042 to the lake and the 60-unit campground. Trial is stocked with rainbow and albino trout, as well as brook trout fingerling. It may also have some cutthroat and grayling.

Trident—Follow the Spring Canyon Road slightly more than 6.25 miles north from Highway 150 to Trident. The shallow lake contains brook trout and receives a lot of pressure.

Lower Twin—This lake is small and situated in rocky terrain immediately south of Upper Twin Lake. Access is 2.25 miles north of the Crystal Lake Trailhead on the Notch Mountain Trail. Leave the trail at the point where it begins the last incline to Notch Pass, and head directly west for 0.125 mile to the Twin Lakes Basin. Lower Twin contains brook and cutthroat trout.

Upper Twin—Very similar to Lower Twin, this lake contains brook trout. The Twins receive heavy to moderate angling pressure.

Wall—This sizable reservoir is 1 mile north of the Crystal Lake Trailhead on the Notch Mountain Trail. Pressure for stocked cutthroat trout is heavy.

Washington—Access is 0.75 mile west of Highway 150 at the Trial Lake Cut-off to the Crystal Lake Road. Proceed west for 0.25 mile over a rough road to Washington. Rainbow trout, brook trout, and cutthroat trout are all planted here. Pressure is heavy.

Watson—Pressure is moderate at this lake 1 mile north of the Crystal Lake Trailhead on the Watson-Clyde Trail. Brook trout are stocked here.

Weir—Directly downstream from Long Reservoir, Weir is 2.5 miles west of the Crystal Lake Trailhead on the Lake Country and Weir Lake Trails. Weir has cutthroat and had grayling at one time.

163 Duchesne River Drainage

Some of the most popular lakes in the Uinta Mountains are found in this drainage. Thirty-eight of the 62 lakes in the Duchesne Drainage support fish. Access is from Highway 150 east of Kamas and Highway 35 north of Hanna. The Highline and

Angler fly fishing for trout at Blue Lake in the Naturalist Basin of the Uinta Mountains.

Mirror Lake are two major trailheads that start off Highway 150. The Sawmill Flat and Grandview Trailheads are accessed from Highway 35.

The Highline Trail is a major access route to the primitive area of the Naturalist Basin and the Packard Lake Trail, as well as the headwater region of the Rock Creek Drainage over the top of Rocky Sea Pass. Waters on the eastern rim are reached primarily from the Grandview Trailhead (reached from Highway 35 near the Stockmore Guard Station on Forest Road 144 to its junction with Forest Road 315). Minor access routes include Olga Lake Trail, Duchesne River Trail, East Fork Trail, Skinner Cutoff Trail, Pinto Lake Trail, Mirror Lake Trail, Blue Lake Trail, and Fehr Lake Trail.

Blue—Brook trout fishing is fast at Blue. The lake is reached on the Highline Trail for 5 miles east to the Blue Lake Trail junction, and then 0.75 mile over steep terrain.

Blythe—Although it has occasional winterkill, Blythe is stocked with brook trout regularly. It is located about 0.5 mile northeast of the Mirror Lake Trailhead. There is no trail, but the lake is easily located.

Bonnie—Located about 150 yards south of Highway 150 near the Scout Lake turnoff on a well-established trail, Bonnie sees a lot of pressure for its brook trout. Access is also possible on 1 mile of trail from the Mirror Lake Trailhead.

Broadhead—Situated on a ledge about 0.75 mile south of the Little Deer Creek Dam, Broadhead is reached by the Duchesne Tunnel Road. Fishing is for brook trout.

Bud—Small brookies make up the fishery at Bud. It is located 75 yards south of Highway 150 near the Butterfly Lake Campground. Most pressure is day use, and the small lake often suffers from winterkill.

Butterfly—At Hayden Pass on Highway 150, Butterfly is immediately across the highway from the Highline Trailhead. Butterfly is stocked heavily with rainbow and albino catchables and brook trout fingerling.

Carolyn—Access is 6 miles south and east on the Highline Pack Trail to about 0.5 mile short of the Olga Lake Trail junction. From there, proceed south 200 yards along the trail. Carolyn maintains a good population of arctic grayling. Pressure is moderate.

Castle—Trails are not present, but Castle is a little more than 0.25 mile west of Butterfly Lake along the base of a talus ridge and past several smaller ponds. There is a small population of cutthroat in Castle.

D-19—This large population of brook trout is commonly ignored by anglers choosing to fish Bonnie Lake instead. D-19 is immediately south of Bonnie.

D-26—Located on a steep talus ridge 0.25 mile north of Echo Lake, D-26 has no trail but it is stocked with brook trout.

Echo—This popular lake is 5.25 miles north on the Murdock Basin Road. At the Echo Lake turnoff, head north for 0.5 mile along a rough road. Echo has a large population of brook trout and some goldens.

Everman—Access is 5.25 miles east on the Highline and Naturalist Basin Pack Trails. Leave the trail at the head of the large meadow below Jordan Lake and

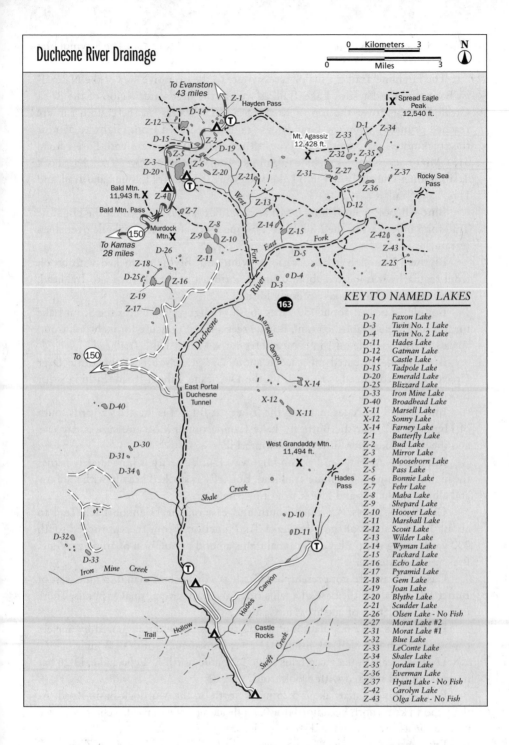

Duchesne River Drainage

Kilometers 0 — 3

Miles 0 — 3

N

To Evanston 43 miles
Z-1
Hayden Pass
D-14
Z-12
D-15
Z-2
Mt. Agassiz 12,428 ft.
D-1
Z-33
Z-34
D-19
Z-5
Z-3
Z-6
D-20
Z-20
Z-21
Z-32
Z-35
Z-31
Z-27
Z-37
Rocky Sea Pass
Z-36
Spread Eagle Peak 12,540 ft.
Bald Mtn. 11,943 ft.
Z-4
West Fork
Z-13
D-12
Bald Mtn. Pass
Z-7
Murdock Mtn.
Z-8
Z-14
Z-15
East Fork
Z-42
Z-43
To Kamas 28 miles
D-26
Z-9
Z-10
Z-25
Z-18
Z-11
D-5
D-25
Z-16
Z-19
D-3
D-4
Z-17
163
150
Marsell Canyon
Duchesne River
X-14
East Portal Duchesne Tunnel
X-12
X-11
D-40
D-30
West Grandaddy Mtn. 11,494 ft.
D-31
D-34
Hades Pass
Shale Creek
D-10
D-11
D-32
D-33
Iron Mine Creek
Hades Canyon
Trail Hollow
Castle Rocks
Swift Creek

KEY TO NAMED LAKES

D-1	Faxon Lake
D-3	Twin No. 1 Lake
D-4	Twin No. 2 Lake
D-11	Hades Lake
D-12	Gatman Lake
D-14	Castle Lake
D-15	Tadpole Lake
D-20	Emerald Lake
D-25	Blizzard Lake
D-33	Iron Mine Lake
D-40	Broadhead Lake
X-11	Marsell Lake
X-12	Sonny Lake
X-14	Farney Lake
Z-1	Butterfly Lake
Z-2	Bud Lake
Z-3	Mirror Lake
Z-4	Mooseborn Lake
Z-5	Pass Lake
Z-6	Bonnie Lake
Z-7	Fehr Lake
Z-8	Maba Lake
Z-9	Shepard Lake
Z-10	Hoover Lake
Z-11	Marshall Lake
Z-12	Scout Lake
Z-13	Wilder Lake
Z-14	Wyman Lake
Z-15	Packard Lake
Z-16	Echo Lake
Z-17	Pyramid Lake
Z-18	Gem Lake
Z-19	Joan Lake
Z-20	Blythe Lake
Z-21	Scudder Lake
Z-26	Olsen Lake - No Fish
Z-27	Morat Lake #2
Z-31	Morat Lake #1
Z-32	Blue Lake
Z-33	LeConte Lake
Z-34	Shaler Lake
Z-35	Jordan Lake
Z-36	Everman Lake
Z-37	Hyatt Lake - No Fish
Z-42	Carolyn Lake
Z-43	Olga Lake - No Fish

proceed east for 200 yards. The lake is subject to winterkill, but it is planted with brook trout and sees little pressure.

Farney—Stocked with cutthroat, Farney is accessed 5 miles north of the Grand View Trailhead on Grandaddy Trail to Fish Hatchery Lake, and then 0.5 mile west through timber. The lake can also be reached by following the Marsell Canyon Creek southeast for 3 miles from the Duchesne River Trail above the East Portal of the Duchesne Tunnel.

Fehr—Access is 0.25 mile east of Highway 150 on the well-marked Fehr Lake Trail that begins across the highway from Moosehorn Lake. Fehr is popular and has heavy day-use pressure for its large population of small brook trout.

Gem—Gem does not appear on USGS topo maps but it is reached by heading 0.5 mile northwest from Echo Lake. Follow the major inlet west of Echo to Joan Lake and then head northeast along Joan's major inlet stream. Brook and cutthroat populations inhabit Gem.

Hades—Located about 0.75 mile northwest of the Grandview Trailhead. It's in Hades Canyon above the Defas Dude Ranch, and it features brook trout.

Hoover—Access is 8 miles north and east of Highway 150 on the Murdock Basin Road to the Hoover Lake turnoff. The lake is about 100 yards to the northwest of the turnoff. Hoover has a good population of brook trout.

Joan—There is no trail to Joan but it is reached over rocky terrain by heading 0.25 mile west of Echo Lake. A good population of brook and cutthroat trout sees moderate angling pressure. Try the stream between Joan and Gem for some good fishing as well.

Jordan—Brook trout inhabit this lake in the Naturalist Basin. Reach it 5.75 miles from the Highline Trailhead on the Highline and Naturalist Basin Trails. The outlet stream also offers some good fishing.

LeConte—Access is 0.5 mile northwest of Jordan Lake over rocky terrain. Cutthroat trout can be found here, but the lake does suffer periodically from winterkill.

Maba—A small population of brook trout inhabit Maba. Access is 50 yards north of Hoover Lake and approximately 75 yards west of the Murdock Basin Road. Pressure is heavy.

Marsell—At the base of West Grandaddy Mountain in the Marsell Canyon Drainage, Marsell is stocked with cutthroat. The lake is reached on the Grandaddy Trail north from the Grandview Trailhead.

Marshall—Access is 7 miles north and east on the Murdock Basin Road from Highway 150 to an unmarked turnoff and then 0.5 mile west. Access is also available on the Fehr Lake Trail from Highway 150. Marshall is stocked with brook trout and may contain some cutthroat.

Mirror—This is the most recognizable of the more than 1,000 lakes in the Uintas. It is 32 miles northeast of Kamas on the Mirror Lake Highway (Highway 150). Fishing and camping pressure is heavy, and there is even a small concrete ramp for launching small craft. The lake is stocked on a regular basis with catchable-size rainbow and albino trout. It also gets some fingerling brook trout. Canoes are popular at Mirror, and the shoreline is often crowded.

Moosehorn—Located at the foot of Bald Mountain 0.5 mile south of Mirror Lake on Highway 150, Moosehorn receives a substantial amount of pressure for its stocked rainbow and albino catchables.

Morat #1—Access is 5 miles east of Highway 150 on the Highline and Naturalist Basin Trails to the Blue-Jordan junction and then 0.5 mile north on the Blue Lake Trail. Morat #1 is stocked with cutthroat.

Morat #2—Immediately east of Morat #1, Morat #2 doesn't have as many cutthroat.

Packard—Perched on a steep ledge overlooking the East Fork of the Duchesne River, Packard has a fair number of brook trout. It is reached 2.5 miles southeast on the Highline Trail to the well-marked Packard Lake cutoff and then 1 mile to the trail's end.

Pass—This lake sits adjacent to Highway 150 0.5 mile north of the Mirror Lake Campground. The lake is stocked regularly with rainbow and albino catchables and receives heavy pressure.

Pyramid—Access is 5.25 miles north and east of Highway 150 on the Murdock Basin Road to Echo Lake. Then proceed north to the first left-hand turn and head west a little more than 0.25 mile for brook trout.

Scout—The lake is 0.5 mile west of Highway 150 on a foot trail beginning at the Camp Steiner turnoff and parking area. Camp Steiner is a Boy Scout summer camp, so expect company when fishing for rainbows.

Shaler—This Naturalist Basin lake is 0.75 mile northeast of Jordan Lake on the Naturalist Basin Trail. It is 6.5 miles from the Highline Trailhead. Fly fishing for cutthroat can be exceptional, especially in the late summer.

Shepard—Located 0.125 mile west of Hoover Lake in the Murdock Basin, Shepard has good populations of brook and cutthroat trout.

Sonny—Although it may winterkill, Sonny is stocked with cutthroat and receives moderate angling pressure. It is 150 yards northwest of Marsell Lake in Marsell Canyon.

Wilder—Access is 2.5 miles southeast of the Highline Trailhead to the Packard Lake Trail and then 0.25 mile south. There is a good population of brook trout here.

Wyman—Located 0.5 mile south of Wilder on the Packard Lake Trail, Wyman sometimes suffers winterkill but is stocked frequently with brook trout.

164 Rock Creek Drainage

This is the largest drainage on the south slope of the Uinta Mountains. It is divided into four drainages: Squaw Basin, Mainstream Rock Creek, Fall Creek, and Grandaddy Basin. The Rock Creek Drainage has more than 120 lakes and is known for its scenic beauty and vast panoramas.

The major point of access is the trailhead at Upper Stillwater Reservoir. It is reached from Highway 87 out of Mountain Home on Forest Road 134, an asphalt road for 22 miles northwest to the reservoir. The reservoir is also reached from

Hanna and Highway 35, which hooks up with FR 134 about 12 miles from the reservoir. The Rock Creek Campground has more than 20 sites.

A trail follows the main stem of Rock Creek up the central drainage basin. Spur trails take off from the main trail and follow the West Fork of Rock Creek and Fish Creek to the Grandaddy Basin, the East Fork of Rock Creek, and Squaw Basin Creek to Squaw Basin and the Rudolph Lake area. Follow Fall Creek to areas in the eastern section of the central basin. The Grandaddy Basin can also be reached from the southwest via the Grandview transfer camp in Hades Canyon. Grandview is reached on Forest Road 315 from Highway 35 (Forest Road 144) between the Hades Campground and Defas Dude Ranch.

Allen—About 0.75 mile east of Bedground Lake, Allen sits in an open meadow. It is populated with arctic grayling. The lake is about 11 miles from the Upper Stillwater Trailhead, 9.5 miles from Mirror Lake, and 9 miles from the Grandview Trailhead. There is no trail from Bedground to Allen Lake.

Amien—This lake, stocked with brook trout, is about 300 yards west of Shamrock Lake in Squaw Basin. It is 9 miles from the Upper Stillwater Dam. Access to the lake for the final 0.25 mile is cross-country and easiest from the southwest.

Anderson—Some 13.5 miles from the Upper Stillwater Trailhead, Anderson is 100 yards east of the trail and 300 yards south of Phinney Lake. The lake gets heavy to moderate pressure on the brook trout stocked there by aircraft.

Arta—Stocked cutthroat make up the catch at this lake, about 0.5 mile west from the end of the logging road along the South Fork of Rock Creek.

Audry—This seldom-visited pond overlooks Rock Creek below the Stillwater Dam. Access is difficult. The lake is reached by taking the Miners Gulch jeep road, FR 134, to Bear Lake (no fish). From there, it is 2.5 miles northwest along the timbered, rocky mountainside. Pressure for aircraft-planted brook trout is light.

Bedground—Between Rainbow Lake and Four Lakes Basin, Bedground is east of the trail, 10 miles from the Upper Stillwater Trailhead. Some large brook trout are caught in this lake.

Betsey—A few hundred yards west of Grandaddy Lake, Betsey gets heavy use. It is stocked with cutthroat.

Black—Fifteen miles up from the Upper Stillwater Trailhead, Black is on a well-marked trail and is popular with scout troops. A large population of brook trout, bolstered with some cutthroat, seems to handle the pressure well.

Boot—On a grassy basin at the head of the Rock Creek Drainage, Boot is 16.5 miles from Upper Stillwater. It is 1 mile north of the main trail across rocky meadows. The lake features a naturally reproducing population of cutthroat.

Brinkley—Aerial stocking sustains moderate pressure for brook trout at this lake west of the trail to Black Lake.

Cabin—An old sheep trail leads from Rudolph Lake over the saddle to Rudolph Mountain. Just over 1 mile on the rough trail, you will come to a cabin. The lake is stocked with brook trout.

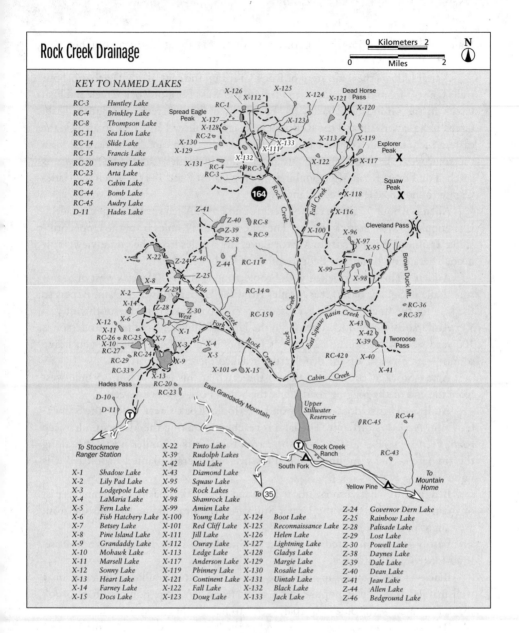

KEY TO NAMED LAKES

RC-3	Huntley Lake
RC-4	Brinkley Lake
RC-8	Thompson Lake
RC-11	Sea Lion Lake
RC-14	Slide Lake
RC-15	Francis Lake
RC-20	Survey Lake
RC-23	Arta Lake
RC-42	Cabin Lake
RC-44	Bomb Lake
RC-45	Audry Lake
D-11	Hades Lake

To Stockmore Ranger Station	X-22	Pinto Lake			
	X-39	Rudolph Lakes			
	X-42	Mid Lake			
X-1	Shadow Lake	X-43	Diamond Lake		
X-2	Lily Pad Lake	X-95	Squaw Lake		
X-3	Lodgepole Lake	X-96	Rock Lakes		
X-4	LaMaria Lake	X-98	Shamrock Lake		
X-5	Fern Lake	X-99	Amien Lake		
X-6	Fish Hatchery Lake	X-100	Young Lake	X-124	Boot Lake
X-7	Betsey Lake	X-101	Red Cliff Lake	X-125	Reconnaissance Lake
X-8	Pine Island Lake	X-111	Jill Lake	X-126	Helen Lake
X-9	Grandaddy Lake	X-112	Ouray Lake	X-127	Lightning Lake
X-10	Mohawk Lake	X-113	Ledge Lake	X-128	Gladys Lake
X-11	Marsell Lake	X-117	Anderson Lake	X-129	Margie Lake
X-12	Sonny Lake	X-119	Phinney Lake	X-130	Rosalie Lake
X-13	Heart Lake	X-121	Continent Lake	X-131	Uintah Lake
X-14	Farney Lake	X-122	Fall Lake	X-132	Black Lake
X-15	Docs Lake	X-123	Doug Lake	X-133	Jack Lake

Z-24	Governor Dern Lake
Z-25	Rainbow Lake
Z-28	Palisade Lake
Z-29	Lost Lake
Z-30	Powell Lake
Z-38	Daynes Lake
Z-39	Dale Lake
Z-40	Dean Lake
Z-41	Jean Lake
Z-44	Allen Lake
Z-46	Bedground Lake

Continent—Southwest of Dead Horse Pass, 15.5 miles from Upper Stillwater, Continent contains cutthroat and brook trout.

Dale—Pressure for stocked brook trout is heavy here. In the popular Four Lakes Basin, it is almost 11 miles from the Upper Stillwater Trailhead and 9 miles from Grandview.

Daynes—This is one of the largest lakes in the Four Lakes Basin. It is a few hundred yards south of Dale Lake. Brook trout and grayling are caught here.

Dean—Just northeast of Jean Lake, Dean is in the extreme corner of the Four Lakes Basin at the base of steep cliffs and talus slopes. Daynes Lake is just to the southwest. The lake is stocked with brook trout.

Diamond—About 0.5 mile off the trail, Diamond can be hard to find. It can be accessed by following the outlet of Mid Lake northwest for 0.5 mile. Diamond, stocked with brook trout by aircraft, is 9 miles from the Upper Stillwater Trailhead.

Docs—This isolated lake can be difficult to find. There are no trails to Doc's, and the best way to find it is by heading 3 miles west of Rock Creek Bridge. Needless to say, fishing for the stocked brook trout is light.

Doug—Less than 0.5 mile south of Boot Lake, Doug is an on-stream pond with pan-size cutthroat. Pressure is light.

Fern—Best access is via the faint trail that cuts off the main trail just south of LaMaria Lake. It is just over 8 miles from the Upper Stillwater Trailhead. Stocked brook trout are the catch.

Fish Hatchery—The large lake in the center of Grandaddy Basin is popular with hiking groups. It is more than 11 miles from the Upper Stillwater Trailhead and about 5.5 from Grandview. Fishing pressure is heavy for stocked cutthroat and some brookies.

Gibby—About 75 yards north of Grandaddy Lake's northwestern arm, Gibby has some brook trout, but fishing is spotty.

Gladys—Pan-size brook trout make up the fishing opportunity at Gladys. The lake is east of the main trail about 16.5 miles from the Upper Stillwater Trailhead and 12.5 from Mirror Lake via the Rocky Sea Pass.

Governor Dern—Along the trail a short distance from Pinto Lake in the Grandaddy Basin, the shallow lake is stocked with brook trout. Occasionally, a cutthroat is landed.

Grandaddy—This is the most popular lake in the Uintas that is not accessible by car. At 173 acres, it is by far the largest natural lake in the Uintas. It is just over 3 miles from the Grandview Trailhead and 13.5 miles from Mirror Lake. Pressure is heavy and the lake is not stocked; naturally sustaining populations of brook and cutthroat trout keep anglers busy. The lake is open to year-round fishing, but its tributaries are closed January 1 to 6:00 a.m. the second Saturday of July.

Heart—West of the trail about 0.5 mile southwest of Grandaddy Lake and 2.5 miles from the Grandview Trailhead, Heart sees moderate to heavy pressure for stocked cutthroat trout.

Helen—Periodically planted with brook trout, Helen is located about 0.25 mile north of Lightning Lake, about 15.5 miles from the Upper Stillwater Trailhead and 12 miles from Mirror Lake. Stocked cutthroat make up the catch.

Horseshoe—About 0.75 mile west of Diamond Lake, fishing pressure is light for stocked brook trout.

Huntley—Just south of Brinkley Lake, Huntley is really a series of three interconnected ponds with a naturally reproducing population of brook trout.

Jack—This lake provides good fishing for stocked cutthroat trout. It is west of Ouray Lake and about 100 yards southeast of Jill Lake, about 15.5 miles from the Upper Stillwater Trailhead.

Jean—Just southwest of Dean Lake in the Four Lakes Basin, Jean is stocked with brook trout and gets moderate to heavy pressure. It is just over 11 miles from the Upper Stillwater Trailhead.

Jill—About 100 yards from Jack Lake, Jill provides similar fishing to her brother lake.

Ledge—Winterkill can be a problem, but Ledge is stocked with brook trout. It is located west of the trail 14.5 miles from the Upper Stillwater Trailhead.

Lightning—At the head of Rock Creek Drainage, this lake is 15.5 miles from the Upper Stillwater Trailhead and 12 miles from Mirror Lake. It has a mixed population of cutthroat and brook trout.

Lily Pad—A few hundred feet southeast of Pine Island Lake, Lily Pad is stocked periodically with brook trout. It is 6 miles from the Grandview Trailhead and 8.5 miles from Upper Stillwater.

Lodgepole—This narrow lake is located on a steep hillside northeast of Grandaddy Lake. Pressure is light for stocked brook trout.

Lost—This lake provides marginal fish habitat and has a history of winterkill. It is planted with brook trout on occasion. It is beside the trail about 0.75 mile northeast of the Brinton Meadows Guard Station in Grandaddy Basin.

Margie—Pressure is light for stocked brook trout at this lake just southwest of Rosalie Lake.

Margo—A trail to the lake begins near the west inlet of Pinto. It is less than 0.5 mile away. The lake is stocked with cutthroat trout.

Mid—In heavy timber due north of Rudolph Lakes, Mid offers good fishing for stocked brook trout.

Mohawk—Just 0.75 mile west of Grandaddy Lake on a well-marked trail, this is one of the most popular lakes in the drainage, especially with Scout groups. Pressure is heavy for stocked brook trout and some cutthroat. It is a large lake, so a raft or float tube may help.

Ouray—This shallow pond is about 0.5 mile west of Jack and Jill Lakes, 15 miles from the Upper Stillwater Trailhead. Fly fishing from shore can be excellent for pan-size cutthroat.

Palisade—This lake is 0.5 mile north of the Brinton Meadows in Grandaddy Basin. Brook trout and cutthroat are caught here.

Phinney—Just 0.25 mile north of Anderson Lake, Phinney is popular with hikers. Fishing can be good for brook trout and some cutthroat.

Pine Island—This large lake is 0.75 mile north of Fish Hatchery Lake in Grandaddy Basin. The lake is stocked with brook trout.

Pinto—In the northwestern corner of Grandaddy Basin, Pinto is a few hundred yards northwest of Governor Dern Lake. It is 10 miles from the Upper Stillwater Trailhead and just over 8 miles from both the Grandview and Mirror Lake Trailheads. There's heavy pressure for brook trout here.

Powell—Cutthroat trout are stocked at this lake in the Grandaddy Basin. It is 0.25 mile east of Lost Lake. A spur trail runs to the lake from the main trail at Lost Lake.

Rainbow—In the northern Grandaddy Basin, near a number of major trail junctions, Rainbow is a popular layover for hikers. About 10 miles from the Upper Stillwater Trailhead, Rainbow is stocked with brook trout and has some cutthroat.

Reconnaissance—There is no trail to the lake for the last mile. It is located at the head of the Rock Creek Drainage about 17 miles from the Upper Stillwater Trailhead and 15 miles from Mirror Lake. A self-sustaining population of brook trout and some cutthroat make up the fishing at Reconnaissance.

Rock 1—In the Squaw Basin 10.5 miles from the Upper Stillwater Trailhead, Rock 1 has no trail for the last 0.5 mile. Follow the East Fork of Rock Creek to Rock 2. Rock 1 is 150 yards northwest across a boulder field. There is an abundant population of brook trout in the lake.

Rock 2—From the junction of Ledge Trail and the Squaw Lake Trail, follow the East Fork of Rock Creek upstream about 0.5 mile. The lake is stocked with brook trout and is almost 11 miles from the Upper Stillwater Trailhead.

Rosalie—Situated at the head of the Rock Creek drainage, about 16 miles from the Upper Stillwater Trailhead, Rosalie is 0.75 mile west of Black Lake and west of the trail to Gladys Lake. Pressure is light for stocked brook trout.

Rudolph 1—This is the largest of the three Rudolph Lakes. It is almost 10.5 miles from the Upper Stillwater Trailhead. It is stocked with brook trout.

Rudolph 2—This is the middle lake of the Rudolph chain. It is stocked with brook trout.

Rudolph 3—This is the smallest and easternmost of the Rudolph Lakes. The lake has a history of winterkill, and fishing can be slow. Some fish may migrate from the lower Rudolph lakes.

Sea Lion—On a high bench overlooking the main stem of Rock Creek, Sea Lion is one of the most inaccessible waters in the drainage. It is best to reach it on a steep trail over Cyclone Pass, east of the Four Lakes Basin. The lake is located 1 mile to the southeast across an extensive boulder field and is easily seen from the pass. The lake is stocked with cutthroat, but it may suffer winterkill in particularly harsh winters.

Shadow—About 0.5 mile southeast of the Brinton Meadows Guard Station, Shadow is reached by following the maintained trail from the guard station to Lost Lake. About 0.5 mile east of the guard station, a spur trail leads south to the lake. There is a large number of brook trout and a few cutthroat in the lake.

Shamrock—This lucky lake is 0.5 mile southwest of Squaw Lake and 300 yards east of Amien Lake in the Squaw Basin. It is stocked with brook trout.

Squaw—This diamond-shaped lake is almost 10 miles from the Upper Stillwater Trailhead. It is a popular place to camp for people hiking the Highline Trail. Stocked brook trout fishing is good.

Survey—This lake is 200 yards to the northwest of Arta Lake on top of a high bench. The lake may winterkill in severe winters, but it is stocked with brook trout.

Thompson—You will rarely find company when fishing for brook trout at Thompson. It is a remote lake 0.75 mile north of Cyclone Pass. In fact, it doesn't show up on most maps.

Uintah—Just south of Margie Lake, there is no trail to the lake. Fishing pressure is light.

Upper Stillwater—Due to its easy access, this reservoir is stocked frequently with rainbow catchables. It also has some cutthroat and brook trout.

Young—This small pond is 10.5 miles from the Upper Stillwater Trailhead by way of Ledge Trail. Stocked cutthroat are the catch.

165 Lake Fork Drainage

This major drainage on the south slope of the Uintas has three main tributaries: Lake Fork, Brown Duck, and Fish. Major access begins at Moon Lake, 15 miles north of Mountain Home. In Mountain Home, follow 2100 West to its end; then, Forest Road 131 leads to the lake. There are two main routes from Moon. The Brown Duck Trail goes 7 miles to the west into Brown Duck Basin, where it splits and continues west into the Rock Creek Drainage north of the Clements Reservoir area and East Basin. The Lake Fork Trail follows the main creek north providing access into Ottoson Basin, Lambert Meadows, and Oweep Creek. Lake Fork has 40 lakes with fish.

Amoeba—Access is from Moon Lake on the Lake Fork Trail for 13 miles into the Ottoson Basin and to the base of Cleveland Peak, then north cross-country for 1 mile. The lake is stocked with cutthroat.

Aspen—This small glacial lake is 9 miles from Moon Lake. It sits 0.5 mile between Atwine and X-62, and there is no trail the last 0.5 mile. Aspen is stocked with brook trout.

Atwine—Access is along the Brown Duck–Clements Lake Trail about 9 miles from Moon. Brook trout are caught here.

Big Dog—This lake contains grayling if it doesn't suffer from winterkill. Hike the 7 miles to Brown Duck Lake, then head south cross-country for 1 mile over a talus ridge.

Brown Duck—This is the first lake on the Brown Duck Trail. It is 7 miles from Moon Lake. Natural and planted cutthroat are caught here.

Clements—Wild cutthroat are bolstered with planted fish at Clements. Reach it on the East Basin Trail, which crosses the Clements Lake Dam about 11 miles from Moon Lake.

Crater—At 147 feet, this is the deepest lake in the High Uintas. It is located at the northeast base of Explorer Peak, 17 miles from Moon Lake on the Lake Fork River Trail, which passes within 2 miles of the lake. Fishing for brook trout is usually good.

East Slide—Brook trout are stocked periodically at this lake, which sits about 1.5 miles east-northeast from the confluence of Lake Fork and Oweep Creeks. This is the most inaccessible lake in the drainage. A USGS map is recommended.

Lake Fork Drainage

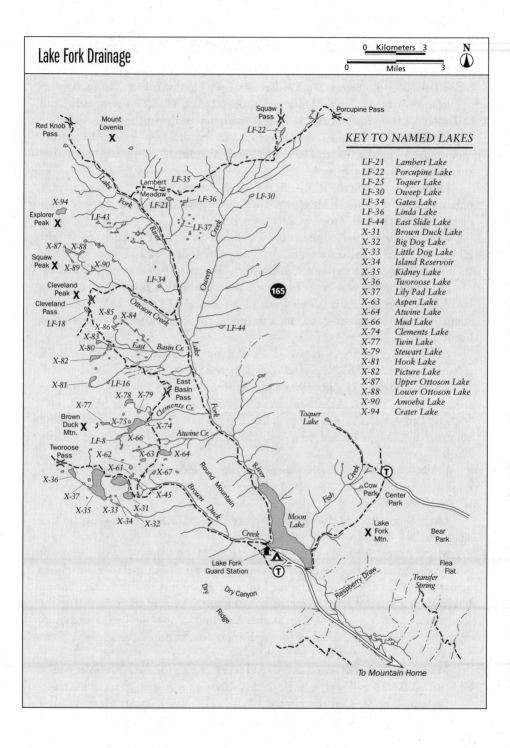

0 Kilometers 3
0 Miles 3

N

KEY TO NAMED LAKES

LF-21	Lambert Lake
LF-22	Porcupine Lake
LF-25	Toquer Lake
LF-30	Oweep Lake
LF-34	Gates Lake
LF-36	Linda Lake
LF-44	East Slide Lake
X-31	Brown Duck Lake
X-32	Big Dog Lake
X-33	Little Dog Lake
X-34	Island Reservoir
X-35	Kidney Lake
X-36	Tworoose Lake
X-37	Lily Pad Lake
X-63	Aspen Lake
X-64	Atwine Lake
X-66	Mud Lake
X-74	Clements Lake
X-77	Twin Lake
X-79	Stewart Lake
X-81	Hook Lake
X-82	Picture Lake
X-87	Upper Ottoson Lake
X-88	Lower Ottoson Lake
X-90	Amoeba Lake
X-94	Crater Lake

Red Knob Pass
Mount Lovenia X
Squaw Pass
Porcupine Pass
LF-22

Explorer Peak X
X-94
Lambert Meadow
LF-35
LF-21
LF-36
LF-30
LF-43
Lake Fork River
LF-37

X-87 X-88
Squaw Peak X
X-89 X-90
LF-34
Oweep Creek
165

Cleveland Peak X
Cleveland Pass
LF-18
X-85 X-84
X-86
X-83
X-80
X-82
East Basin Cr.
LF-44
Lake
X-81
LF-16
East Basin Pass
Fork

X-77
Brown Duck Mtn. X
X-78 X-79
Clements Cr.
X-75
X-74
LF-8
X-66
Atwine Cr.
Toquer Lake

Tworoose Pass
X-62
X-63 X-64
X-36
X-61
X-67
X-45
Round Mountain
River
Cow Park
Center Park
T

X-37
X-35 X-33 X-31
X-34 X-32
Brown Duck
Fish Creek
Moon Lake
Lake Fork Mtn. X
Bear Park

Creek
Lake Fork Guard Station
T
Flea Flat
Transfer Spring

Dry
Dry Canyon
Raspberry Draw

Ridge

To Mountain Home

Gates—Brook trout fishing is light at Gates. Access it from a small trail where the Ottoson Basin Trail crosses the creek. In another 1.5 miles you will be fishing.

Hook—Located 1 mile south of Picture Lake, Hook is about 18 miles from Moon Lake over the Brown Duck–Clements Trail. Hook has brook trout.

Island—Between Brown Duck and Kidney Lakes, Island is on the main trail about 8 miles from Moon Lake. Fishing pressure for cutthroat can be heavy.

Kidney—This is the second-largest lake in the drainage. It is 9 miles from Moon Lake along the Brown Duck Basin Trail. Cutthroat are the main catch, but some brookies are here as well.

Lambert—This alpine lake is on the upper end of the Lake Fork Drainage, 1 mile southeast of Lambert Meadows. Total distance from Moon Lake is 17 miles on the Lake Fork Trail. Brook trout are stocked.

LF-16—The lake is 0.5 mile due east of Hook Lake in the southern part of the East Basin. No trail exists, but it can be reached by following a series of meadows 0.5 mile from the main trail in a southwesterly direction. Brook trout are stocked.

LF-35—This small spring-fed pond has an outlet that flows 150 yards east into Linda Lake. Access is 0.5 mile east on a trail from Lambert Lake, then turn south and go cross-country 0.25 mile to Linda. LF-35 has a small population of brook trout.

LF-37—Located about 1 mile south of Linda Lake, access is via the outlet stream from Linda. The lake is stocked with brook trout.

LF-43—About 1.25 miles east-southeast of Crater, LF-43 sits just north of the saddle near the long ridge that separates Ottoson Basin. The lake has brook trout.

Lily Pad—A small meadow pond, Lily Pad has a small population of brook and cutthroat trout. It is located on the stream that connects Tworoose and Kidney Lakes.

Linda—Access is via the Highline Trail east 0.5 mile from Lambert Lake, then cross-country due south 0.25 mile to a boggy meadow where the lake sits. Pressure is light for brook trout.

Little Dog—About 0.5 mile southwest of Brown Duck Lake off the main trail sits Little Dog. Brook trout inhabit Little Dog.

Moon Lake—Situated in a deep glacial valley, Moon Lake is popular because it is so easily accessed from Mountain Home. Head north out of Mountain Home across the Indian reservation. The road turns to gravel just past Mountain Home, but is paved again just after it enters national forest. The road leads directly to the lake, about 15 miles from Mountain Home. A 57-unit campground and lodge serves visitors at Moon Lake. Fishing is for rainbow, brook, cutthroat, and splake. Trout limit is four, but only two may be splake.

Mud—Stocked with brook trout, Mud is reached by following the inlet stream of Atwine Lake 0.5 mile west. Mud is the first lake on the stream. It has brook trout.

Oweep—Access is on the Highline Trail west from Lambert Meadow for 4 miles, then south 1 mile off the trail to the long talus ridge. It has a population of brook trout.

Ottoson, Lower — On the upper end of Ottoson Basin, this lake has a good population of cutthroat trout. It lies 0.25 mile south of Upper Ottoson.

Ottoson, Upper — This lake is 15 miles on the Lake Fork Trail from Moon Lake into the Ottoson Basin. There is no trail for the last 2 miles over open tundra. Pressure is light for cutthroat trout.

Picture — Access is via the Brown Duck–Clements Lake Trail over East Basin Pass. It is 17 miles from Moon Lake, and the trail is vague for the last mile. Fishing is good for stocked rainbow trout.

Porcupine — On the southern base of Squaw Pass, Porcupine provides headwaters to Oweep Creek in the Upper Lake Fork Drainage. It is reached by a 16-mile hike via the Lake Fork Trail to Lambert Meadows from Moon Lake. Follow the trail east over tundra toward Squaw Pass for about 8 miles. Pressure is light for brook trout.

Stewart — Access is through the timber about 0.5 mile northwest of the Clements Lake Dam. Brook trout are stocked here.

Toquer — Brook and cutthroat are caught at this lake that is the headwater of Fish Creek. Access is 7 miles via the Fish Creek National Recreation Trail from Moon Lake, or 3 miles via the Hell's Canyon Trail from the west end of Center Park.

Twin — It suffers from winterkill, but is stocked with brook trout. Follow the inlet stream of Clements Lake due west for 1 mile to access it.

Tworoose — This lake sits at the base of Tworoose Pass, 11 miles up the Brown Duck Trail from Moon Lake. The lake has a natural cutthroat trout population.

X-61 — This lake is the second in a series of three meadow ponds located about 0.25 mile northeast of Island Reservoir Dam in Brown Duck Basin. Access is north 0.5 mile on the Clements Reservoir Trail from the trail junction below Brown Duck Reservoir. Follow the stream past X-45 to X-61. There is a small cutthroat population.

X-62 — About 0.5 mile north and west of X-61, this is the third of the three meadows lakes. It also has cutthroat.

X-75 — About 250 yards west of Clements Reservoir, X-75 has a few cutthroat trout.

X-78 — Access is northwest from Clements Reservoir Dam, 1 mile through timber past Stewart Lake. Pressure is light for limited cutthroat.

X-80 — Brook trout and cutthroat call X-80 home. It is in the East Basin, 16 miles on the Brown Duck–Clements Lake Trail from Moon Lake.

X-84 — Access is cross-country 0.25 mile northeast from X-86. Brook trout fishing pressure is light.

X-85 — This is the northernmost of three lakes grouped in the north part of East Basin. Access is along the trail from X-80 in East Basin, 0.5 mile northwest, then northeast 0.5 mile cross-country. Brook trout are caught here.

X-86 — This is the largest of the three lakes grouped in the north part of the East Basin. It has brook trout and is reached on a trail 0.5 mile northwest from X-80, then cross-country northeast for 0.5 mile.

166 Yellowstone Drainage

Located in the middle of the Uinta Mountain Range, the Yellowstone River Drainage drains down the south slope. Kings Peak (13,528 feet) borders the northeast corner of the drainage. Access to the Yellowstone Drainage is via two routes. The first is at the Swift Creek Campground and Trailhead on the Yellowstone River, about 4 miles north of the Yellowstone Guard Station on the Yellowstone River Road (Forest Road 119 out of Mountain Home). The other access point is at the bottom of Long Park about 7 miles up the Hell's Canyon Road (Forest Road 227) from its junction with the Yellowstone River Road. The 25 lakes are actively managed for trout populations. Stream fishing is good in this drainage as well.

Bluebell — Follow the east inlet stream from Spider Lake southwest 0.25 mile to Bluebell. There is an abundant population of brook trout and some cutthroat here.

Doll — Pan-size brook trout are found in Doll. It is accessed 0.75 mile west-northwest of Five Point Lake up a trailless ridge and is 13 miles from Swift Creek Campground.

Drift — Access is 1.25 miles southwest of Five Point Lake or 0.5 mile west from Spider Lake. A small population of brookies is found here.

Five Point Lake — Numerous pan-size brook and cutthroat trout inhabit Five Point. It is reached from the Swift Creek or Hell's Canyon Trailheads with a 12-mile hike.

Gem — Follow the outlet stream from Five Point for 0.5 mile southeast and you will reach Gem. It has brook and cutthroat trout.

Kings — At the southwest base of King's Peak, this lake with cutthroat is reached by following the trail northeast for 3 miles from Tungsten Pass, then turning south cross-country for 2 miles around a talus ridge extending southwest from King's Peak.

Little Superior — Access is 1 mile north of Five Point Lake. There is an abundant population of brook trout here.

Milk — Fishing pressure for brook trout is light. Access is 14 miles via the marked trail that follows the Yellowstone River from Swift Creek Campground or about 11 miles via the Swift Creek drainage trail. Milk sits about 1 mile due north of Bluebell Pass.

North Star — Brook trout are caught here. Reach North Star with a 16.5-mile hike north on the trail from Swift Creek Campground or Hell's Canyon.

Spider — Access is 11 miles north from the Hell's Canyon Trailhead at Long Park. There are a few brook trout and cutthroat in Spider, but pressure is heavy.

Superior — One mile north of Five Point Lake, Superior has brook trout. It is 13 miles from the Swift Creek Trailhead.

Swasey — Pressure is heavy here. Access is from the Hell's Canyon Trailhead for 6 miles. Cutthroat and brook trout are caught here.

Tungsten — Access is about 16 miles north from either the Swift Creek Trailhead or Hell's Canyon. The lake contains brook and cutthroat trout.

X-57 — Access is from Swasey Lake, 1 mile due west up a slope. Small brook trout inhabit the lake.

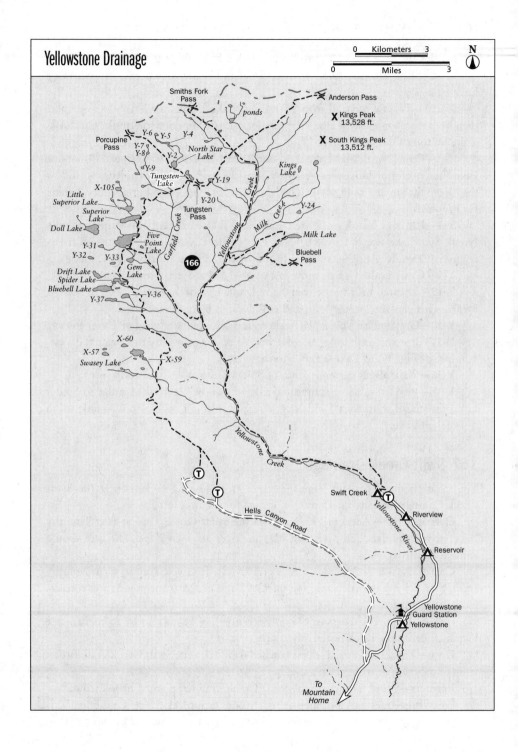

Yellowstone Drainage

0 Kilometers 3

0 Miles 3

N

Smiths Fork Pass

ponds

Anderson Pass

X Kings Peak 13,528 ft.

X South Kings Peak 13,512 ft.

Porcupine Pass

Y-6
Y-5
Y-4
Y-7
Y-8
Y-2

North Star Lake

Y-9

Tungsten Lake

Y-19

Kings Lake

X-105

Little Superior Lake

Superior Lake

Doll Lake

Five Point Lake

Tungsten Pass

Y-20

166

Garfield Creek

Yellowstone

Milk Creek

Y-24

Milk Lake

Bluebell Pass

Y-31
Y-32
Y-33

Gem Lake

Drift Lake
Spider Lake
Bluebell Lake

Y-37

Y-36

X-60

X-57

Swasey Lake

X-59

Yellowstone Creek

Swift Creek

T
T

Hells Canyon Road

Yellowstone River

Riverview

Reservoir

Yellowstone Guard Station

Yellowstone

To Mountain Home

X-59—Brookies are the primary species here, but there are some cutthroat as well. Access is 6 miles north along the Hell's Canyon Trail into Swasey Hole, then northwest following the stream to Swasey Lake. X-59 sits just south of the lake.

X-60—This lake is stocked with cutthroat and is 0.33 mile northwest of Swasey Lake up a slope.

X-105—Follow the trail from Five Point Lake 1 mile north to Superior Lake, then head north-northwest along the inlet past Little Superior for 1 mile. Cutthroat make up the fishing at X-105.

Y-2—From North Star Lake head northeast 1 mile on a trail toward Porcupine Pass, then head northeast cross-country for 0.25 mile. Another choice is to follow the North Star inlet 1 mile north. The lake is seldom visited and offers good fishing for brook trout.

Y-4—Pan-size brook trout are the catch of the day here. Follow the trail from North Star Lake north 1 mile toward Porcupine Pass, then go northeast cross-country 0.25 mile. Another route is to follow the inlet of North Star 1.25 miles.

Y-5—One hundred yards northeast of Y-4, Y-5 also has brook trout.

Y-19—Located next to the trail 0.5 mile due east of Tungsten Lake, the lake is loaded with pan-size brook trout and is 16.5 miles from the trailhead.

Y-20—Grayling have been planted here. It is 0.25 mile southeast of Tungsten Pass.

Y-31—Pressure is light for brook trout. Access is gained by following the western inlet of Five Point Lake 0.5 mile to the west.

Y-36—Walk about 0.3 mile south of Spider Lake. Y-36 has brook trout.

Y-37—From the Hell's Canyon Trailhead, follow the trail 11 miles to Spider Lake, then head southwest 1 mile over rugged terrain. Y-37 is also 0.33 mile south of Bluebell Lake.

167 Swift Creek Drainage

The main trailhead for this drainage starts in Yellowstone Canyon at the Swift Creek Campground, about 15 miles north of Mountain Home.

Carrol, East —Access is 9.5 miles via the Swift Creek Trail to East Timothy Lake, across the dam and northeast 0.5 mile over an open ridge. The lake should contain cutthroat.

Carrol, Lower —Access is 9 miles on the Swift Creek Trail to East Timothy Lake, then 0.5 mile north along the inlet. A large brook trout population receives moderate pressure.

Carrol, Upper —Access is 0.75 mile due north of East Timothy Lake. Pan-size brook trout are the catch of the day.

Deer—This heavily used lake is reached 6 miles up the Swift Creek Trail. Brook trout and cutthroat trout are planted here.

Farmers—Head 8 miles up the Swift Creek Trail for planted brook trout.

Grayling—A small population of brook trout reside at Grayling. It is reached 5 miles up the Swift Creek Trail to Swift Creek, then 1 mile north along Swift Creek.

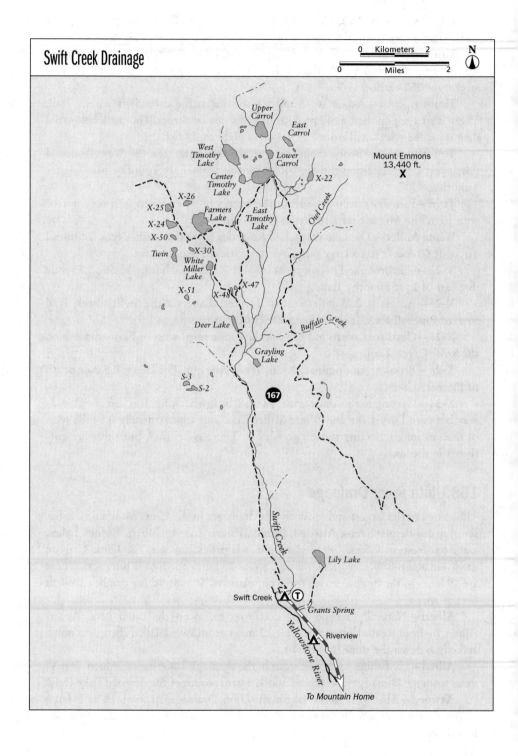

Swift Creek Drainage

0 Kilometers 2
N

0 Miles 2

Upper Carrol

East Carrol

West Timothy Lake

Lower Carrol

Center Timothy Lake

X-22

Mount Emmons
13,440 ft.
X

X-26

X-25

Farmers Lake

East Timothy Lake

Owl Creek

X-24

X-50

X-30

Twin

White Miller Lake

X-51

X-47

X-48

Deer Lake

Buffalo Creek

Grayling Lake

S-3

S-2

167

Swift Creek

Lily Lake

Swift Creek

T

Grants Spring

Riverview

Yellowstone River

To Mountain Home

Lily—A steep but well-defined trail northeast from Grants Spring in Yellowstone Canyon leads to Lily. Stocked brook trout make up the catch.

Timothy, Center—Pressure is heavy for natural brook trout here. It is reached 9.5 miles up the Swift Creek Trail to East Timothy, then due west along the inlet stream for 250 yards.

Timothy, East—Access is 9.5 miles from the trailhead on Swift Creek Trail. There is a large population of brook trout and some cutthroat. The creek below the dam is loaded with small trout and is a great place to fly fish.

Timothy, West—Brook trout make up the fishing at Timothy West. Access is northwest 0.5 mile along the west inlet stream from East Timothy past Center Timothy.

Twin—Pan-size cutthroat lurk in the waters of Twin about 0.75 mile northwest of White Miller over a rocky and timbered ridge.

White Miller—The lake is reached 6.5 miles from the Swift Creek Trailhead on Swift Creek. It has a large population of stocked brook trout.

X-22—Cutthroat and brook trout inhabit X-22. Reach it by hiking 0.75 mile due east of East Timothy Lake.

X-24—Access is 0.75 mile west of Farmers Lake via the Swift Creek Trail toward Bluebell Pass. It is stocked with cutthroat trout.

X-25—Cutthroat are found here. Walk 1 mile northwest of Farmers Lake on the Swift Creek Trail.

X-26—Brook trout dominate X-26. Take some out. The lake is 0.5 mile north of Farmers Lake.

X-51—Getting to this one requires a little bushwhacking. It is just about midway between Deer Lake and White Miller Lake and approximately 0.5 mile west of the stream connecting those two waters. There is no trail, but there are cutthroat in the lake.

168 Uinta River Drainage

This is one of the largest and most diverse drainages in the Uinta Mountains. It has seven major basins: Krebs, Atwood, Painter, Painter Lakes, Gilbert, Kidney Lakes, and Fox Crescent Lakes. Two major trailheads provide access. The Uinta Canyon Trailhead and the Whiterocks Drainage, about 25 miles north of Whiterocks. There are 49 lakes in the drainage with trout populations. Stream fishing can be excellent here as well.

Albert—Naturally reproducing cutthroat make up the catch here. Access Albert by heading northwest up a ridge 2 miles from Bollie Lake, then turn north and climb down the slope into the basin.

Allred—Fly fishing for brook trout in the evenings is nonstop at Allred. It is 18 miles from the Uinta River Trailhead and 225 yards south of the Atwood Lake Dam.

Atwood—This is the largest lake in the Uinta Drainage. Access is 18 miles from U-Bar Ranch over a well-marked trail. Brook trout and the rare golden trout are found here.

B-29—Reach B-29 by going east 0.25 mile from Carrot Lake after crossing Carrot Creek on the Lake Atwood Trail. It about 17.5 miles from the Uinta River Trailhead.

Beard—At the eastern base of Kings Peak, this lake is 22 miles through the Atwood Basin to Trail Rider Pass. Follow the trail an additional 0.125 mile into Painter Basin, turn southwest, and go 150 yards into the basin where the lake sits. Pressure is light for stocked brook trout.

Bowden—Half a mile southeast of the Kidney Lakes, Bowden is stocked with brook trout and periodically winterkills.

Brook—Brook and cutthroat trout inhabit Brook, which is 1 mile east by trail from Fox Lake. It can also be reached by following the Highline Trail west from Whiterocks over the North Pole Pass.

Carrot—Total distance from the U-Bar Ranch is 17.5 miles. The lake is 0.5 mile southwest of the big meadow where the trail crosses Atwood Creek. Fishing is good for stocked brook trout.

Chain, Upper—Fishing pressure is heavy early in the summer for pan-size brook trout. The lake is 11.5 miles from the U-Bar Ranch Trailhead on a well-marked trail.

Chain, Middle—A half mile above Upper Chain, this lake has an abundant brook trout population.

Chain, Lower—Just 100 yards above Middle Chain, Lower Chain may offer the best fly fishing of the Chain Lakes for brook trout.

Chain, Fourth—Cutthroat are planted in this lake, the last of the Chains.

Craig—Access is from the U-Bar Ranch for 14 miles on a well-marked trail to North Fork Park, where the North and Center Forks of the Uinta River converge. Head south 2 rough miles on a vague trail next to a small stream into Painter Lakes Basin. Cutthroat and some brook trout are found here.

Crescent—Popular with Scout groups, Crescent is reached from the West Fork Whiterocks River Trailhead over Fox-Queant Pass (8 miles), or 15.5 miles on a marked trail from the U-Bar Ranch. The catch is cutthroat and brookies.

North Davis—About 1.25 miles north of the Kidney Lakes and 250 yards due north of South Davis, this lake contains stocked brook trout.

South Davis—The fish can freely move between North and South Davis, so try one if the other isn't producing.

Divide—Access is 2 miles north from Fox Lake via a trail that goes over the pass to Island Lake. Cutthroat trout are regularly stocked here.

Dollar—Sometimes called Dime, this lake has a naturally reproducing population of brook trout. The lake is about 1 mile northwest of Fox Lake and about 15 miles from the U-Bar Ranch.

Fox—Brook and cutthroat trout are caught here. Use is primarily by large groups. Fox is 15 miles from the U-Bar Ranch, or 8.5 miles from the West Fork Whiterocks River Trailhead.

George Beard—Access is 2 miles via a rocky trail from Atwood Lake. George Beard is located just below Trail Rider Pass. There is a large population of brook trout.

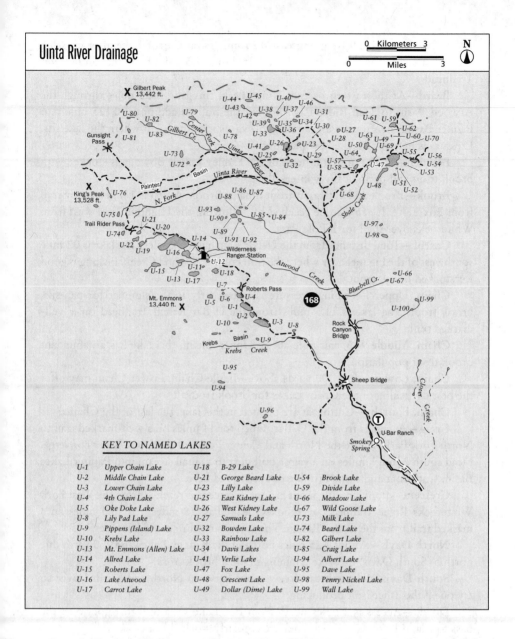

Uinta River Drainage

0 Kilometers 3
0 Miles 3

N

Gilbert Peak
13,442 ft.

Gunsight Pass

Gilbert Cr.

King's Peak
13,528 ft.

Painter

Uinta River

Basin

N. Fork

Trail Rider Pass

Uinta River

Wilderness
Ranger Station

Atwood Creek

Mt. Emmons
13,440 ft.

Roberts Pass

168

Shale Creek

Bluebell Cr.

Rock
Canyon
Bridge

Krebs Basin

Krebs Creek

Sheep Bridge

Clover Creek

Smokey
Spring

T

U-Bar Ranch

KEY TO NAMED LAKES

U-1	Upper Chain Lake	U-18	B-29 Lake		
U-2	Middle Chain Lake	U-21	George Beard Lake	U-54	Brook Lake
U-3	Lower Chain Lake	U-23	Lilly Lake	U-59	Divide Lake
U-4	4th Chain Lake	U-25	East Kidney Lake	U-66	Meadow Lake
U-5	Oke Doke Lake	U-26	West Kidney Lake	U-67	Wild Goose Lake
U-8	Lily Pad Lake	U-27	Samuals Lake	U-73	Milk Lake
U-9	Pippens (Island) Lake	U-32	Bowden Lake	U-74	Beard Lake
U-10	Krebs Lake	U-33	Rainbow Lake	U-82	Gilbert Lake
U-13	Mt. Emmons (Allen) Lake	U-34	Davis Lakes	U-85	Craig Lake
U-14	Allred Lake	U-41	Verlie Lake	U-94	Albert Lake
U-15	Roberts Lake	U-47	Fox Lake	U-95	Dave Lake
U-16	Lake Atwood	U-48	Crescent Lake	U-98	Penny Nickell Lake
U-17	Carrot Lake	U-49	Dollar (Dime) Lake	U-99	Wall Lake

Gilbert—At the head of Gilbert Creek, Gilbert Lake is reached by heading northwest from North Fork Park for 6.5 miles. It is about 20.5 miles from the U-Bar Ranch. The lake is stocked with brook trout.

Kidney, East—Accessed by 15 miles of trail from the West Fork Whiterocks River Trailhead, or 18 miles from the U-Bar, East Kidney has rainbow and brook trout. Camping and fishing pressure can be heavy.

Kidney, West—One hundred yards west of East Kidney, this lake helps absorb pressure. Brook, rainbow, and cutthroat trout are caught here.

Lilly—Lilly is 0.5 mile northeast of the Kidney Lakes. Brook trout are stocked here.

Lily Pad—This is the first lake reached on the Chain Lakes Trail. It is about 8 miles from the U-Bar Ranch. It is 0.25 mile off the trail, about 1 mile east of Upper Chain and about 0.33 mile north of the Krebs Creek Trail crossing. Brook and rainbow trout naturally reproduce here.

Milk—Milk is about 5 miles west of North Fork Park or 7 miles northeast of Trail Rider Pass. The last mile is rocky. Pan-size brook trout and cutthroat are prevalent.

Mt. Emmons (Allen)—Brook trout are common and golden trout are sometimes caught at this lake, 0.25 mile south of Allred Lake in the Atwood Basin. It is about 18.5 miles from the U-Bar Ranch.

Oke Doke—Cutthroat trout are stocked in Oke Doke. It sits at the eastern base of Mt. Emmons, 1 mile due west of Roberts Pass. It is 15 miles from the U-Bar Ranch and provides an excellent place for a small group.

Penny Nickell—There is no trail to the lake, and a map is highly encouraged. It sits next to a steep slope 3.5 miles due south of Fox Lake. The lake is stocked with cutthroat.

Pippen—This is a good fly-fishing lake for brook trout. Go west about 1 mile through the large meadow located 0.5 mile southwest of Upper Chain.

Rainbow—Brook and rainbow trout inhabit this lake, 1.25 miles northwest of the Kidney Lakes on a well-marked trail.

Roberts—Cutthroat and some brook trout are caught at Roberts. Follow a small trail 1.5 miles west of Mt. Emmons Lake through a meadow, and then climb the steep ravine to the lake.

Samuals—Between Fox and Kidney Lakes at the head of Samuals Creek, Samuals Lake has an abundant population of brook trout and is a good escape from the crowds at nearby lakes.

U-19—Near the head of the Atwood Basin, this lake is 0.5 mile south of George Beard Lake past U-22, or 2 miles due west of Atwood Lake Dam. Pressure is light for brook trout.

U-35—Just over 100 yards from Rainbow Lake, U-35 holds a few stocked cutthroat and brook trout.

U-36—One hundred yards south of U-35, this lake contains a natural brook trout population.

U-37—About 0.5 mile northeast of Rainbow Lake and 0.5 mile southeast of U-38, this lake is stocked with brook trout.

U-38—Half a mile due north of Rainbow, U-38 has cutthroat trout.

U-39—About 0.5 mile due north of Rainbow, U-39 may have stocked brook trout.

U-42—One mile northwest of Rainbow Lake and 0.5 mile west of U-38, U-42 has cutthroat.

U-45—About 2.5 miles northwest of the Kidney Lakes, this lake has a few cutthroat.

U-50—Brook trout inhabit this lake 0.25 mile northwest of Dollar Lake.

U-75—One mile northwest of Trail Rider Pass, U-75 sees few anglers for its pan-size brook trout.

U-76—At the southeast base of Kings Peak in the Upper Painter Basin, U-76 is about 2 miles northwest of Trail Rider Pass. The lake contains pan-size brook and cutthroat trout. Pressure is light.

U-88—A natural population of brook trout inhabits the largest lake in the Painter Lakes Basin. It sits 1 mile due west of Craig Lake.

U-89—About 100 yards southwest of U-88, this lake has brook trout.

U-93—At 11,402 feet, this is the highest lake in the Painter Lakes Basin. It is 1.5 miles west of Craig Lake and is stocked with cutthroat trout.

Verlie—About 1 mile due west of the Kidney Lakes, Verlie has a natural population of brook trout and some cutthroat.

169 Whiterocks River Drainage

Because of its close proximity to Vernal, the Whiterocks Drainage is one of the most heavily used on the south slope of the Uintas. There are 45 lakes or ponds supporting fish here.

From Highway 121 near Lapoint, a road heads north to Forest Road 104, which takes you to Paradise Park Reservoir. Trailheads at Paradise Park provide access to lakes on the east side of the Whiterocks Drainage.

Another point of access can be reached by following the main road in the town of Whiterocks north to a road that leads up Pole Mountain and ends at Chepeta Lake. This serves as a good place to start trips to the Reader Lakes Basin and lakes by the East Fork of the Whiterocks River.

Angel—Fishing pressure is light at Angel, which sometimes winterkills. It is stocked with cutthroat and is less than 1 mile south of the West Fork Trailhead.

Ann—Four miles up the West Fork Trail near the head of the Rasmussen Lakes Basin, Ann Lake is subject to winterkill but is planted with cutthroat. There are no trails, but the lake is 0.5 mile northwest of Eric Lake.

Becky—Stocked with brook trout, Becky gets little pressure. Becky is 1.5 miles west of the Rasmussen Lakes.

Chepeta—This is by far the largest lake in the Whiterocks Drainage. A dirt road (first Forest Road 117, then Forest Road 110) begins at the Elkhorn Guard Station at the bottom of Whiterocks Canyon, and after 24 miles, it terminates 200 yards south of the lake. The lake is stocked with brook trout and has a naturally reproducing population of cutthroat.

Cirque—May contain grayling. It is less than 0.5 mile southwest of Rasmussen Lakes and 2 miles due west of the West Fork Trailhead.

Cleveland—Open shoreline makes fly fishing possible for brook trout and cutthroat. The lake lies just west of the trail to Fox-Queant Pass and is 4 miles from the West Fork Trailhead.

Cliff—The lake is 5.5 miles by trail from Chepeta Lake, but vehicle access is possible by taking FR 104 at Paradise Park Campground west. The road eventually con-

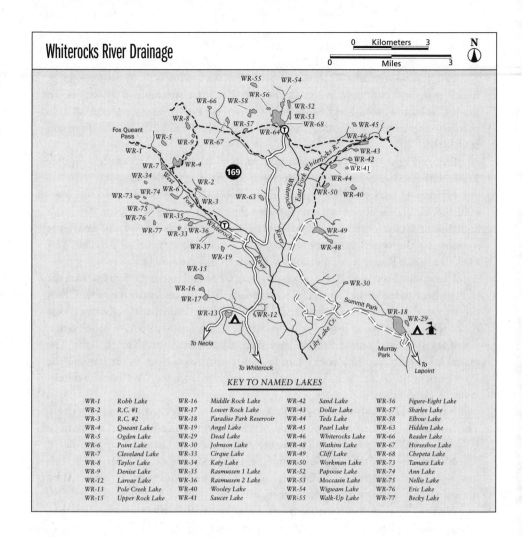

KEY TO NAMED LAKES

WR-1	Robb Lake	WR-16	Middle Rock Lake	WR-42	Sand Lake	WR-56	Figure-Eight Lake
WR-2	R.C. #1	WR-17	Lower Rock Lake	WR-43	Dollar Lake	WR-57	Sharlee Lake
WR-3	R.C. #2	WR-18	Paradise Park Reservoir	WR-44	Teds Lake	WR-58	Elbow Lake
WR-4	Queant Lake	WR-19	Angel Lake	WR-45	Pearl Lake	WR-63	Hidden Lake
WR-5	Ogden Lake	WR-29	Dead Lake	WR-46	Whiterocks Lake	WR-66	Reader Lake
WR-6	Point Lake	WR-30	Johnson Lake	WR-48	Watkins Lake	WR-67	Horseshoe Lake
WR-7	Cleveland Lake	WR-33	Cirque Lake	WR-49	Cliff Lake	WR-68	Chepeta Lake
WR-8	Taylor Lake	WR-34	Katy Lake	WR-50	Workman Lake	WR-73	Tamara Lake
WR-9	Denise Lake	WR-35	Rasmussen 1 Lake	WR-52	Papoose Lake	WR-74	Ann Lake
WR-12	Larvae Lake	WR-36	Rasmussen 2 Lake	WR-53	Moccasin Lake	WR-75	Nellie Lake
WR-13	Pole Creek Lake	WR-40	Wooley Lake	WR-54	Wigwam Lake	WR-76	Eric Lake
WR-15	Upper Rock Lake	WR-41	Saucer Lake	WR-55	Walk-Up Lake	WR-77	Becky Lake

nects with Forest Road 140, which terminates at Cliff Lake, about 11.5 miles from Paradise Park. The road is rough and four-wheel drive is required. Brook trout and an occasional cutthroat are caught.

Denise—Reach Denise by heading about 2 miles northeast of Queant Lake. Denise is about 6 miles from the West Fork Trailhead. The lake can also be reached from Chepeta Lake across the shallow saddle on the high ridge west of Reader Lake Basin. Fishing pressure for stocked brook trout is light.

Dollar—This lake sits about 0.5 mile south of Whiterocks Lake. Follow the trail from Chepeta Lake east along the south flank of Rose Peak. Dollar Lake lies cross-country at the base of the ridge. It has a naturally reproducing population of brook trout. Cutthroat are also numerous.

Elbow Lake—Elbow is 1 trailless mile west of Chepeta, at the base of a steep cliff. The best way to ensure finding Elbow is to head for the northwest corner of

Chepeta at the inlet. Traveling along the inlet from Elbow is rough, but is more reliable than going cross-country. Elbow is stocked with brook trout.

Eric Lake—Actually a pair of ponds, Eric Lake is a good place for fly fishing. Brook trout and cutthroat live in the ponds, which are surrounded by marsh. To reach Eric by the most direct route, follow the West Fork upstream about 0.8 mile to its confluence with the outlet from Eric Lake. Follow the outlet up the slope and to the lake.

Figure-Eight—Only a few hundred yards northwest of Chepeta lies Figure-Eight, with its large naturally reproducing population of cutthroat.

Hidden—Located at the base of a rocky knob 400 yards off the road to Chepeta Lake, Hidden is about halfway between the turnoff to the West Fork Trailhead and Reader Creek. A trail to Hidden begins on the south side of the first large meadow on the west side of the road, about 3 miles past the turnoff to the West Fork Trailhead. Pressure on the stocked brook trout here is light.

Horseshoe Lake—This lake is 3 miles from Chepeta Lake and 2.5 miles from the trailhead at Reader Creek. To reach Horseshoe, follow the outlet from Reader Creek north to the lake from the Reader Basin Trail. The last 0.5 mile is cross-country across rocky terrain. Horseshoe is stocked with cutthroat, but it may also have brook trout.

Katy—Stocked with cutthroat, pressure at out-of-the-way Katy is light. The glacial lake is situated in a rocky cirque 1 mile northwest from Point Lake in the West Fork of the Whiterocks Drainage. Total distance from the West Fork Trailhead is just under 5 miles.

Larvae—This lake sometimes winterkills, but it is stocked with brook trout. The lake is 0.3 mile east of the junction of the Chepeta Lake Road and the road to Pole Creek Lake. It is just over 1 mile due east of the Pole Creek Campground.

Moccasin—Less than 1 mile east of Chepeta, Moccasin is easily accessed by following the first stream inlet to Chepeta on the east side. Moccasin is supported by naturally reproducing brook and cutthroat trout.

Nellie—This small on-stream pond is stocked with cutthroat and is less than 0.5 mile west of Eric Lake. It is just over 3.5 miles from the West Fork Trailhead.

Ogden—Access is northwest from Queant Lake, cross-country up a slope. The lake is stocked with cutthroat, but has suffered winterkill.

Papoose—Just 500 yards north of Chepeta, Papoose is a good place to fly fish for naturally reproducing brook trout.

Paradise Park Reservoir—The reservoir is reached from a dirt road (FR 104) 26 miles north of the town of Lapoint. A 15-unit campground and guard station is located at the reservoir. Paradise is planted with catchable rainbows and fingerling brook trout.

Pearl—This lake lies at the head of the East Fork of the Whiterocks Drainage in a small basin of the Uinta Divide, east of Chepeta Lake. It is 4.5 miles from Chepeta, and the last 0.5 mile is cross-country through long, narrow meadows. The lake is stocked with cutthroat and has some brook trout as well.

Point—There is no trail to Point, but it is reached by following the West Fork Trail to the confluence of the West Fork and the outlet of Point Lake, and up a rocky slope. Total distance from the West Fork Trailhead is just over 3 miles. It is stocked with brook trout and gets light to medium fishing pressure.

Pole Creek—Annually stocked with catchable-size rainbows, Pole Creek Lake gets heavy pressure. It is reached via FR 117 from the Elkhorn Guard Station north of the town of Whiterocks. It is a 15-mile drive to the lake. Pole Creek Campground has 18 sites.

Queant—The lake is reached from the West Fork Trailhead with a 4-mile hike. Pressure is heavy for stocked brook trout. This is perhaps the most popular lake not accessible by vehicles in the Whiterocks Drainage.

Rasmussen 1—Slightly larger than its sister to the southeast, Rasmussen 1 is stocked with brook trout. There is no trail to reach the Rasmussen Lakes. They are accessible about 2 miles west of the West Fork Trailhead.

Rasmussen 2—Brook trout are planted here.

R.C. # 1—The outlet stream of R.C. # 1 crosses the West Fork Trail about 1.5 miles from the trailhead. Follow it to the lake. It is about 2.5 miles from the trailhead. The lake is stocked with cutthroat.

R.C. # 2—Just west of R.C. # 1, # 2 offers more marginal fish habitat and is only rarely stocked with cutthroat.

Reader—At the head of the Reader Basin, this lake is accessible by the Reader Basin Trail before it climbs over the divide. Total distance from Chepeta Lake and the Reader Creek Trailhead is about 4 miles. Reader has suffered from winterkill. Brook or cutthroat may be caught.

Robb—This lake is located along the trail at the head of the West Fork of the Whiterocks Drainage just below Fox-Queant Pass. Total distance from the West Fork Trailhead is just under 6 miles. Winterkill can be a problem, but Robb is planted with brook trout.

Rock, Lower—Fishing pressure for stocked brook trout is light, considering its proximity to the Pole Creek area. Lower Rock is best reached by following the inlet of Pole Creek Lake upstream to the large meadow 0.5 mile from the road. Skirt the south side of the meadow and follow the outlet of Lower Rock Lake through heavy timber.

Rock, Middle—This is the smallest of the Rock chain lakes. It is 200 yards north of Lower Rock and has brook trout stocked in its waters.

Rock, Upper—This is the largest of the Rock chain lakes. Upper Rock is less than 0.5 mile north of Middle Rock. Winterkill is a problem, but cutthroat are planted here.

Sand—Bring hip boots if you plan on fishing Sand. The shoreline is wet and muddy, but fishing for large populations of brookies and cutthroat may make it worth the effort. Sand is just over 0.5 mile northeast from Ted's Lake.

Saucer—Stocked with brook trout, Saucer periodically has winterkill. It is less than 0.5 mile east of Ted's Lake.

Sharlee—Pretty Sharlee sits on a high bench on the north side of Reader Lakes Basin. It is about 2 miles on a good trail west of Chepeta Lake. Open shorelines make fly fishing for cutthroat and brookies easy.

Tamara—From Eric Lake, continue up the bottom of the basin past Nellie and up a steep, rocky slope through timber. Total distance from the West Fork Trailhead is just over 4 miles. Pressure is light for stocked cutthroat.

Taylor—The Queant Trail passes within a few hundred yards of Taylor just before the Highline Trail junction. Total mileage from the West Fork Trailhead is about 6.5 miles. Fishing for stocked brook trout is good.

Teds—This popular lake lies in the middle of a series of meadows in the East Fork of the Whiterocks Drainage. Travel east from the Chepeta Lake Trailhead on the Whiterocks Trail to a point just south of Rose Peak. An old trail cuts off the main trail and heads south, eventually crossing the East Fork. Continue up the slope until you reach a trail junction at the base of a wet meadow. Ted's is a short distance to the northeast. Pressure for stocked brook trout is moderate to heavy.

Walk-Up—This lake sits in a deep bowl with cliffs of 1,000 feet around it. It is 2.5 miles northwest of Chepeta Lake. A rocky cleft leads from Figure-Eight Lake due north to Walk-Up. It is stocked with brook trout.

Watkins—Just 100 yards southeast of Cliff Lake, Watkins sees little pressure for stocked brook trout.

Wigwam—Stocked with brook trout, Wigwam's outlet flows 150 yards south into Chepeta Lake. The lake sees moderate pressure.

Wooley—This lake is about 1 mile east of Workman Lake. Wooley has a self-sustaining population of brook trout.

Workman—This lake is just over 0.5 mile south of Ted's Lake in the East Fork Drainage. It is accessible from Paradise Park and Chepeta Lake. Workman has viable populations of brook and cutthroat trout.

170 Dry Gulch Drainage

This is the smallest drainage on the south slope of the High Uintas. It is located between the Uinta River and Swift Creek drainages, about 15 miles northeast of Altamont. The drainage is divided into two basins: Heller and Crow.

Access to Heller Basin is north from Neola or Altamont to the Dry Gulch Road (Forest Road 122) near the Forest Service/Indian Reservation boundary. Access to the Crow Basin is via the Timothy Creek Road (Forest Road 120) for 6 miles to Jackson Park.

Dry Gulch/Crow Basin Lakes

Crow—From Jackson Park, climb down the steep slope. Follow the outlet stream south 0.75 mile to Crow. Pressure is moderate for cutthroat trout.

DG-6—Head north from Jackson Park 1.5 miles, then drop over the canyon rim to the meadow. DG-6 is stocked with cutthroat. DG-7 and DG-8 suffer winterkill and only have fish if they have migrated from DG-6.

DG-9—Follow the inlet from DG-6 north 0.5 mile. This lake has a small population of cutthroat trout.

DG-10—Follow the inlet from DG-9 1 mile north. Cutthroat inhabit DG-10.

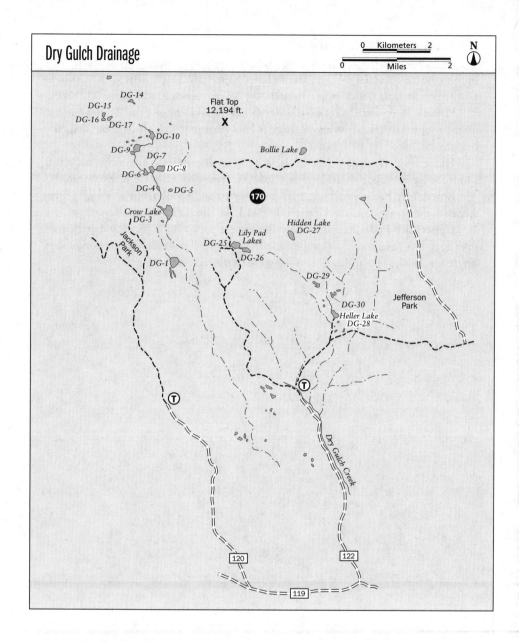

0 Kilometers 2

0 Miles 2

N

DG-14

DG-15

DG-16 DG-17

Flat Top
12,194 ft.
X

DG-10

DG-9 DG-7

DG-6 DG-8

DG-4 DG-5

Crow Lake
DG-3

Jackson Park

DG-1

Bollie Lake

170

Hidden Lake
DG-27

Lily Pad
Lakes
DG-25

DG-26

DG-29

DG-30

Heller Lake
DG-28

Jefferson
Park

Dry Gulch Creek

T

T

120

122

119

DG-14—There is no trail to this lake, but it sits at the northeast head of the canyon about 0.75 mile north of DG-10. It has a fair population of cutthroat.

DG-15—This lake sits in the northwest head of the canyon, south and west of DG-14. The water level fluctuates at DG-15, and the cutthroat here are subject to winterkill.

DG-16—One hundred feet south of DG-15, this lake also has cutthroat.

DG-17—A large population of cutthroat makes this one of the best lakes to fish in the Crow Basin. It is 100 yards east of DG-16.

Dry Gulch/Heller Basin Lakes

DG-29 — This small beaver pond is subject to winterkill. It is stocked with brook trout and can be reached from Heller Reservoir. From there, it is 0.25 mile northwest to a long park. Follow the park for 0.5 mile, then head east for 0.125 mile.

Heller — Access is 4 miles up the Dry Gulch Road to its end and 2 miles by foot on the trail to the lake. Fishing pressure is heavy for pan-size brook trout and cut-throat.

Hidden — This isolated lake at the head of Heller Basin contains brook trout. From Heller Reservoir, head 2 miles north-northwest on a poorly marked trail.

Lower Lily Pad — Small numbers of cutthroat and brook trout are caught here. Access is via a vague trail to Upper Lily Pad Lake then 0.2 mile due east.

Upper Lily Pad — Access is 7.5 miles via the Dry Gulch Road and pack trail over Flat Top Mountain, or 2 miles northwest of Heller Reservoir, cross-country. There are small populations of brookies and cutthroat here.

Index

About the Author

Brett Prettyman grew up learning to fish on a small stream in central Utah and in the high-elevation lakes of the Uinta Mountains. Trout fishing in these cold waters was Brett's first love. More recently, as an outdoors writer for the Salt Lake Tribune, Brett has traveled Utah, exploring and writing about the countless and diverse fisheries the state offers. He has learned to appreciate the unique opportunities of each of the disciplines of angling and enjoys them all, but a fly rod is the one he reaches for first. Brett lives in Salt Lake City with his wife, Brooke, and their two children, William and Lucie, with whom he finds great pleasure in rediscovering the wonders of angling.